ODDBALL
WISCONSIN

ODDBALL WISCONSIN

A Guide to Some Really
STRANGE PLACES

JEROME POHLEN

CHICAGO
REVIEW
PRESS

Library of Congress Cataloging-in-Publication Data

Pohlen, Jerome.
    Oddball Wisconsin : a guide to some really strange places / Jerome Pohlen.
        p. cm.
    Includes bibliographical references and indexes.
    ISBN 1-55652-376-9
    1. Wisconsin—Guidebooks. 2. Wisconsin—History, Local—Miscellanea.
    3. Curiosities and wonders—Wisconsin—Guidebooks. I. Title.
    F579.3 .P64 2001
    917.7504'44—dc21

                                                    2001017322

Cover design: Mel Kupfer

The author has made every effort to secure permissions for all the material in this book.
If any acknowledgment has inadvertently been omitted, please contact the author.

All photographs courtesy of Jerome Pohlen unless otherwise noted.

Published by Chicago Review Press, Incorporated
814 North Franklin Street
Chicago, Illinois 60610
ISBN 978-1-55652-376-2
Printed in the United States of America
10 9 8 7 6 5

TO MY PARENTS,
JOSEPH & BARBARA POHLEN,
FOR ALL THE FAMILY TRIPS
IN THE BIG ORANGE DODGE

CONTENTS

INTRODUCTION

*L*et's be honest. Wisconsin is a state of oddballs. Where else do citizens proudly wear foam cheese wedges on their heads? In which state are there not one, but two, men who have had their names legally changed to Elvis Presley? Where have voters elected the infamous Senator Joseph McCarthy and the nation's longest-running Socialist big-city mayor? And which state's official song is owned by Michael Jackson? The answer to all these questions is the same: Wisconsin.

And what do these odd folk do with their time? They build elaborate concrete shrines in their front yards or erect enormous fiberglass figures of fish, corkscrews, chickens, and cows. They open museums to honor mustard, hamburgers, angels, honey, toy tops, and cheese. And towns organize festivals to celebrate pot roasts, UFOs, rutabagas, watermelon-seed spitting, and cow chip tossing. These weird folk are willing to break free of Midwestern conformity. They are the people I admire.

Where other travel guides might bore you with scenic driving tours, homey bed and breakfasts, and where to find the fall colors, *Oddball Wisconsin* offers you road trip information you're not likely to find any-where else. Where was Liberace born? How do you catch a Hodag? Who invented the hamburger, and what is his hometown doing to honor this visionary man? What is Ed Gein best known for, and where is he buried? Which rodent is a better weather forecaster, Jimmy the Groundhog or Punxsutawney Phil? And will a Polka Hall of Fame ever be built?

So forget antiquing in Door County, fly-fishing in the North Woods, and bicycling along the Mississippi. You've eaten far too many waffle cones in Lake Geneva. It's time to live a little, and laugh a lot, on your vacation.

While I've tried to give clear directions from major streets and land-marks, you could still make a wrong turn. Bigfoot might be out there, so it's not a time to panic. Remember these Oddball travel tips:

- Stop and ask! For a lot of communities, their Oddball attraction might be their only claim to fame. Locals are often thrilled that you'd drive out of your way to marvel at their underappreciated shrine. But choose your guides wisely; old cranks at the town cafe are good for information; pimply teenage clerks at the Gas-n-Go are not.
- Call ahead. Few Oddball sites keep regular hours, but most will gladly wait around if they know you're coming. Wisconsin is a seasonal travel state, and sites can be closed for the winter season at a moment's notice, especially if the fish are biting. Always call.
- Don't give up. Think of the person who's sitting in a tiny museum dedicated to an obscure topic, and know that they're waiting just for you. Actually, they're waiting for anyone—but you'll do.
- Don't trespass! Don't become a Terrible Tourist. Just because somebody built a sculpture garden in their front yard doesn't mean they're looking for visitors.

Do you have an Oddball site of your own? Have I missed anything? Do you know of an Oddball site that should be included in a later version? Please write and let me know: Chicago Review Press, 814 N. Franklin St., Chicago, IL 60610.

ODDBALL WISCONSIN

Northern Wisconsin

When you think of Northern Wisconsin, think big. Paul Bunyan B-I-G. Everywhere you turn are enormous monuments to everyday objects and wildlife. A giant corkscrew. A colossal penny. A two-story loon. A massive badger. A titanic chicken. A Chrysler-sized white-tail deer. Huge black bears, man-made and stuffed. And the World's Largest Fiberglass Structure, a gargantuan muskie at the National Freshwater Fishing Hall of Fame in Hayward.

To properly display these mammoth structures, they've been placed great distances from one another; they are not the kind of things you can visit on an afternoon drive in the country. You need a full tank of gas, a good map, and an alarm clock to hit the road early—it's going to be a full weekend.

And you won't just see fiberglass monstrosities. There are things up in those woods, things you'll never see anywhere else: UFO parades, death-defying goats, crowds of concrete people, card-playing raccoons, hippie colonies, a Bong memorial, and the Exact Geographic Center of the Northern Half of the Western Freakin' Hemisphere. What are you waiting for?

Amery
The Haunted Lutheran Church

If you're driving along Route 46 south of Amery and you hear the toll of a church bell, stop! But only if the tolling comes from a Lutheran church atop a hill.

Old Norwegian ghosts from the church's adjoining cemetery have refused to go to their final rest, choosing instead to congregate in the chapel after hours. Oftentimes they ring the bell to call their otherworldly neighbors to their spirit services.

Many parishioners have heard the noisy throng over the years, only to have the voices fade as they approached the building. Others have heard murmurs in the basement, and one church trustee had a light fixture reassemble itself when he turned his back for a moment. As of yet, the dead have not harmed anyone . . . though there is no guarantee that they won't!

East Immanuel Lutheran Church, 207 120th St., Amery, WI 54001

(715) 268-9291

Hours: Always visible

Cost: Free

Directions: Five miles south of town on Rte. 46, turn west on 30th Ave., turn south on 120th St.

Aniwa
Behn's Game Farm

Lest you think Wisconsin farms raise only cows, stop by Behn's Game Farm. Although it looks like a working farm, its animals are a bit more exotic. They've got emus and pygmy goats, long-horn bulls and lions, turkeys and tigers, and most are approachable. As part of your entrance fee you're given a cupful of corn to feed the goats who, rather than pester you for a handout, actually work for their meals. Put a few kernels in a tin can tied to a clothesline pulley, and the goats will climb a staircase and yank the rope to collect the food. Amazing!

The menagerie is the collection of Wilbert Behn, self-taught animal trainer. Throughout the day, Behn or his son Clyde put on animal shows. Watch goats jump through hoops and pigs skid down slides. See a tiger walk the high wire, or dogs perform a slapstick routine. Shows are usually choreographed to tunes like *Yakkety Sax* or *Dueling Banjos*. Occasionally,

Clyde serenades the critters with a gospel melody played on a handsaw with a cello bow. Clyde also rides a unicycle. Have those cameras ready.

Though Wilbert is in his eighties, he's still going strong, and the animals still know who's boss. Behn's Game Farm is one of a dying breed of entrepreneurial tourist attractions once common in America. But sadly, it's tough to find alligator wrestlers or bears on motorcycles anymore. You should see Behn's while you still can.

Rte. 52, Aniwa, WI 54408

(715) 449-2971

Hours: May–October, daily 8A.M.–6P.M.

Cost: Adults $3, Kids(5–12) $1

Directions: Just west of the Rte. 52 intersection with Rte. 45.

Birnamwood

Big Chicken

Talk about sleeping with the enemy! This traitorous clucker shamelessly lures hungry travelers along Route 45 to a killing field two blocks west of the highway where its feathered kin are roasted, fried, and carved into breaded strips. Sure, the food at Chet & Emil's is tasty, and yes, they do offer a broad selection of non-poultry meals. But it's the notion that this large, white, fiberglass chicken would participate in this carnage—it's nothing short of cannibalism!

In the chicken's defense, it is obviously wired to the top of its sign and probably couldn't escape if it wanted to, and if it didn't act as the restaurant's spokes-hen, whose head do you think would be next on the chopping block? This bird could feed the whole town!

Chet & Emil's Broasted Chicken, 388 Main St., Birnamwood, WI 54414

(715) 449-2226

Hours: Always visible

Cost: Free

Directions: Sign at the intersection of Rte. 45 and Elm St.; Chet & Emil's is two blocks west on Main.

BIRCHWOOD

A mammoth bluegill statue has been erected in Birchwood, the "Bluegill Capital of Wisconsin."

Wisconsin's Godzilla.

Remains of the World's Largest Badger

He's not what he used to be, but he's still ferocious. The World's Largest Badger once loomed over a mound-shaped gas station north of Birnamwood. The station's pumps were located inside a large hollow log with an equally impressive squirrel crawling on top. Customers could park their cars inside the log while they filled up, then snap a picture to tell their friends, "Honey, I shrunk the Chevy!"

But the gas station closed several years ago. The new owners pulled the badger off the roof and buried him neck deep, closer to the road, emerging from the ditch to startle drivers on Route 45. The badger mound was leveled. The log was converted to a storage shed, though the squirrel is still up there. In its place an architecturally uninspired exotic dance "club" has been erected.

Things could be worse. The badger and squirrel could have been bulldozed or the joint could have reopened as a McDonald's. Count your roadside blessings.

Badger Country Exotic Dancers, N11004 Rte. 45, Birnamwood, WI 54414

No phone

Hours: Always visible

Cost: Free

Directions: Just north of the Rte. ZZ intersection, north of town.

Couderay
The Hideout

When things got too hot for Al Capone in Chicago, he often fled to the Wisconsin woods for a "vacation." Not one to mince words, he called the place "The Hideout," and that's what it is named today. The lakeside home still has machine-gun portals, a blockhouse, gun tower, and 18-inch-thick walls, just in case you question if this is the real thing. It kind of sounds like Idaho.

But there are other clues to let you know you're in Capone Country. A garage has been used to re-create the St. Valentine's Day Massacre, something you'll never see in Chicago. A restaurant now housed in what used to be Capone's eight-car garage serves Italian fare, as well as seafood and prime rib. And last year, The Hideout added a Roaring '20s Museum with mobsters, flappers, and bootleg booze.

12101 W. Rte. CC, Couderay, WI 54828

(715) 945-2746

E-mail: hideout@win.bright.net

Hours: May, Friday–Sunday Noon–7p.m.; June–August, daily Noon–7p.m.; September, daily Noon–5p.m.; October, Friday–Sunday Noon–5p.m.

Cost: Adults $8.50, Kids(6–11) $4

wistravel.com/hideout/alcapone.htm

Directions: Six miles north of town on Rte. CC, off Rtes. N and NN.

WHERE DOES A GANGSTER FISH? ANYWHERE HE WANTS!

Thugs led by Chicago mobster Joe Saltis put a contract out on the life of Game Warden Ernie Swift after he arrested them for illegal fishing at the Winter Lake Dam in 1928. The gang was fly-fishing in a restricted area below the dam and ended up paying a $50 fine. Swift was tipped off, and he escaped before he ended up on the bottom of the lake—in cement overshoes.

COLBY

Colby cheese was invented in Colby by Joseph Steinwand in 1885.

World's Largest Wooden Chain. Photo by author, courtesy of Carl's Wood Art Museum

Eagle River
Carl's Wood Art Museum

Bavarian immigrant and onetime trapper Carl Schels, Sr., loved the forests of Northern Wisconsin, but not in the modern, take-only-photos-leave-only-footprints sense. When he found an interesting burl, he'd pull out a saw, cut it off, and bring it home for his collection. His dream was to one day open a museum to show off his wood specimens, carvings, and translucent veneer panels. That vision has finally become a reality.

This museum's late namesake would be proud of the institution that bears his name, now operated by his son, Ken. Carl's veneer panels are now displayed in the Translucent Room, backlit to expose the intricate wood grains of various species. Scattered through the main building you'll find Paul Bunyan's Pinball Machine, a miniature working sawmill, carvings, and other works of art. The museum grounds are covered with totem poles, a large wood chain whose links each weigh 30 pounds, over-sized chairs and boots to pose in, and cars that would look more at home in Bedrock than Eagle River. It's all guarded by a 5,000-pound grizzly carved with a chainsaw by Ken Schels. The adjoining Gift Shop has other works of wood art, only these ones are for sale.

1230 Sundstein Rd., Eagle River, WI 54521

(715) 479-1883

Hours: June–October, Monday–Saturday 9a.m.–5p.m., Sunday 10a.m.–4p.m.

Cost: Adults $4, Seniors(63+) $3.50, Kids(6–12) $3.50

www.carlswoodart.com

Directions: At the intersection of Rtes. 51 and M.

A CLOSE ENCOUNTER IN EAGLE RIVER

Few UFO sightings quite compare to a widely reported encounter in Eagle River on April 18, 1961. Local resident Joe Simonton discovered a chrome-plated saucer near his farmhouse south of town. While inspecting the craft, three aliens emerged. They were five feet tall, wore black turtlenecks, and "resembled Italians." One held a two-handled jug and motioned to Joe that he would like it filled. Upon returning, Joe noticed the aliens were cooking pancakes on a barbecue grill. In exchange for the water, Joe received four steaming-hot flap-jacks. He ate one, claiming it tasted like cardboard. The remaining three were later analyzed by the U.S. Food Laboratory and found to contain common baking materials . . . but absolutely no salt. Were these health-conscious Martians, sent to warn us of our impending cardiac doom, or Italian midgets out for a low-sodium picnic in their hovercraft? We may never know.

SUPER SNOWMOBILES

True snowmobile fanatics make the trek to Eagle River each January for the **World Championship Snowmobile Derby**, the North Woods equiv-alent of the Indy 500. Rather than race through the forests, contes-tants compete on a permanent oval track. Winners are inducted into the Snowmobile Racing Hall of Fame. The Hall of Fame Museum is cur-rently being moved from Eagle River to nearby St. Germain, where it will have a proud new home on Route 70.

Ice Palace

This is the type of oddball attraction that can be standing one day and gone the next, literally. Depending on the weather and the ice pack, the Eagle River Fire Department builds an Ice Palace after Christmas using blocks cut from local lakes. When finished, the structure is illuminated from the inside for a sparkling nighttime display. If the temperature cooperates, they try to finish it by New Year's Day.

But then there's the problem of global warming. Not only will the world's coastal regions be flooded as our atmosphere heats up, but the Ice Palace might go the way of the dodo bird. And even if the thing is erected, there's no guarantee it will stay up for long; once the melting palace appears unstable, the walls are knocked in so nobody gets injured.

Eagle River Chamber of Commerce, PO Box 218, Eagle River, WI 54521
(800) 359-6315
E-mail: info@eagleriver.com
Hours: Depends on the weather; call ahead
Cost: Free
www.eagle-river.com
Directions: Call ahead for this year's location.

Eau Claire
Paul Bunyan Statue

Many states, from Maine to California, claim Paul Bunyan as their native son. Given his size and roaming area, and his role in digging the Grand Canyon, pushing up the Rocky Mountains, and filling the Great Lakes, many states could make a case. The guy got around. Some say when he died he was buried beneath Rib Mountain near Wausau, but the people who tell this tale are usually from the Badger State.

Whatever. Putting aside the Great Bunyan State Debate, it bears noting the largest tribute to Paul within Wisconsin is in Eau Claire. It was erected in 1982 outside the Interpretive Center that bears his name. Babe the Blue Ox is by his side.

The Paul Bunyan Logging Camp has plenty to offer those with lumberjack fetishes. You get a feel for the industry in the Bunkhouse, Cook Shanty, and Blacksmith Shop. And for more on Paul, stop by the Tall Tales Room, where you'll see a replica of Paul's full-sized boot. It dwarfs the statues outside, and you know what they say about big boots: Big boots? Big feet!

Paul Bunyan Logging Camp, Carson Park, 1110 Carson Park Dr., PO Box 221, Eau
Claire, WI 54702

(715) 835-6200

E-mail: info@paulbunyancamp.org

Hours: April–August, daily 10A.M.–5P.M.; September, Tuesday–Friday 1–4:30P.M.,
Saturday–Sunday 10A.M.–4:30P.M.

Cost: Adults $3, Kids(5–17) $1.50

paulbunyancamp.org

Directions: Take Menominie St. east from Claremont Ave. (Rte. 12), turn north into
Carson Park and follow the signs.

He's a lumberjack, and he's okay.

Elmwood
UFO Capital of the World

Stop through Elmwood at any other time of year than the last full weekend in July, and you'll think the aliens have already come and gone—and took everyone with them! Not much seems to be happening in this sleepy little burg. But that hasn't always been the case.

The first UFO sighting near Elmwood occurred on March 2, 1975. A star-shaped light chased a local woman and eventually landed on her car's hood when she stopped to get a better look. A year later, in April 1976, another fireball, this one the size of a football field, shot out a blue light beam that blasted all the plugs in a police cruiser driven by officer George Wheeler. Little green men seem to have set their laser sights on Elmwood.

And Elmwood welcomes the extraterrestrial attention. A few years ago, Tomas Weber of the UFO Site Center Corporation in Chippewa Falls proposed a two-square-mile UFO landing pad be built near town. The project has yet to get off the ground, or on the ground. Nobody talks much about it anymore, perhaps due to some type of "shadow government" cover-up.

In the meantime, the town throws an annual "UFO Days" celebration to let the Martians know they're still invited. UFO Days has earthly events like beer tents, bands, and a fun run (we might see a not-so-fun run if a flying saucer shows up!), but they also crown a UFO Queen and have a parade with kids dressed up as aliens.

Elmwood Village Office, PO Box 26, Elmwood, WI 54740

(715) 639-3792

Hours: When you least expect it; UFO Days, last full weekend in July

Cost: Free

www.pressenter.com/org/elmwood/

Directions: All over town; watch the skies.

CUMBERLAND

Cumberland calls itself "The Rutabaga Capital." Each August it holds a Rutabaga Festival where the town crowns a Rutabaga Queen.

DANBURY

Danbury recorded the state's coldest temperature on January 24, 1922: -54°F.

Keep a close eye on the bunny. Photo by author, courtesy of the Moccasin Bar

Hayward
Moccasin Bar & Wildlife Museum

The Moccasin Bar is one of those rare private institutions bold enough to explore uncharted territory for the benefit of humankind. And where have they ventured? The world of anthropomorphic taxidermy!

Four dioramas pose North Woods animals in human situations as never seen before. Two bear cubs play a game of poker. One cub slips a carrot to a bunny in an apron for an ace to complete a royal flush. The other, eyes glazed in a drunken stupor, is served beer by an otter. In another scene, a beaver referee declares one boxing raccoon the victor while another lies outside the ring in a bloody pool. A skunk manager cries over the limp body. The third diorama depicts dozens of chain-smoking Tyrolian chipmunks in a beer garden. The final diorama is a North Woods kangaroo court, yet there are no kangaroos in Wisconsin. Instead, Judge Wolf comes down hard on a handcuffed badger who has been hunting out of season. Who caught the poaching badger? Sheriff Bobcat, that's who!

The dioramas almost detract from the fifth wonder of the Moccasin Bar, the world-record muskie mounted over the pool table, a 60.25-inch, 67.5-pounder caught by Cal Johnson. Just imagine this fish swimming around your legs the next time you take a dip in a local lake.

The Moccasin Bar has a sister establishment with a wildlife museum attached, but unlike the Moccasin, this place puts the animals in traditional settings. They've got even larger muskies, but these ones died of natural causes and are not as impressive as Cal Johnson's. The World's Largest Dead Muskie was found floating in the nearby Chippewa Flowage. The Wildlife Museum does have a few oddities, including a stuffed, now-extinct passenger pigeon, and albino specimens of a peacock, skunk, mink, pheasant, squirrel, and raccoon.

Moccasin Bar, 124 First St., Hayward, WI 54843

(715) 634-4211

Hours: Daily 9 A.M.–2 A.M.

Cost: Free

Directions: At the intersection of Rtes. 27 and 63, downtown.

Wildlife Museum & Bar, 15708 Rte. B, Hayward, WI 54843

(715) 634-3386

Hours: Daily 9 A.M.–2 A.M.

Cost: Bar free; Museum, Adults $3, Kids $2

Directions: South of the intersection of Rtes. 27 and B.

National Freshwater Fishing Hall of Fame

Bob Kutz had a vision in 1960 to build an Angler's Shrine in the heart of the upper Midwest and, to humankind's benefit, has achieved his dream. The most impressive part of this shrine to freshwater fishing is the 143-foot-long, 500-ton muskie that rises above a pool filled with live fish and snapping turtles.

As you might suspect, this is no ordinary muskie. It was built in 1976 and proudly (and accurately) claims to be the World's Largest Fiberglass Structure. Inside is a collection of artifacts related to the sport. A stairway ascends to the fish's gaping mouth, where you can stand on the observation deck and view the rest of the museum complex. Six couples have been married up here. On your way back down, keep your eyes peeled for Herman the Worm, the World's Largest Nightcrawler; he's in there (a real worm!) . . . but long since dead. Herman appeared on the *Tonight Show*, where he shot baskets and rolled over on his master's command.

Outside, on the grounds of the shrine, are even more large fiberglass models. Several are outfitted with poles and fishing line for gag photos and unbelievable "Fish Stories." A large building houses the bulk of the Hall of Fame's collection of 6,000+ lures, 350 outboard motors, Polaroids of record holders, rods and reels, and a couple of Bigfoot-like statues of early fishermen. Even if you have no interest in fishing, you'll enjoy this place.

1 Hall of Fame Dr., PO Box 33, Hayward, WI 54843

(715) 634-4440

Hours: April–October, daily 10A.M.–5P.M.; November–March, Monday–Friday 9A.M.–4P.M.

Cost: Adults $5, Kids(11–18) $3.50, Kids(10 and under) $2.50, Membership $25

freshwater-fishing.org

Directions: At the intersection of Rtes. 27 and B.

You're not visitors, you're bait.
Photo by author, courtesy of the Freshwater Fishing Hall of Fame

---

HAYWARD
The town of Hayward hosts the **Lumberjack World Championships** each July, with competitions in ax-throwing, log rolling, chainsaw carving, and other woodcutter events.

Screw this!

Hurley
World's Largest Corkscrew

Sometimes, size isn't everything. While this 15-foot corkscrew is impressive, where would anyone ever find a 40-foot wine bottle to open with it? Certainly not at the liquor store that bears its name. You couldn't fit the corkscrew inside, much less the bottle!

Even without a bottle this is a good place to stop for a gag photo. If you're limber enough to stand within the spiral cork-puller, you can tell all your friends, "I went to Hurley and was totally screwed!"

Corkscrew Liquors, 5819 W. Rte. 2, Hurley, WI 54534

(715) 561-5645

Hours: Always visible

Cost: Free

Directions: Just west of the intersection of Rtes. 51 and 2, north of town.

La Pointe
Tom's Burned Down Cafe

Where have all the hippies gone? In La Pointe, you can find them at Tom's Burned Down Cafe, and many locals are none too happy about it.

Shortly after buying Leona's Bar in 1992, Tom Nelson's investment went up in flames. He had long dreamed of opening a restaurant and bar. Rather than call it quits, he opened the Phoenix Gallery in the ashes of the former structure. The gallery transformed into Tom's Burned Down Cafe, sometimes called the Bar Tent, a combination of eatery, concert hall, and gallery for local artists. And because it's one of the few places on this oh-so-quaint island to deviate from the prevailing Midwestern-Maine decorating theme, some people got upset.

"It's an eyesore!" True. "It attracts bikers, old hippies, and other weirdos!" True. "The bands are too loud!" True.

It also siphons off all the fun people from the rest of Madeline Island, which, barring Tom's, isn't worth the time or ferry fare to get to. If you must go, proceed directly to the primary eyesore off Main Street (not counting the T-shirt shops) and you're at Tom's. Odds are you can find somebody in the ruins that will proudly tell you they were at Woodstock, even if they weren't, and ramble on about how things have changed, man.

PO Box 222, La Pointe, WI 54850

(715) 747-6100

Hours: Call ahead; it varies, man

Cost: Free

www.tomsburneddowncafe.com

Directions: Accessed via the Madeline Island Ferry Line (www.madferry.com, (715) 747-2051); from the Dock, turn right on Big Bay Rd. (Rte. H), then left on the first road.

Manitowish Waters
Dillinger Is Almost Nabbed!

In April 1934, after being embarrassed across the nation, the FBI was tipped off that John Dillinger and his gang (which then included "Baby Face"

Missed me, copper!
Photo by author, courtesy of Little Bohemia

Nelson) were hiding out in the North Woods at Wisconsin's Little Star Lake. J. Edgar Hoover put Melvin Purvis on the case and a swarm of agents descended on the Little Bohemia Resort. What happened next became the 1930s equivalent of Waco; despite (or because of) overwhelming numbers on the side of the feds, things went horribly wrong.

On April 22, soon-to-be-innocent-victim Eugene Boiseneau and two CCC coworkers were leaving the resort after a chicken dinner. Their car was ambushed. Trigger-happy G-men riddled the car with bullets, killing Boiseneau and injuring the others. Dillinger's gang heard the shots and dove out a second-story window, escaping north along the lake.

Nelson fired at agents from his cabin next to the lodge, then fled south along the shore. During the battle, the FBI riddled Little Bohemia with machine-gun fire, but never hit Nelson or the rest of the already-departed gang.

Nelson took several hostages at a nearby home, then was confronted by three agents in a car. Nelson jumped on their running board and fired his machine gun into the cab, killing agent W. Carter Baum and wounding two more. They ran off and he fled in their car.

The walls of Little Bohemia still bear the holes. Shattered windows were left in place with new panes placed over them. Personal items Dillinger forgot in his hasty retreat are now on display, including his clothes, underwear, toothpaste, and laxatives. At one time, Dillinger's father operated a museum in the adjoining cabin where Nelson stayed.

Little Bohemia is still a working restaurant and bar. Be sure to ask your server about the $700,000 in securities supposedly buried 500 yards north of the lodge next to two pine trees and an oak.

Little Bohemia Restaurant, Rte. 51, Manitowish Waters, WI 54545

(715) 543-8433

Hours: April–January, Thursday–Tuesday 11:30A.M.–2P.M., 5–10P.M.

Cost: Free

www.geocities.com/Athens/Olympus/4172/litbo.html

Directions: Two miles south of town on Rte. 51, on Little Star Lake, southeast of the airport.

Mercer
World's Second Largest Loon

Mercer claims to be "Loon Capital of the World," and Claire de Loon is its spokes-loon—not that she talks much. Oh, she used to give a three-minute chat about her fellow loons when you pushed a button on her belly. That was back in 1981 when she was erected by the local Chamber of Commerce, but today the 16.5-foot, 1-ton fiberglass bird sits silently beside the highway, bill upturned.

Maybe she knows there's another, larger loon in Minnesota, and that it floats on a lake where any self-respecting loon should be. Could she be suffering from loon-envy? If she's upset, she's not discussing it.

Mercer Area Chamber of Commerce, PO Box 368, Mercer, WI 54547

(715) 476-2389

E-mail: mercer.chamber@centurytel.net

Hours: Always visible

Cost: Free

www.mercerwi.com

Directions: On Rte. 51 in the center of town.

MEDFORD

Astrologer/psychic **Jeane Dixon** was born in Medford on January 5, 1918. She once claimed a gypsy told her as a child she would go into this line of work.

The world's first **Tombstone Pizza** was made by the Joe Simek family of Medford in 1962 and served at their Tombstone Tap.

Minocqua
Eat Like Paul Bunyan

You can work up a mighty powerful hunger from hours of miniature golf, antiquing, and paddle-boating. Take that tall appetite to Paul Bunyan Meals, located just behind a 25-foot lumberjack sign in Minocqua. They aren't big on formalities. No individual tables, just mess hall seating. No menus to speak of, just take what they serve you in "home style" bottomless bowls. Don't expect any peace and quiet, either. Paul Bunyan's is popular with large families who want to avoid the time-consuming process of having the children decide on what to order.

The restaurant is decorated in a North Woods motif and almost every wall hanging, grizzly bear lamp, or maple syrup jug has a price tag on it. No, this isn't a typical Cook Shanty—it's a gift shop that serves meals! Before you know it, you're walking out with a mounted critter head that you won't realize looks goofy over your sofa until you arrive home. By then you'll be hundreds of miles from being able to return it.

Paul Bunyan Meals, 8653 Rte. 51, Minocqua, WI 54548

(715) 356-6270

Hours: Breakfast, daily 7A.M.–Noon; Lunch, Monday–Saturday 11:30A.M.–2P.M.; Dinner, daily Noon–9P.M.

Cost: Meals $7–$12

www.paulbunyans.com

Directions: Just south of the Rte. 70 intersection on Rte. 51.

Phillips
Wisconsin Concrete Park

Fred Smith didn't slow down when he retired from lumberjacking. For a while he occupied himself as a one-man band at the bar he owned, the Rock Garden Tavern, playing the fiddle and jingling bells on his knees as he jumped from table to table. But then he got an idea to honor people, famous and not, with concrete sculptures he made himself. The Concrete Park was born. It was 1950, and he was 65 years old.

His first piece was a barbecue pit with two Indian heads, one for the Cleveland Indians and one for the Boston Braves, both of whom had been in the previous year's World Series. Fred made many figures of Indians whom he felt, correctly, had been mistreated by the immigrant population around him. He built 203 figures in all, cowboys, "coolies," Indians, soldiers, loggers, brides and grooms, and occasionally the well-known: Ben Hur, Abraham Lincoln, the Statue of Liberty, and Paul Bunyan. His final piece was a life-sized Budweiser Clydesdale team pulling a beer wagon.

Smith eventually couldn't continue his work and in 1968 landed in a nursing home; he died in 1976. Volunteers had been trying to restore the figures that had fallen prey to the elements. Then, on July 4, 1977, a violent windstorm blew down trees and damaged 70 percent of the figures. The Kohler Foundation, which had acquired the site, undertook a full and remarkable restoration.

Friends of Fred Smith, c/o Price County Forestry and Tourism Department, 104 S. Eyder St., Phillips, WI 54555

(800) 269-4505, (715) 339-4505, or (715) 339-6371

Hours: Daylight hours

Cost: Free

outsider.art.org/fred/

Directions: One-half mile south of town on Rte. 13.

Fred's friends. Photo by author, courtesy of Friends of Fred Smith

Poniatowski
Center of the Northern Half of the Western Hemisphere

There is nothing particularly unique about the community of Poniatowski, save for the fact that it's located at the exact center point of the northern half of the Western Hemisphere, according to cartographers.

What does that mean? Just northwest of town is a stone marker to indicate you are 90° west of the Greenwich Meridian, halfway to the International Date Line, and 45° north of the equator, halfway to the North Pole. And as you gaze around from this point you'll realize one thing: Halfway from all these places is right in the middle of nowhere.

Rte. U and Cherry Lane, Poniatowski, WI 54426

No phone

Hours: Always visible

Cost: Free

Directions: Just north and west of the Rte. U and Cherry Lane intersection.

Poplar and Superior
Bong Memorial

No, not that kind of bong memorial. Richard I. Bong of Poplar shot down 40 enemy planes in the South Pacific during World War II, two on his first combat mission, becoming America's Ace of Aces. For the most part, he flew *Marge*, a Lockheed P-38 Lightning named after his wife. Bong's skills as a pilot eventually got him transferred stateside to test experimental aircraft in Burbank, California. He died one week before the end of the war on August 6, 1945, while taking off on a test flight in a P-80 Shooting Star. His body was returned to Poplar for burial.

Both of Bong's Marges are still around. Marge the plane was once mounted on a pedestal in Poplar, but the cold winters and hot summers were damaging the aircraft, and a more permanent memorial was proposed. It now sits, restored, in an Anoka County Airport hangar in Blaine, Minnesota. The other Marge tours the country on speaking engagements to fund a Heritage Center to be erected in her husband's honor.

When finished, the Heritage Center will overlook the port of Superior, Wisconsin (305 Harbor View Parkway), and both Marges will return to honor the brave men and women who won the war. The plane will rest in a replica of a South Seas landing strip, with palm trees, thatched huts, and machine gun turrets.

Memorial Room, Poplar Elementary, 4956 S. Memorial Dr., Poplar, WI 54864

(715) 364-2766

Hours: June–August, daily 9A.M.–5P.M.; September–May, Monday–Friday 9A.M.–3:30P.M.

Cost: Free; donations encouraged

www.cp.duluth.mn.us/~bong/

Directions: One block north of Rte. 2 on Memorial Dr.

Poplar Cemetery, Cemetery Rd., Poplar, WI 54864

No phone

Hours: Daylight hours

Cost: Free

Directions: Take Cemetery Rd. southeast from the intersection of Rtes. 2 and D.

Rhinelander
Dead John Heisman

John Heisman had many football accomplishments. He supposedly invented the term *hike* as well as the snap from the center. Some believe he thought up the forward pass, but don't dare say that around a Knute Rockne fan. He was also part of the greatest blowout in collegiate sports history, the 222–0 victory of Georgia Tech over Cumberland in 1916. At what point did Georgia Tech decide enough was enough?

Heisman went on to coaching, piling up an impressive 184-67-18 record. To honor his achievements, each year the New York City Athletic Club gives college football's highest award, the Heisman Trophy, to the best player at the amateur level. The coach died in 1936 and was buried in Rhinelander. Cumberland alumni who still hold a grudge are not invited to the gravesite.

Forest Home Cemetery, 650 Washington St., Rhinelander, WI 54501

(715) 362-4172

Hours: Daily 9A.M.–5P.M.

Cost: Free

Directions: One block south of Rte. 8 Business, eight blocks east of Rte. G.

ST. CROIX FALLS

Women may not wear red in public in St. Croix Falls.

River Falls
Mollie Jensen's Art Exhibit

Although there is little left of Mollie Jensen's work, she deserves recognition for her independent spirit and wacky vision.

Mollie Jensen was determined to make her Wisconsin farm a thing of wonder for people to visit. She began by collecting a menagerie of misfit and cast-off animals. The most popular of her 150 pets was Ma, a performing black bear who had lost a paw in a car wreck and could no longer ride a bike in the sideshow. Ma would follow the Jensens to the local tavern, where she would drink bottled beer and shatter the empties on the brass rail.

The broken glass must have given Mollie an idea or two, because she began smashing her old dishes in the family's tub. She used the pieces to create elaborate mosaics on the living room floor during the winter that she embedded outside in concrete during the spring. Her first creation was a working windmill that powered colored light bulbs on its glass-encrusted base.

The most elaborate structure Mollie built was a "fireplace," a large outdoor barbecue where the family held picnics and parties during the summer. It quickly grew to form an enclosed shell, its outer surface covered with animal and plant mosaics. Inside, Jensen mounted her former zoo animals that had been stuffed by the local taxidermist.

Because her "fireplace" was covered with broken glass, it proved to be a hazard for drunks at her gatherings. Mollie's offspring tore down the structure after her death. The windmill is all that remains, falling in upon itself, a monument to a woman ahead of her time. For the complete story, check out Jensen's biography in *Sacred Spaces and Other Places* by Lisa Stone and Jim Zanzi (Chicago: School of the Art Institute of Chicago Press, 1993).

1684 County Rd. M, River Falls, WI 54022

Private phone

Hours: Private property; view from the road

Cost: Free

Directions: 8.5 miles east on Rte. M, just west of 170th St. on the north side of the road.

STURGEON BAY

Carol Lorenzen spotted a silver, egg-shaped UFO while standing on the corner of 3rd and Michigan Sts. in Sturgeon Bay on May 21, 1952.

Sayner
World's First Snowmobile

Carl Eliason built the world's first snowmobile in 1924 to putt around Star Lake. The vehicle was a hit, and Eliason inaugurated the Ski-Doo line of snowmobiles. He applied for a patent in 1927, but sold the patent to the FWD Company of Clintonville when orders from Finland became more than he could handle.

His original models are still around, and you can find them at the Vilas County Museum, all lined up in a row, among the 48,000+ other items on display. For true snowmobile nuts, you can visit the museum in the winter on your machine. The museum's windowed display is kept lit at night, adjacent to a local snowmobile path, and you can zoom by the shrine to see how it all began.

Vilas County Historical Museum, 217 Main St., Sayner, WI 54560

(715) 542-3388

Hours: June–September, daily 11A.M.–5P.M.

Cost: Free; donations encouraged

Directions: On Rte. 155 (Main St.).

Shell Lake
The Last Supper

Joseph T. Barta took four and a half years to carve this life-sized re-creation of Leonardo Da Vinci's masterpiece, but he wanted to do it right since, according to him, it had to "outlast (the) delicate painting which is flaking away from the plaster of the wall in Milan, Italy." Each figure is chiseled from glued two-by-fours bought at a local lumberyard. It is an impressive centerpiece to the Museum of Woodcarving, the World's Largest Collection of Wood Carvings by a Single Individual. Barta created 100+ life-sized figures and 400 miniatures over a 25-year period.

Barta's interest in carving began while attending the Art Institute of Chicago. After viewing his first composition, his instructors told him (according to Joe), "Your carving is perfect. Young man, go out into the world and make a name for yourself!" Joe wandered the United States and beyond, whittling small figures as he went, eventually settling in Spooner, north of Shell Lake. It was there, in 1947, that he began creating his larger pieces, most having to do with the life of Jesus.

Who thought lumber could be so spooky?
Photo by author, courtesy of the Museum of Woodcarving

Barta added features to his scenes that weren't always in the New Testament. For example, his crucifixion scene has a horned Devil taunting Jesus as he hangs on the cross. A midget stands nearby, giving him the "thumbs down." The face of the lion in Daniel in the Lion's Den is supposed to be Joseph Stalin's. Herod's face is actually that of Adolf Eichmann. Barta claimed he channeled the spirits of the persons he carved, which was trouble when he portrayed Judas hanging from a noose. "I never felt so mean; in fact, it was difficult to live with myself," he confessed.

Barta was not only an artist, but a poet, though it could be said his verse lacks a certain *je ne sais quoi*. For example, his poem "Our Mom" begins, "Our mom is fat, there is no doubt / She's plenty broad but also stout." Stick to the chisel, Joe.

Museum of Woodcarving, Rte. 63 North, PO Box 371, Shell Lake, WI 54871

(715) 468-7100

Hours: May–October, daily 9A.M.–6P.M.

Cost: Adults $4, Kids(12 and under) $2

museum.com/jb/museum?id=31775

Directions: One-half mile north of town on Rte. 63.

Spooner
Spooner Cowboy

What's a 30-foot cowboy doing in the North Woods? Not a lot. This hombre in tight bluejeans sports a big white Stetson on his disproportionately large skull and silently guards a go-cart track and water park north of town. One of his hands is turned downward, as if to make a fist. The other is palm up, looking for a handout.

Go-Kart Track, Rte. 63, Spooner, WI 54801

No phone

Hours: Always visible

Cost: Free

Directions: At the north end of town on Rte. 63.

Spring Valley
Crystal Cave

From the outside, Crystal Cave seems like a typical privately owned cave attraction. A rustic stone building. A gift shop full of geodes. A surface picnic area. But there's so much more beneath the surface.

Compared to other caves, Crystal Cave is short on stalactites and stalagmites. It makes up for this with bat colonies and goofy tour guides spouting strange tidbits about the cave. Need a little good luck? Walk once, counterclockwise, around a stone pillar in the first room at the bottom of the stairway. Do it twice and your fortune reverses. Over in the corner are the remains of a caved-in room where early owners tried to excavate beneath a nonrock ceiling. Perhaps they walked around the pillar twice.

Step into the Ballroom, the scene of two weddings over the years. Visit the Ghost and Goblin Room, where the frightening faces of Frankenstein, the Roadrunner, and Ronald Reagan have been spotted in the formations. See where thousands of bats hibernate in the winter and learn about the tons of droppings that were cleaned out before the cave was presentable for visitors. Experience total darkness at the cave's deepest point, 70 feet below the surface, and pray the guide doesn't lose track of the switch. And come prepared with a coin and a secret desire for the Make-a-Wish Room. It is said if you press the coin into the muddy walls and it sticks, your wish will come true.

Want more? Come back in the autumn for the Adventure Tour. Several years ago, the owners discovered new passageways to larger, undiscovered caverns. The new caves expanded the attraction three-fold, making it Wisconsin's largest cave. Rather than blast away for walkways as their predecessors had done, they decided to offer special tours for spelunkers. If you want to sign up for one of the three-hour tours, you must be able to squeeze through "The Box" in the Gift Shop. This journey is not for the claustrophobic or the overweight.

W2465 Rte. 29, Spring Valley, WI 54767

(800) 236-CAVE or (715) 778-4414

E-mail: cavebats@win.bright.net

Hours: May 15–August, daily 9A.M.–6P.M.; September–October, daily 9A.M.–5P.M.; April–May 14, Saturday–Sunday 9A.M.–5P.M.

Cost: Adults $8, Kids(4–12) $4.50, Adventure Tour $25

www.cavern.com/crystalcave/

Directions: One mile west of town on Rte. 29; follow the signs.

Washburn
Art Colony

There seem to be few communities in Northern Wisconsin where someone with a chainsaw isn't churning out black bear statues for the disposable-income crowd. The Art Colony is something unique, however. Their pieces have personality. Several local artists exhibit their creations in what looks like a New Age commune crossed with an Old Age logging camp. Most days you can find organizer Bill Vienneaux working on his sculptures outdoors, first with a chainsaw and then with a chisel. Most of the pieces on display "a smile south of Washburn" have been made to order and are not for sale, but you're welcome to look through Vienneaux's photo album and commission your own.

1825 W. Bayfield St., PO Box 154, Washburn, WI 54891

(715) 373-2708

Hours: Call ahead

Cost: Free

Directions: On Rte. 13 south of town.

Woodruff
World's Largest Penny

A penny isn't a lot, but don't tell that to Dr. Kate Newcomb, The Angel on Snowshoes. One penny might be worth only 1¢, but a million pennies really add up.

Newcomb devised a fund-raising effort for the Lakeland Memorial Hospital called the "Million Penny Parade." It started with kids at the Arbor-Vitae-Woodruff Grade School and eventually raised $10,000. Her efforts to bring health care to the folks of this region were featured on *This Is Your Life* in 1954, and thousands of pennies flooded in from around the nation. Before it was over, the hospital had received $105,000.

In Newcomb's honor, a huge concrete penny was erected in a local park. It weighs 17,452 pounds and stands 10 feet tall—not exactly able to fit in a gumball machine. Paul Bunyan might be able to use it, but Kate was out of luck.

It ought to buy a mighty big gumball.
Photo by James Frost

World's Largest Penny, 3rd Ave. and Hemlock St., Woodruff, WI 53568

No phone

Hours: Always visible

Cost: Free

Directions: One block west of Rte. 51, two blocks south of Rte. 47.

Dr. Kate Pelham Newcomb Museum, 923 2nd Ave., Woodruff, WI 53568

(715) 356-6896

Hours: Monday–Friday 11a.m.–4p.m.

Cost: Donations encouraged

Directions: At the corner of 2nd Ave. and Rte. 51.

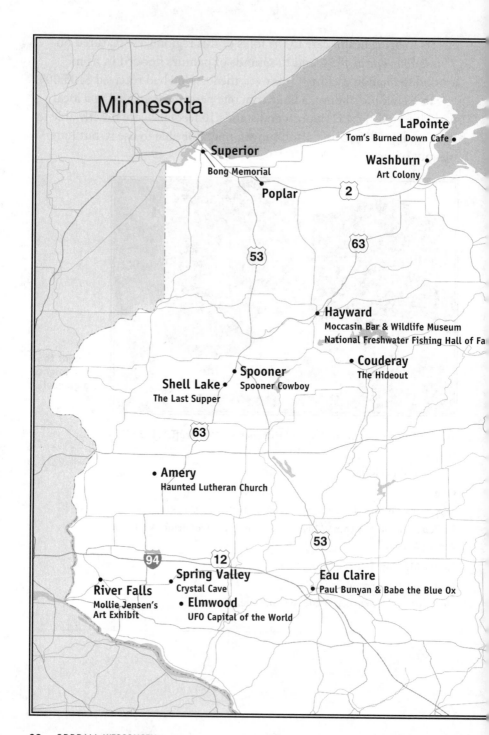

Minnesota

LaPointe
Tom's Burned Down Cafe •

Superior •
Bong Memorial

Washburn •
Art Colony

Poplar •

2

53

63

Hayward •
Moccasin Bar & Wildlife Museum
National Freshwater Fishing Hall of Fa

Couderay •
The Hideout

Spooner •
Spooner Cowboy

Shell Lake •
The Last Supper

63

Amery •
Haunted Lutheran Church

53

94

12

Spring Valley •
Crystal Cave

Eau Claire
• Paul Bunyan & Babe the Blue Ox

River Falls •
Mollie Jensen's
Art Exhibit

• Elmwood
UFO Capital of the World

Hurley
World's Largest Corkscrew

Michigan

Mercer
World's Second Largest Loon

Manitowish Waters
Dillinger Almost Nabbed!

Sayner
World's First Snowmobile

51

Woodruff
World's Largest
Penny

Eagle River
Carl's Wood Art Museum
Ice Palace

Minocqua
Eat Like Paul Bunyan

Phillips
Wisconsin Concrete Park

Rhinelander
Dead John Heisman

45

51

Aniwa
Behn's Game Farm

Poniatowski
Center of the Northern Half
of the Western Hemisphere

Birnamwood
Big Chicken
Remains of the World's Largest Badger

CENTRAL WISCONSIN

*D*on't let the Door County snobs tell you otherwise: Central Wisconsin is where the artists are. No, they don't paint shoreline landscapes of Lake Michigan lighthouses, knit cozy and expensive sweaters, or fashion wooden chimes out of teak and mahogany. Central Wisconsin artists use blowtorches and trowels, not paint-brushes and looms. Who needs beeswax and charcoal when you have cement, empty bottles, and junked cars?

And though most of these artists are weekend warriors, their works are not insignificant. On the contrary, they're massive. The Rudolph Grotto and Wonder Cave stretches a fifth of a mile through an artificial mountain of stone. The Prairie Moon Sculpture Gardens & Museum covers an acre of Mississippi flood plain. Each miniature building at LaReau's World in Pardeeville took weeks, and some-times months, to construct. The Paul and Mathilda Wegner Grotto, The Painted Forest, Tony's Fan Fair, Paul Hefti's Yard Environment—the list goes on.

A few of these artists gained recognition and respect during their lifetime, including Lester Schwartz and his Gloria Hills Sculpture Garden, and Clarence Shaler, whose works are scattered all around Waupun. Clyde Wynia is a relative newcomer to the Central Wisconsin industrial art scene with his Jurustic Park north of Marshfield, but he has already turned dozens of Dodges into dinosaurs.

The funky art would be reason enough to head to the middle part of the state. Throw in cranberry museums, motels guarded by Vikings, and restaurants shaped like pyramids, and you've got yourself a road trip!

Appleton
Houdini Historical Center

If you didn't know better, you'd swear that you'd stumbled into an S&M supply house—handcuffs, shackles, leg irons, collars with chains—but these restraints are only the instruments of Harry Houdini's trade. The Outagamie Museum has over 120 artifacts and 150 photos from the life

Escape from Appleton!

of the world's most renowned escape artist, handed down through Harry's brother, Theodore Hardeen, to fellow magician Sidney Radner.

You'll see the tub where Houdini was submerged in milk, handcuffed and bound, only to emerge unscathed with glowing, supple skin. Check out his early beefcake publicity photographs, wearing little more than chains and a determined glare. Or see the pair of handcuffs that once held Charles Guiteau, President McKinley's assassin. Houdini escaped from them without any trouble. Lesson? If you want to shoot the president, it would help to be an escape artist.

Houdini was born Ehrich Weiss in Budapest, Hungary, on March 24, 1874, but he grew up in Wisconsin. Contrary to claims made by his mother, he was NOT born in Appleton on April 6, 1874; she wanted his fans to believe he was American-born and chose their family's immigration date as his birthday. Harry's father, Samuel Weiss, was the rabbi for Zion Congregation (Durkee and Harris Sts.) and the family lived in a storefront apartment (Appleton St. south of College Ave.), long since torn down for a parking lot. Adjacent to the lot is a sculpture entitled *Metamorphosis* by Richard Wolter. The open, unchained box was dedicated by Doug Henning in 1985 and bears the name of the first escape act Houdini ever performed in public. Be sure to pick up "The Houdini Historic Walking Tour" pamphlet at the museum for a stroll past several Houdini sites downtown.

Outagamie Museum, 330 E. College Ave., Appleton, WI 54911

(920) 733-8445

Hours: September–May, Tuesday–Saturday 10A.M.–5P.M., Sunday Noon–5P.M.;

June–August, Monday–Saturday 10A.M.–5P.M., Sunday Noon–5P.M.

Cost: Adults $4, Seniors(65+) $3.50, Kids(5–17) $3

www.foxvalleyhistory.org/houdini/index.html

Directions: At Drew St., one block north of the river.

Joseph McCarthy's Home and Grave

Appleton is one of the few places in the nation where you can still find Joseph McCarthy supporters, and it's the only spot where you can still find Joseph McCarthy—he's buried here! Born in Grand Chute, the Senator was an Appletonian later in life, having a small home here from 1942 until his death fifteen years later.

McCarthy's life and legacy were built on a mountain of lies. He claimed he earned the nickname "Tail Gunner Joe" during his service in the South Pacific in WWII. True. But his fellow GIs gave him the moniker after he fired 47,000 ammo rounds at a coconut grove, just for fun. And that limp he supposedly sustained in combat? McCarthy actually injured his leg in a drunken fall from a ladder during a shipboard equator-crossing party.

McCarthy was a circuit judge before being elected an unremarkable U.S. Senator. To attract attention and improve his standing with the GOP, he came up with the idea of hunting Communists wherever he didn't quite find them. Trouble was, he could never get his numbers correct. How many "subversives" were there in the State Department? 205, 57, 81, 10, 116, 121? The number changed each time he wagged his folded laundry list.

Many Wisconsinites want you to believe McCarthy didn't have the full support of their state, but in his 1952 senatorial election he carried all but two Wisconsin counties. Conservative toady William F. Buckley, Jr., praised McCarthy for "a movement around which men of good will and stern morality can close ranks." But within two years, following the disastrous Army hearings, the U.S. Senate "condemned" him in a 67–22 vote on December 2, 1954. Dwight Eisenhower joked, "Did you hear the latest? McCarthyism is now McCarthywasm."

Joe crawled into a bottle. Just before his death he confided in a friend, "No matter where I go, they look on me with contempt. I can't take it any more." He didn't have to. Joe died of liver failure on May 2, 1957, at Bethesda Naval Hospital in Maryland. During his final days he had detox hallucinations and imagined that snakes were after him.

So what's left of McCarthy? "McCarthyism" is in *Webster's Dictionary* and Joe's tombstone overlooks the Fox River. Each year, on November 14, the anniversary of his birth, members of the John Birch Society, which is based in Appleton, hold a vigil at the grave of this twisted, misguided bully. They reaffirm their commitment to Commie-hunting, thinly veiled bigotry and all-around mean-spiritedness. It is, thankfully, a small gathering.

McCarthy's Final Home, 514 S. Story St., Appleton, WI 54914

No phone

Hours: Private residence; view from street

Cost: Free

Directions: Four blocks south of College Ave., three blocks east of Mason St.

McCarthy's Grave, Cemetery of St. Mary's Roman Catholic Church, 2019 W. Prospect Ave., Appleton, WI 54914

No phone

Hours: Daily 9A.M.–5P.M.

Cost: Free

Directions: East from Rte. 47, on the first street north of the river.

World's First Electrically Lighted House

Who would have thought this small Midwestern city could be the starting point of the greatest technological revolution in the modern world? Still, it's true. The Hearthstone, built by Henry Rogers and powered by the nearby Vulcan Street Plant (600 Vulcan St., since demolished), was the World's First Electrically Lighted House. The plant began generating hydroelectric power on September 30, 1882, and supplied enough electricity to illuminate 250 50-watt bulbs.

Four years later, on August 16, 1886, the Appleton Electric Street Railway Company (807 S. Oneida) began operation, connecting the previously unilluminated towns of Appleton, Kaukauna, Neenah, and Menasha. It was the Nation's First Electric Trolley System.

The Hearthstone is open to the public, and though gentrification of old mansions is common, this place still has its original Edison switches and chandeliers. Historians have kept the rehabbers' hands off this old house.

625 W. Prospect Ave., Appleton, WI 54911

(920) 730-8204

Hours: Tuesday–Friday 10a.m.–4p.m., Sunday 1–4p.m.

Cost: Adults $4, Kids(7–17) $2

Directions: At the corner of Prospect and Memorial, at the river.

It's packed on Mummy's Day.

Beaver Dam
Pyramid Supper Club

Have you ever sipped a Yummy Mummy, a Black Lily, or a Pyramid Punch? You're not likely to find them on many drink menus unless you frequent the Pyramid Supper Club—these Royal Nile Cocktails are the house specialty! But make sure you've got a designated driver, or you could end up in a sarcophagus.

The Pyramid Supper Club's dinner menu is less creative but still tasty. Though the decor is Egyptian, the food is 100 percent American: surf and turf. No Tasty Tut beef jerky, Cleopatra burgers, scarab salad, or Chicken a-la-Valley-of-the-Kings. The only Middle Eastern–sounding item is the "Spearamid" on a bed of rice. Don't forget, you're still in Wisconsin.

Inside this asphalt-shingled tan pyramid you'll find hieroglyphics, fake mummies, and a ceiling that gets lower around the perimeter. For larger parties, call ahead and reserve the King Tut Room.

Rte. 33E, Beaver Dam, WI 53916

(920) 885-6611

Hours: Monday, Thursday–Saturday 4:30p.m.–10p.m., Sunday 11:30a.m.–9p.m.

Cost: Meals $10–$18

Directions: On Rte. 3 between Beaver Dam and Horicon, just east of Rte. I.

Black River Falls
Orange Moose, Jumping Deer, and Sailor Mouse

It must be something in the Black River Falls water. It's turned two moose bright orange, caused a deer to expand to gigantic proportions, and persuaded a giant mouse to dress up in a sailor suit. You can find them all at the Black River Crossing Oasis, scattered around a man-made pond, silently guarding the semis and minivans.

These fiberglass creatures are great for kid photos while Mom or Dad is filling up the gas tank. Who cares if none of these animals belong together? In the future, the town plans to erect another statue, but this one's designed for the parents: the World's Largest Beer Stein.

Arrowhead Lodge Best Western, Black River Crossing Oasis, 600 Oasis Rd., Black River Falls, WI 54615

(715) 284-9471

Hours: Always visible

Cost: Free

Directions: Behind the Perkins Restaurant on the east side of I-94 at the Rte. 54 exit.

Where are my feet?

Buffalo
Big Viking

The large Viking statue outside the Viking Motel in Buffalo was not originally built for this establishment; it spent most of its early life selling "Kitchen Carpets by Viking." The company's slogan is still emblazoned on his shield. The 15-foot horny Scandinavian was fabricated in 1963, and when he retired he was shipped to this sleepy resort community along the Mississippi. To keep him from falling over, washing away in a flood, or being nabbed by rowdy teens as a prank, his feet were encased in cement. It gives the impression he ticked off a mob boss.

Viking Motel, 1675 N. River Rd., Buffalo, WI 54622

(608) 248-2590

Hours: Always visible

Cost: Free

Directions: At the intersection of River Rd. and 17th St.

Cataract
Paul & Mathilda Wegner Grotto, aka A Landscape for Peace on Earth

Paul and Mathilda Wegner saw the Dickeyville Grotto in 1929 (see Chapter 4) and were inspired to build one for themselves, and perhaps raise a little money, too. Admission to the Wegners' attraction was free, but photographs were not permitted. This allowed them to make money from picture postcards, as well as concession sales of sodas and food.

As part of their gardens, the Wegners chose to make a statement about the growing religious intolerance in Europe and elsewhere during the 1920s and 1930s, so they built the Glass Church. The Glass Church depicts 11 different buildings on its outside walls, each from a different religion, and has a Star of David over the front entrance.

And there was more they wished to commemorate. They constructed an enormous steamship, a model of the *Breman*, which carried the Wegners to America in 1885. For their 50th anniversary, the Wegners "baked" a stone wedding cake. After Paul died in 1937, Mathilda made a headstone for him and one for herself at the Cataract Cemetery. Mathilda died in 1942. The site was restored by the Kohler Foundation in 1986–87.

Contact: Monroe County Local History Room, 200 W. Main St., PO Box 419, Sparta, WI 54656-0419

(608) 269–8680

Hours: Daily, sunlight hours

Cost: Free

Directions: Just west of Rte. 27 on Rte. 71, 1.5 miles south of Cataract.

Clintonville
Four-Wheel Drive Museum

What would Wisconsin be without four-wheel drive trucks? Probably just a bunch of drunk guys standing around in bright orange hunting suits. And a lot of happy deer.

But thanks to Otto Zachow and William Besserdich, the deer are on the run. In 1908 the pair designed the first vehicle powered by all four wheels in this machine shop. They dubbed it "The Battleship" because it would go anywhere, and over anything, they chose. A year later they founded the Badger Four-Wheel Drive Auto Company, which was later shortened to the FWD Corporation.

Zachow and Besserdich's vehicles were widely used by the military, while other car companies supplied bubbas, and eventually today's urban professionals, with the off-road vehicles they so desperately need. The Four-Wheel Drive Museum is one of the few locations where these folk find common ground.

Walter Olen Park, 11th St. and Memorial Circle, Clintonville, WI 54929

(715) 823-2141

Hours: June–August, Saturday–Sunday Noon–4P.M.

Cost: Donations encouraged

Directions: One block east of Rte. 22, two blocks north of the river.

"A good way to kill old-age boredom." Photo by author, courtesy of Town of Milton

Cochrane
The Prairie Moon Sculpture Gardens & Museum

The Prairie Moon Museum was opened in 1955 by 71-year-old farmer Herman Rusch to put his tools on display and as a "good way to kill old-age boredom." He housed his collection in the old Prairie Moon Dance Pavilion and added other fantastic finds, such as a goat-powered washing machine and a tree that had grown around a scythe.

Three years into the project he decided the surrounding landscape needed something more and began building one of 45 different sculptures that eventually made up the Prairie Moon Sculpture Gardens. In the Gardens are a Hindu temple, animal sculptures, dinosaurs, a giant jug, two obelisks, an Indian on horseback, and a 260-foot wagon wheel fence running the length of the property. In addition, Rusch preserved and planted many rare native species of flowers.

When Rusch decided to hang it up, the place was sold and used as a dog kennel. The sculptures began to fall apart and lost their painted finishes. Then, in 1992, it was bought and restored by the Kohler Foundation and donated to the Town of Milton. The museum is long gone, but the sculptures have been repaired and repainted. The old dance hall has been converted to an interpretive center.

Town of Milton, S2921 County Rd. G, Fountain City, WI 54629

(608) 687-9874

Hours: Daily 9A.M.–6P.M.

Cost: Free

Directions: Two miles south of Cochrane on Prairie Moon Rd. (Rte. OO), just off Rte. 35.

Fountain City
Fountain City Rock Garden

John and Bertha Mehringer saw Paul and Mathilda Wegner's Peace Monument in Cataract (who had, in turn, seen Father Wernerus's Dickeyville Grotto), and built their own concrete and glass creation in the 1930s. The retired couple constructed the Fountain City Rock Garden over six years along the old Route 95 "dugway." It contains a windmill, birdhouse, wishing well, and fountain among its terraced gardens. The entrance is framed by two mirrored pillars adjacent to the vaulted sidewalk.

As with many private roadside creations, the Fountain City Rock Garden did not fare well over the years. The family currently renting the Mehringers' home are doing their best to clean it up and cut back the weeds, but it's a big task. The best time to see it is after the snow but before the grass starts growing.

Eagle Bluff, Old Rte. 95, Fountain City, WI 54629

Private phone

Hours: Daylight; view from sidewalk

Cost: Free

Directions: Old Rte. 95, just north and west of downtown.

Rock in the House

Talk about making lemonade from lemons! On April 24, 1995, Maxine Anderson was working in her home at the bottom of a Mississippi River bluff when a 55-ton boulder shaped like a Ding-Dong snack cake rolled in her back door. Or, more accurately, through her back door—and everything else. Surprisingly, the boulder stopped midway through the building and didn't end up on the highway or in the river on the other side.

Maxine and her husband, Dwight, sold their home to Fran and John Burt of Fountain City, who ran out the numbers and found it would be

Don't look at us—we didn't do it!
Photo by author, courtesy of Rock in the House

cheaper to open the house as a tourist attraction at one dollar a head than to pay somebody to remove the rock. Rock in the House was born! The Burts left the house in the same condition as it was the day the rock arrived. The TV is still on, and you're welcome to have a seat on the living room couch. The structure is stable, and you wouldn't know there was a problem when viewing it from the outside. The gaping rock-filled hole is more impressive from the inside.

Look through this hole and admire the awesome strength of Mother Nature. Remember how others have not been as lucky as the Andersons, like a certain Mrs. Dubler, who was squished by a tumbling boulder in 1901—in the home next door. Realize there are plenty of other rocks just itching to fall from the same bluff, through those trees. Then get in your car, and get the hell out of the way.

440 N. Rte. 35, Fountain City, WI 54629

No phone

Hours: Daily 10A.M.–6P.M.

Cost: $1

Directions: On Rte. 35 at the north end of town; watch for the signs (you won't see the rock).

CAMBRIA

Actress **Gena Rowlands** was born in Cambria on June 19, 1934.

Green Lake
Gloria Hills Sculpture Garden

Lester Schwartz sure liked white paint. Virtually all of the pieces in his enormous sculpture garden overlooking Green Lake are white. Gutted Chevy jumping through the air? White. Prancing horse silhouettes? White. Chameleons riding bicycles? White on white. The works are mostly made of cast-off industrial items and scrap sheet metal cut into interesting shapes—painted white, of course.

If there is a rhyme or reason to the collection, it's not immediately apparent. Someone keeps the grassy hill well mowed around the pieces, and you're welcome to stroll around and figure out what it all means. Don't worry too much if you don't get it; just enjoy the visit.

Schwartz assembled his garden between 1980 and 1996; he has since passed away. The Gallery he established on the site of his studio/home is still open and managed by his family.

W908 Scott Hill Rd., Green Lake, WI 54941

Contact: Schwartz Gallery, PO Box 10, Ripon, WI 54971

(920) 748-3720

Hours: Daily 10A.M.–4P.M.

Cost: Free

Directions: Just west of Rte. A on Rte. K (Scott Hill Rd.).

Hatfield
Thunderbird Museum

There aren't many museums like the Thunderbird around any more, and the world is a lesser place because of it. This privately owned collection of North Woods and Western artifacts is impressive enough, but its lack of institutional pretension makes it extra special.

Would you ever expect to see an eight-legged pig mounted and on display at a big-city natural history museum? How about a stuffed albino squirrel? A closet with an Indian mannequin propped up in a chair? On the Thunderbird's top floor the stuff is crammed in themed rooms with windowed doors, making you feel like a voyeur wandering through a boarding house. If you can guess the number of dolls in the Doll Room, you get a candy stick. In the basement are several dimly lit dioramas of local history, depicting Hatfield back when it was a logging camp. Somewhere in the place is an original copy of the Declaration of

Independence, but it's hard to locate, given the display cases jammed with arrowheads, antiques, and Western kitsch.

N9517 Thunderbird Lane, Hatfield, WI 54754

(715) 333-5841

E-mail: tbirdm@win.bright.net

Hours: June–August, daily 9A.M.–5P.M.

Cost: Adults $2.50, Kids $1.50

www.win.bright.net/tbirdm

Directions: Just west of Rte. K on the south end of town.

La Crosse
Heap Big Hiawatha

The 25-foot Hiawatha statue outside the La Crosse Area Convention & Visitors Bureau in Riverside Park once greeted travelers with a plaque that read "Me welcome you to Visitor Center." The concrete statue of the stereotyped chief was built in 1962 by Anthony Zimmerhakl. It weighs 25 tons, which, if you're calculating, is a ton a foot.

Hiawatha is there to remind visitors of a vision the famous Native American once had: No tragedy would ever come to the spot where the three rivers meet. Since the Mississippi, La Crosse, and Black Rivers converge in La Crosse, people sleep soundly at night. This vision remained true—until the World's Largest Six-Pack was painted over.

La Crosse Area Convention & Visitors Bureau, Riverside Park, 410 E. Veterans Memorial Dr., La Crosse, WI 54601

(800) 658-9424 or (608) 782-2366

E-mail: lacvb@centuryinter.net

Hours: Statue always visible; Information Center June–August, daily 10A.M.–5P.M.

Cost: Free

www.explorelacrosse.com

Directions: Where the La Crosse River meets the Mississippi River, at the end of State St.

EMBARRASS

The town of Embarrass draws its name from the French word for tangle: *embarrass*. French trappers thought the river running through it was "tangled."

The Six-Pack before being desecrated.

World's Biggest Six-Pack?

For many years this monument stood proud on the south end of town. These six tanks held up to 22,000 gallons of beer for the Heileman Old Style Brewery—7,340,796 regular cans' worth. If you drank a six-pack a day, it would have taken you 3,351 years to finish it all off. The Six-Pack was the crowning jewel on the Old Style Brewery Tour, unique in the industry for serving samples *before* you were escorted through the plant. They knew their customers!

But Stroh's bought the brewery in 1999 and stopped the tours. The Six-Pack was painted over and may even be demolished. Is there no respect for tradition, or beer? What would King Gambrinus, the 15-foot statue who guards the Six-Pack from across the street, say? Well, if he said anything, and you heard him, you'd know you'd taken one tour too many.

You can still see the white tanks and imagine them as Generic Beer. If City Brewery (the newest owner) receives enough encouragement, the tanks could be repainted with a new beer can's design. Let's hope so.

1111 S. Third St., La Crosse, WI 54602

No phone

Hours: Always visible

Cost: Free

Directions: At Jackson (Rte. 33) and Third Sts.

Paul Hefti's Yard Environment

Paul Hefti's brother once told him he should never do anything to attract attention. For many years, Paul took his advice. But long into retirement, Paul figured he had nothing to lose and started making whirligigs out of plastic bottles to put on his lawn. Soon he was building bottle fences, bottle people, and bottle Christmas trees covered in old stuffed animals. He made signs to announce holidays and to wish passersby well.

Paul has been attracting a lot of attention.

It is difficult for neighbors to object to the display because Hefti is likable and keeps the grass around his hundreds of creations neatly trimmed. If you're lucky enough to run across Hefti working in his yard he'll likely give you the guided tour. Each doodad has a corny joke or pun associated with it, and Hefti is patient enough to wait until you "get" each and every one. No doubt Paul's brother would disapprove.

515 Adams St., La Crosse, WI 54601

Private phone

Hours: Daylight hours; view from street

Cost: Free

Directions: At the corner of Adams and Fifth Sts., two blocks south of Rte. 33.

Recycling run amok.

Keep Up the Good Work—Just in Case

The Franciscan Sisters of Perpetual Adoration have been praying for world peace since August 1, 1878. Praying hard. Twenty-four-hours-a-day hard, seven days a week, 365 days a year, and more on leap years. Two sisters are always at the altar and are relieved in shifts, like a tag-team match. That's how their order earned its name.

Does it matter that during the last 120+ years the world has seen two World Wars, dozens of civil conflicts, and more senseless destruction than anyone cares to remember? No, because it isn't fair to judge these nuns by what *has* happened, only by what *hasn't*, and that's difficult to gauge. God only knows how much more could have gone wrong had these women not been on the case.

Franciscan Sisters of Perpetual Adoration, St. Rose Convent, 715 S. Ninth St., La Crosse, WI 54601

(608) 784-2288

Hours: Monday–Saturday 9–11A.M., 1–3:30P.M., Sunday 1–3:30P.M.

Cost: Free

Directions: At Market and 9th Sts., just north of Rte. 33.

Marshfield
Chevy on a Silo

No, a tornado didn't pass just south of Marshfield. That car is on top of that silo for a reason. In addition to being a working farm, this place warehouses cars for local residents. The one on the silo is a 1967 Chevy, and it's been up there since 1983. Owner Curt Evans hoisted it up with a crane. It's hard to beat the advertising value of a mis-parked vehicle.

When Evans isn't plowing his fields or stranding automobiles 40 feet in the air, he tries his hand at chainsaw art. A small roadside gallery houses sculptures of black bears standing around, rearing on their hind legs, and rowing cute little canoes.

8627 S. Rte. 13, Marshfield, WI 54449

(715) 676-3659

Hours: Always visible

Cost: Free

Directions: South of town on Rte. 13.

Jurustic Park

Something strange is going on in McMillan Marsh. Artist/paleontologist Clyde Wynia has been extracting extinct creatures from the mud that has trapped them since the Iron Age. Or at least that's what he tells you.

Some of these critters look suspiciously industrial, not biological. Take, for example, the dragon with the massive, spinning helicopter blade on its back. Dinosaurs' heads appear to have been fashioned out of oil pans. Storks and cranes have springy necks and claws that resemble gardening tools. What's going on here?

Ask Clyde's wife, Nancy. She'll tell you he's a retired lawyer, a part-time welder, and a full-time jokester. Hundreds of creatures inhabit his Jurustic Park, tucked between the trees along the Little Eau Plaine River. Dragons dangle from branches, huge spiders creep along paths, and birds with bell-bodies clang when the wind kicks up. Jurustic Park is best appreciated when taking a tour with Wynia, but only if you've sharpened your wit.

Be sure to visit Hobbit House, Nancy Wynia's studio inside the park. She's an accomplished glass sculptor and fiber-worker. Her work includes marbles, glass fish, eyes for Clyde's sculptures, knit sweaters, and full-sized soft sculptures of friends and family.

M222 Sugarbush Lane, Marshfield, WI 54449

(715) 387-1653

E-mail: clyde@tznet.com

Hours: "Most days"

Cost: Free

www.jurustic.com

Directions: North of town on Rte. E, then left on Sugarbush Lane just north of Marsh Rd.

Montello
The Boy Who Would Not Tell a Lie

In 1850, Mr. and Mrs. Samuel Norton, foster parents of orphan Emmanuel Dannan, murdered a traveling peddler on their farm southeast of Montello, then stole his horse. But they made the mistake of allowing Emmanuel to witness the deed. When law enforcement officials became suspicious, the Nortons tried to coach Emmanuel to substantiate their alibis.

But Emmanuel had been taught to tell the truth by his deceased English parents. The Nortons tortured the eight-year-old until he perished on November 30, 1851, then buried him on the farm. The police never had enough evidence to charge the couple with the peddler's murder, but they were able to convict them of first-degree manslaughter in Emmanuel's death.

The boy's body was moved to Greenwood Cemetery in 1858. Early efforts to erect a monument fell through when the man hired to raise funds for the honest child ran off with the donations. Not until 1954 was a granite marker placed over the grave of "The Boy Who Would Not Tell a Lie." It was dedicated on all-too-seldom-celebrated "Truth Day," September 14.

Greenwood Cemetery, Rte. B, Montello, WI 53949

No phone

Hours: Daily 8A.M.–6P.M.

Cost: Free

Directions: South on Rte. 22, east on Rte. B to 18th Rd.

Wisconsin's Largest Tree

There are many different ways to measure a tree. You could measure its height or its width or count the number of leaves on its branches. But the easiest method is to measure the circumference of its trunk at the base. Using that method, the enormous cottonwood on the courthouse lawn in Montello is Wisconsin's Largest at 23.2 feet.

That's what it measured in 1978 when a plaque was erected to celebrate the tree's accomplishment. At the time it was 138 feet tall with a 132-foot crown, but has no doubt grown since then. To see if it retains the title, bring a tape measure, record its new dimensions, then compare it to every other tree in the state.

77 W. Park St., Montello, WI 53949

No phone

Hours: Always visible

Cost: Free

Directions: On the courthouse lawn, one block east of Rte. 23, at the lake.

FOND DU LAC

Don Gorske of Fond du Lac has eaten at least one Big Mac every day of his life but seven since 1973.

Necedah
Virgin Mary Apparitions

Mary Ann Van Hoof began having religious visions on November 12, 1949, and didn't stop until she died in 1984. She would see the Nativity on the Friday before every Christmas. She witnessed the Passion of Christ each Easter. She saw Jesus open the Iron Gates of the Soviet Union, 18 years before Mikhail Gorbachev got around to it. In 1951 and 1952 the wounds from a crown of thorns appeared on her forehead during Lent. And strangest of all, Mother Cabrini showed up in 1975 and promised to "go with us" if we drove 55 mph, and not over 60, before the national speed limit became law!

The present-day Necedah Shrine (its official full name is Queen of the Holy Rosary, Mediatrix of Peace, Mediatrix Between God and Man Shrine) is filled with dioramas, statues, and mini-grottos, most of them based on Van Hoof's holy visions and proclamations channeled from on high. The Last Supper, Joan of Arc, George Washington, Abe Lincoln—they're all here!

The most interesting is the Crucifixion Shrine. During Lent 1955, Van Hoof was instructed to find a white crucifix and red and purple crayons. A week later, another vision guided her as she marked up the corpus with colorful wounds. Mary Ann had a field day, and sculptors translated her vision into the shrine you see today. The result is one of the most horrific, bloody, gouged, and battered crucifixions you're ever likely to see.

The best days to visit the Shrine are the anniversaries of Van Hoof's major visions: April 7, May 28, 29, and 30, June 4 and 16, August 15, October 7, and November 12. You're welcome any time, but if you come, you are asked to dress modestly, not to wear shorts, and if you're a woman, not to wear slacks, either. Wraparound skirts are available to hide your immodest 21st-century attire. As the entrance sign says, "As the women go, so goes the nation!"

Queen of the Holy Rosary, Mediatrix of Peace, Mediatrix Between God and Man Shrine, Rte. 21, Necedah, WI 54646

(608) 565-2617

Hours: Open 24 hours; tours daily 9:30A.M.–9P.M.

Cost: Free

Directions: One-half mile east of Rte. 80 on Rte. 21, follow the signs.

Neenah
Bergstrom-Mahler Museum

Neenah is one of the Great Lake's biggest paper-producing towns, so it seems only logical that it have one of the world's largest collections of paperweights, too. Remember the rock you painted for your father's birthday when you were strapped for cash as a child? Well, you won't find that type of crud here. The 1,800+ pieces at this museum are far too dazzling to hold down a pile of unpaid invoices.

The Bergstrom-Mahler's focus is on Germanic Glass, where small designs, like flowers, are magnified by the rounded contour of the spherical weight. Each paperweight is displayed in a lighted case to get the full effect of the pattern, and to keep out of the hands of the little ones. If you want to see how they're created, come in the summer when artisans braze weights while you watch.

165 N. Park Ave., Neenah, WI 54956

(920) 751-4658

Hours: Tuesday–Friday 10A.M.–4:30P.M., Saturday–Sunday 1–4:30P.M.

Cost: Free; donations accepted

Directions: Main St. Exit from Rte. 41, east to Riverside Park, turn north on Park Ave.

Is that all you talk about? Cheese?!?

Neillsville
Chatty Belle, the World's Largest Talking Cow and Replica of World's Largest Cheese

Wisconsin's reputation as the cheese state is well deserved . . . just ask Chatty Belle, the World's Largest Talking Cow. She just might be the world's only talking Holstein, for even her son, Bullett, is silent. But perhaps Bullett just can't get a word in edgewise. His 30-foot mother shamelessly plugs the local cheese-based economy and tries to dispel all those nasty rumors that the stuff is chock-full of cholesterol.

If Chatty were a real cow she would produce 270 pounds of milk each day and, at that rate, would take 40 months to deliver the 170,000 quarts necessary to produce The World's Largest Cheese, which is on display beside her. That's 43 years of udder-time for a real cow.

Sorry to say, the block of cheese you see is an inedible replica. But it is housed in the actual air-conditioned semi, the Cheesemobile, "constructed to cart the 34,591-pound block to the [1965 Cheese Convention]." The 14.5 foot x 6.5 foot x 5.5 foot fake block sits on its glass-enclosed bed. What happened to the original? It was devoured in Eau Claire in 1966, and many who ate it are still alive to tell the tale.

If Chatty and the Cheesemobile aren't interesting enough, come when the Wisconsin Pavilion is open to see a rock that resembles the Cheese State, "exactly [that] shape when it was dug out of the ground."

WCCN Wisconsin Pavilion, 1201 E. Division St., Neillsville, WI 54456

(715) 743-3333

Hours: Always visible; Pavilion open daily 9A.M.–5P.M.

Cost: Free

Directions: On Rte. 10 near WCCN studios, east of Rte. 73.

SAY "BIG CHEESE!"

Sadly for Neillsville, their replica cheese no longer holds the world's record. Wisconsin farmers topped their mark in 1988 with a 40,060-pound brick. It, too, had its own Cheesemobile, and it, too, has been consumed.

HILLSBORO

A mysterious hairless raccoon attacked a Hillsboro dog in 1992. Nobody could figure out why it was without fur.

MONTELLO

The granite for **Grant's Tomb** was quarried near Montello.

Richard Hanson's version of a lawn gnome.

Nelson
Warner Brothers in Cement

Richard Hanson has what many people rightly feel is the ideal life. He built a home for himself off a quiet road near the Mississippi River and spends a good part of the day reading old dime-store Westerns and doing odd jobs around the property. The oddest job he does is build a new concrete statue every year. He's been at it since 1986 and has amassed a nice collection of people and cartoon critters, all standing in his front yard.

Closest to the road are several pieces with Native American themes. Indians on horseback. Indians around a campfire. An Indian teaching his son to shoot a bow and arrow. A very large Indian doing nothing in particular. And one lone cowboy with a sheriff's badge to whom the Indians pay no mind. Back farther, closer to the house, are Bugs Bunny, Yosemite Sam, the Road Runner, and Wile E. Coyote, as well as traditional kid favorites like Little Red Riding Hood and the Big Bad Wolf.

What's next? Come back next year and see for yourself. Hanson is in no particular hurry.

S1509 Mill Rd., Nelson, WI 54756

Private phone

Hours: Private property; view from road

Cost: Free

Directions: One mile north of town on Mill Rd., just east of the intersection of Rtes. 25 and 35.

Oshkosh
Apostles on Parade

German immigrant Mathias Kitz was a furniture maker by trade, but the Great Oshkosh Fire of 1875 put an end to all that, and his shop, and the rest of the town's business district. So Kitz turned to making cigar boxes and tinkering with clocks in his spare time. His vision of an elaborate mechanical cuckoo clock based on Jesus and the twelve apostles began to take shape in 1889, and six years later the Apostles Clock was completed.

Every hour, on the hour, Jesus throws open the central doors (where the cuckoo normally is), and the twelve apostles march out in a circular route. As each figure passes directly in front of the Messiah, he turns toward Jesus and bows his head. With one exception. Judas, the last in the parade, turns his back when he gets to the front so you can see the sack of coins in his hand. Jesus lifts his arms toward his betrayer, but when Judas doesn't respond, Jesus' head drops.

You can catch this Biblical steeplechase at the Oshkosh Public Museum, a place with even more to offer than this remarkable timepiece. But a visit would not be complete without witnessing this holy cuckoo drama. Hour after hour, year after year, decade after decade, Judas never learns.

Oshkosh Public Museum, 1331 Algoma Blvd., Oshkosh, WI 54901

(920) 424-4731

E-mail: info@publicmuseum.oshkosh.net

Hours: Tuesday–Saturday 9A.M.–5P.M., Sunday 1–5P.M.

Cost: Free

www.publicmuseum.oshkosh.net

Directions: At the intersection of Rtes. 21 and 110 (Algoma Blvd.).

The EAA AirVenture Museum

This place was formerly called the Experimental Aircraft Museum but today goes by the name AirVenture. The enormous aircraft collection is equally split between well-known popular planes and experimental one-of-a-kind models.

Homemade craft are the heart and soul of the museum. Planes like the Aerocar I, a prototype of an all-purpose land and air vehicle, or the Stits "Skybaby" biplane with three-foot-long wings. How did these things ever get into the air and back down in one piece? Others look airworthy, but strange nonetheless, like the Crosley "Flying Flea," dubbed La Cucaracha by its creator, the JM-2 Formula Racer "Pushy Galore," and the Rutan Varieze "Very Easy." AirVenture has dozens of these funky fliers filling its hangar berths.

And then they've got the planes you all know and love. See replicas of the Wright brothers' Kitty Hawk model, a working *Spirit of St. Louis* copy winging over a diorama of nighttime Paris, and a Voyager cockpit (first round-the-world, nonstop flight) poured in the same mold as the original. For originals, they have the Double Eagle V gondola, the first balloon to cross the Pacific.

In the adjoining Eagle Hangar there's a salute to WWII aircraft with planes from both sides of the conflict. Inside the "Classified Area" you'll see where engineers are dissecting Axis aircraft beside a replica of the Fat Man atomic bomb. Part of an aircraft carrier's flight deck has smashed through a wall in the U.S. Navy display, yet the department store mannequins on its balconies seem unconcerned.

The newly added Hangar X contains the military's prototype F22 and a Podracer from *Star Wars: Episode I*—that's really in the experimental stage! Outside the buildings are more planes, including barnstormers and craft too large to park inside. If you come during the late-July AirVenture Fly-In, you'll see even more. The Oshkosh Airport becomes the world's busiest with 15,000 planes from around the globe. Many are experimental or built from kits by hobbyists, so keep watching the sky for something strange to happen.

EAA Aviation Center, Whittman Airfield, 3000 Poberezny Rd., Oshkosh, WI 54903-3065 (920) 426-4818

Hours: Monday–Saturday 8:30A.M.–5P.M., Sunday 11A.M.–5P.M.

Cost: Adults $8, Seniors(62+) $7, Kids(8–17) $6.50

www.eaa.org

Fly-In: www.airventure.org

Directions: East off Rte. 41 at Rte. 44/Knapp St. Exit, first right on Koeller St., and first right on Poberezny Rd.

OSHKOSH
By law, you can play neither fife nor drum on the streets of Oshkosh.

Save on airfare—come to LaReau's! Photo by author, courtesy of LaReau's World

Pardeeville
World of Miniature Buildings

Paul and Clarice LaReau use their free time well. The couple has constructed a miniature wonderland of 130+ famous buildings, with more every year. The most recognizable are the German Castle, the White House, the Statue of Liberty, Monticello, the Lincoln Memorial, the U.S. Capitol, and Mount Vernon. They also have the Chartres Cathedral, the Pyramids of Giza, and a Kentucky Fried Chicken restaurant. Most are made from Styrofoam, though some are wood.

Most models have a plaque to tell you how long the LaReaus spent building it. Add up the figures and you'll see 4,640 hours (580 eight-hour days) worth of work, and that's not including the time spent on the House of the Seven Dwarfs or the Miniature Life of Christ!

Lareau's World opens up a broad variety of photo opportunities. You can pose as a modern King Kong, ready to scale America's tallest building. Or are you Godzilla, rising from the East River to attack the United Nations?

LaReau's World of Miniature Buildings, Rte. 22, PO Box 548, Pardeeville, WI 53954

(608) 429-2848

Hours: June–September, daily 10A.M.–5P.M.

Cost: Adults $4, Kids(7–16) $2

Directions: On Rte. 22, south of town.

Pepin
Little House in the Big Woods

Before there was the *Little House on the Prairie* there was the *Little House in the Big Woods*, the home in which Laura Ingalls Wilder was born on February 7, 1867. Within three years of her birth the Ingalls family would move from their cabin in Wisconsin and bounce around the upper Midwest. Laura wrote a book about every last place they lived, starting with the Big Woods. She wrote her first story when she was 65 years old.

The original cabin Pa built is long gone, as are most of the Big Woods. You have to use your imagination to cover the rolling farmland with trees around this reconstructed cabin. You also have to picture the place without picnic tables and modern pit toilets.

In town, at the Pepin Historical Museum, are Ingalls family artifacts, a family quilt, and a letter written by Laura, as well as common household items and farm implements from her era. Each September the town throws a festival for their famous Native Daughter.

Ingalls Cabin, Rte. CC, Pepin, WI 54759

No phone

Hours: Daily 8A.M.–5P.M.

Cost: Free

Directions: Seven miles north of town on Rte. CC.

Pepin Historical Museum, 306 Third St., Pepin, WI 54759

(715) 442-3161

Hours: May–October, daily 10A.M.–5P.M.

Cost: Donations encouraged

Directions: At the intersection of Rtes. N and 35 (Third St.).

PARDEEVILLE

Pardeeville hosts the **U.S. Watermelon Seed–Spitting and Speed-Eating Championships** the second Sunday of each September.

Plover
Get Out, You Drunks!

When the Mulderink family converted historic Sherman House to a restaurant in the early 1980s, the former owners were not happy. But how were they to know? The former owners were long dead.

The Mulderinks found out just the same. It all began when the wine glasses began exploding. Doors and windows would open and close by themselves and there were footsteps in the halls. Why were the spirits upset? Apparently the original owners were staunch teetotalers. When the Mulderinks converted the master bedroom into a bar, it was too much for them to stay silent.

Eventually the Mulderinks sold the business; whether the ghosts had anything to do with it is anyone's guess. Today it's known as The Cottage. You can have a glass of wine at The Cottage but be sure to wear your safety goggles.

The Cottage, 2900 Post Rd., Plover, WI 54467

(715) 341-1600

Hours: Wednesday–Saturday 5–10P.M.

Cost: Meals $8–$15

Directions: On Rte. 51 Business (Post Rd.).

PORTAGE
Pulitzer Prize–winning author and dramatist **Zona Gale** lived at 506 W. Edgewater St. in Portage from 1906 to 1928. Another of Gale's homes, at 804 MacFarlane St., is currently the Portage Public Library. She was born here in 1874.

RIPON
Suffragist **Carrie Chapman Catt** was born in Ripon in 1859. She helped found the League of Women Voters.

SPARTA
Astronaut **"Deke" Slayton** was born in Sparta in 1924.

The GOP's newest recruit.

Ripon
Birthplace of the Republicans

When a group of Ripon citizens gathered on March 20, 1854, at the Little White Schoolhouse (then standing at the corner of Fond du Lac and Thorne Sts.), they had an admirable goal: to oppose the newly passed Kansas–Nebraska Act that allowed slavery to be extended north through the territories from its Southern stronghold to the Canadian border. Fifty-four locals, mostly Whigs and Free-Soilers but including a few Democrats, formed a new local party, and they called themselves Republicans. They were led by Ripon attorney Alvan E. Bovay, who had the ear of Horace Greeley. Bovay and Greeley had been tossing around the idea of a Republican Party for a few years.

Greeley, editor of the *New York Tribune*, encouraged others to join in this fledgling movement. The first Republican State Convention was held in Jackson, Michigan, on July 6, 1854. The first National Convention was convened in Pittsburgh on February 22, 1856. And four years later, Abraham Lincoln was elected President of the United States. So far, so good.

Though you'll never hear it recalled at this museum, Wisconsin's GOP history has slipped some since its founding. On the 100th anniversary year of the Ripon get-together, another Wisconsin Republican was condemned by the U.S. Senate for the tactic that still bears his name: McCarthyism. Ouch! That's got to put a damper on the centennial celebrations!

The Little White Schoolhouse has been moved three times before its current location in front of Ripon's 1857 Republican House. This historic structure operates today as a Chinese restaurant.

Little White Schoolhouse, 303 Blackburn St., Ripon, WI 54971

(920) 748-4730 or (920) 748-6764

Hours: June–August, daily 10 A.M.–4 P.M.; May, September–October, Saturday–Sunday 10 A.M.–4 P.M.

Cost: Free

www.ripon-wi.com

Directions: On Rte. 23/49, in the middle of the two-block "jog" downtown.

Rudolph

Rudolph Grotto and Wonder Cave

Unlike the redemption killjoys who usually seem to populate the shrine-building community, those who constructed the Rudolph Grotto intended it to be fun, even if it was a holy place. While training to be a priest in Europe, Fr. Philip Wagner was injured in an athletic accident. As did many of the faithful in 1912, he journeyed to Lourdes for the healing waters. Here he cut a deal with the Virgin Mary: If he was healed, he'd build her a shrine.

Mary came through, and so did Wagner. When he was transferred to the Rudolph parish (St. Philomena's) in 1917, he started working on his promise. First, he built a sledding hill for the Catholic school. This made a big impression on student Edmund Rybicki, who ended up doing most of the heavy work for Wagner in later years.

In 1918, construction started on a new church, and directly behind it a year later, Wagner began planting trees for the shrine. In 1927, the Rudolph Grotto started going up. Not everyone, however, was impressed by Father Wagner's extracurricular efforts. His bishop ordered the project stopped in 1949, angry that the parish church had not been finished "while the most elaborate developments are going on in this series of caves which are to me perfectly nonsensical." Thankfully, Wagner returned to his nonsensical work after completing the chapel.

The Wonder Cave stretches one-fifth of a mile through a fake rock hill. Recorded organ music is pumped into the cave to add an air of holiness as you contemplate the "needlepoint virtue" lessons along the path. Each lesson is a large tin sheet punctured thousands of times with a nail, spelling out a Bible verse or depicting a narrative scene. All are backlit with colored bulbs, giving the sense you're viewing a Holy Lite-Brite. There are 26 shrines inside the Wonder Cave, each more astounding than the previous. At the center of it all is a two-story grotto of Christ in the Garden of Gethsemane. Jesus prays, the apostles sleep, and an angel flies overhead.

Whether you're religious or not, you'll believe the Wonder Cave is a miracle. To honor Wagner, the parish was rechristened St. Philip's in 1961.

St. Philip the Apostle Church, 6957 Grotto Ave., Rudolph, WI 54475-9706

(715) 435-3120

E-mail: StPhilip@TZNet.com

Hours: Daily, daylight hours; Gift Shop and Cave, June–August, daily 10A.M.–5P.M.

Cost: Adults $2.50, Kids(12–17) $1.25, Kids(6–11) 75¢

www.tznet.com/rudolphgrotto

Directions: Behind St. Philip the Apostle Church, off Second St.

Sparta
F.A.S.T. Corporation

Few American corporations have done as much for the roadtripping public as F.A.S.T. If you've ever putted around a miniature golf course, locked up your brakes at the sight of a hotdog-shaped wiener stand, licked ice cream beneath an enormous fiberglass cone, or stolen a Big Boy statue as a senior prank, chances are you were dealing with a F.A.S.T. product.

F.A.S.T. stands for Fiberglass Animals, Shapes & Trademarks and it's the nation's largest producer of outdoor sculpture—and they're all fiberglass! Marble dissolves. Granite is too hard. But fiberglass makes roadside wonders affordable. F.A.S.T. is responsible for many of the giant roadside attractions listed in this book, including Hayward's Giant Muskie and Delevan's Circus Elephant.

Because these sculptures are formed in molds, the fields around this production facility are littered with hundreds of former projects. Come see where your local taco stand was born. It can be creepy running across the Jolly Green Giant mold broken into a dozen body parts, but you're likely to do just that. If you want to look around, ask a worker for permission before wandering off.

This facility is a working factory, so you'll see several new sculptures being finished for shipping around the country. If you're interested in something for the person who has everything (but probably not a 25-foot gorilla), ask for their current price list. A Chicken Swing will set you back $8,900, a Pirate (in a tub) $7,300, a Mexican Bandito Concession Stand $24,200, and that Big Boy? Only $5,000. Relatively speaking, he sounds like a bargain.

F.A.S.T. Corporation, Rte. 21, PO Box 258, Sparta, WI 54656

(608) 269-7110

E-mail: fastkorp@centurytel.net

Hours: Daylight hours

Cost: Free

www.fastkorp.com

Directions: One-half mile east of town on Rte. 21.

Stevens Point
Tony's Fan Fair

Tony Flatoff, by virtue of his art, is one of Stevens Point's movers and shakers—or at least movers. On his south-side property he's built and perfected a spinning, twisting artwork for almost half a century. He named it *Fan Fair*, and it is easy to miss if you pass by on a calm day. But if a breeze is blowing, you'll find it without any trouble.

Fan Fair is a large structure covered with more than 80 fan blades, many from old appliances. Flatoff, a survivor of WWII's Battle of the Bulge, has painted the fans and supports to grab your attention. Many have reflective surfaces and sparkle in your headlights as you come to a stop at the nearby intersection.

Flatoff has been working on his *Fan Fair* for more than 40 years. Because it has so many moving parts, the work today is as much maintenance as it is creation. Though it is a modest work, you'll probably come away a *Fan Fair* fan.

556 W. Harding Ave., Stevens Point, WI 54481

Private phone

Hours: Always visible; best when windy

Cost: Free

Directions: Just northwest of the intersection of Rtes. 10 and P.

Tomah
Gasoline Alley

Though cartoonist Frank King was born in nearby Cashton in 1883, he always considered Tomah his home. It was this small Wisconsin community that inspired his world-famous comic strip, *Gasoline Alley*. Several local landmarks, like Humboldt Hill and Fieting's Store, appeared in the strip, should anyone question that these toon folk lived in Tomah.

Gasoline Alley was an offshoot of a strip King was writing for the *Chicago Tribune, The Rectangle*. It was the first comic to feature a single dad (Walt Wallet finds the infant Skeezix on his front step on Valentine's Day) and the first to age its characters. Unlike Bart Simpson, Skeezix actually grows up. In the jargon of the comic strip world, the aging phenomenon has become known as "King's Law." So, as the readership fattens and sags, so do its favorite characters: Slim and Pudge, Adam and Eve, Joel and Rufus, and their donkey, Becky, are all headed to the Great Big Strip in the Sky someday.

Greater Tomah Area Chamber of Commerce, 306 Arthur St., PO Box 625AG, Tomah, WI 54660

(800) 94-TOMAH

Hours: Always visible

Cost: Free

www.tomahwisconsin.com/tidbit.htm

Directions: "Gasoline Alley" is the honorary name for Superior Ave.

Valton
The Painted Forest

The Painted Forest was built to be the sacred meeting space (Camp 6190) of the Modern Woodmen of America, a secret society much like the

Masons. Its plain white exterior hides the amazing piece of folk art inside. Every square inch of the interior walls is covered in a wraparound woodland mural painted between 1897 and 1899 by Ernest Hüpedon, a wayward artist. He was put up in a local hotel in exchange for his artistic services and managed to drag the job out for two years.

The mural depicts, both literally and figuratively, the initiation rites and benefits of joining this fraternal order. The Woodmen's main purpose was to provide burial fees for its members, but it was also a social club. To join, you were put through a series of wacky rites with great mystical significance. For example, inductees were blindfolded and placed on a mechanical goat, then bucked about in an attempt to knock each rider to the floor. This rite was depicted on the mural by a man with an arm in a sling riding a runaway goat. You can see it just above the door.

The Modern Woodmen are still around as a Fraternal Life Insurance Company, and you don't have to ride a goat, robotic or not, to get a policy.

Contact: Gordon Johnson, S-2110 Woolever Rd., Wonewoc, WI 53968
(608) 983-2352
Hours: June–August, Saturday 1–3:30P.M., or by appointment
Cost: Free; donations accepted
Directions: Off Rtes. EE and G, on Painted Forest Drive.

Warrens
Cranberry Expo, Ltd.

Wisconsin's biggest fruit export is . . . (drum roll) . . . cranberries! That's right, and this state has recently surpassed Massachusetts as the nation's largest cranberry producer. Cranberry Expo, Ltd., run by the fifth-generation Potter family bogs, is a monument to the farmers who make Thanksgiving tart each year.

You'll learn a lot of interesting facts at Cranberry Expo, the best-smelling museum around. Did you know *cranberry* is a bastardization of *craneberry*, the name given to the crane-shaped blossom of the flower? Were you aware cranberries are one of only three fruits native to North America, blueberries and Concord grapes being the others? And how many chances is a cranberry given to bounce on a picker to demonstrate its freshness? Seven bounces, no more, no less.

Cranberry farming is a specialized industry, and as such, the machinery and tools used to plant, grow, and harvest cranberries have to be custom made in Warrens. You'll see vine trimmers, cutting pushers, fruit pickers, berry sorters, and plastic baggers at the museum.

At the end of the tour you'll be given free sample of cranberry ice cream, pie, or jelly beans to entice you to buy cranberry-related items in the gift shop. And each year in September, Warrens holds a Cranberry Festival, where a Cranberry Queen is crowned with a ruby tiara.

28388 County EW, Warrens, WI 54666-9501

(608) 378-4290

Hours: April–October, daily 10A.M.–4P.M.

Cost: Adults $5, Seniors(55+) $4.50, Kids(6–12) $3.50

www.cranberryexpo.com

Directions: Four miles east of town on Rte. EW.

Waupun
Sculptureville

Do you ever feel you're being watched?

Clarence Addison Shaler was an accomplished inventor. Ever repair a tire with a Vulcanizer or slip a cover on an umbrella? If so, your life was touched by this creative genius. When Shaler retired at the age of 70, he tried his hand at sculpture. Waupun's public parks show the result.

Today, Waupun calls itself the "City of Sculpture." Most of the works were done by Shaler, though some were collected by him and donated. The local Chamber of Commerce offers a free map of all the town's pieces. Here are three of the best:

• *The Citadel.* A young woman cries on the steps of the Waupun Historical Museum while a fiendish devil looks over her shoulder.

No, she hasn't lost her library card. This 1939 Shaler piece is a comment on the rise of Fascism. The woman represents Europe. Guess who the devil is?

- *Dawn of Day*. Carved by Shaler in 1931, this statue of a nude woman appears to be running toward the entrance to City Hall. Is she applying stag for a marriage license? Has she lost all her belongings to high property taxes? Is she just a common streaker? You be the judge.
- *The End of the Trail*. The world-famous sculpture by James Earle Fraser might be the third generation of the masterpiece, but it's the oldest version existing today. The piece shows a Native American slumped over on his horse, both of which have seen better days. It was first created in 1894 at the Art Institute of Chicago, then Fraser re-created it in 1915 for San Francisco's Panama-Pacific Exposition. Both incarnations were plaster and were destroyed. The Waupun statue is bronze.

The Citadel, Waupun Heritage Museum, Madison and Jefferson Sts., Waupun, WI 53963
Directions: On the east side of the museum, on Rte. 26.
Dawn of Day, City Hall, 201 E. Main St., Waupun, WI 53963
Directions: On Route 49 (Main) and Forest, on the north side of the courthouse.
The End of the Trail, Shaler Park, Madison St., Waupun, WI 53963
Directions: Rte. 26 at the river, across from the high school in Forest Mound Cemetery, north of Rte. 49.
Chamber of Commerce, 121 E. Main St., Suite A, Waupun, WI 53963
(920) 324-3491
E-mail: info@waupunchamber.com
Hours: Always visible
Cost: Free
www.waupunchamber.com

Westfield
A Lost Wagon Train

The enormous "pioneer" in the parking lot of the Pioneer Motor Inn in Westfield looks both out of place and out of proportion. First of all, with his coonskin cap and long musket, he looks more like a French trapper than a pioneer, and secondly, he's twice the size of the oxen pulling his covered wagon. And what are those concrete deer doing at his feet, and why aren't those oxen hitched to the wagon? This whole arrangement begs more questions than it answers, which is a good reason you should never draw historical conclusions from commercial displays.

Westfield Pioneer Motor Inn, 242 N. Pioneer Park Rd., Westfield, WI 53964

(608) 296-2135

Hours: Always visible

Cost: Free

Directions: Just west of the Rte. J exit from Rte. 51.

Winneconne
Winneconne Secedes

You've no doubt studied the Civil War, but did you know there has been a recent attempt to break away from the Union, or at least the state of Wisconsin?

The trouble began when Winneconne was left off the official Wisconsin highway map in 1967. The outraged citizenry concluded if Wisconsin didn't want them, they didn't want Wisconsin. They drafted a Declaration of Independence and sent it to the governor. On June 22, they seceded and erected a toll bridge on Route 116 over the Wolf River.

These actions got the governor's attention and soon he issued an order that Winneconne be returned to the state map. Satisfied their demands had been met, Winneconne rescinded its declaration on June 23 and the toll booth came down. A bloody war pitting brother against brother was avoided, but let this be a cautionary tale to mapmakers everywhere.

Winneconne Area Chamber of Commerce, PO Box 126, Winneconne, WI 54986

(920) 582-4775

E-mail: chamber@winneconne.org

Hours: Always visible

Cost: Free

www.winneconne.org

Directions: The toll booth sat on the Rte. 116 bridge in the middle of town.

Pepin
Little House in the Big Woods

Nelson
Warner Brothers in Cement

Cochrane
The Prairie Moon Sculpture Gardens & Museum

Buffalo
Big Viking

Fountain City
Fountain City Rock Garden
Rock in the House

12

Neillsville
Chatty Belle & World's Largest Cheese

Marshfield
Chevy on a Silo
Jurustic Park

Hatfield
Thunderbird Museum

94

53

Black River Falls
Orange Moose, Jumping Deer, and Sailor Mouse

Warrens
Cranberry Expo,

Cataract
Paul & Mathilda Wegner Grotto

Sparta
F.A.S.T. Corporation

Tomah
Gasoline Alley

12

La Crosse
Heap Big Hiawatha
World's Biggest Six-Pack?
Keep Up the Good Work—Just in Case
Paul Hefti's Yard Environment

Minnesota

Valton
The Painted Fore

Iowa

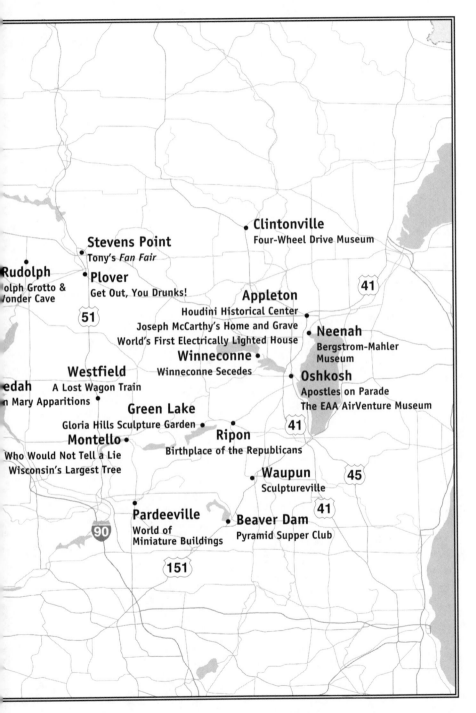

Clintonville
Four-Wheel Drive Museum

Stevens Point
Tony's *Fan Fair*

Rudolph
olph Grotto &
/onder Cave

Plover
Get Out, You Drunks!

Appleton
Houdini Historical Center
Joseph McCarthy's Home and Grave
World's First Electrically Lighted House

Neenah
Bergstrom-Mahler
Museum

Winneconne
Winneconne Secedes

Westfield
A Lost Wagon Train

edah
n Mary Apparitions

Oshkosh
Apostles on Parade
The EAA AirVenture Museum

Green Lake
Gloria Hills Sculpture Garden

Montello
Who Would Not Tell a Lie
Wisconsin's Largest Tree

Ripon
Birthplace of the Republicans

Waupun
Sculptureville

Pardeeville
World of
Miniature Buildings

Beaver Dam
Pyramid Supper Club

3

THE DELLS

*F*irst, the good news. There is still no place in the Cheese State with a higher concentration of weirdness than the Wisconsin Dells. If you prefer staying in one place on vacation, come to the Dells and crack open the savings account—this type of fun doesn't come cheap. You'll find museums for robots, UFOs, and snakes; waterski thrill shows and haunted mansions; amphibious troop carriers and bungee towers; and more go-carts, miniature golf courses, and water slides than you can shake a block of fudge at.

Now for the bad news: The Dells used to be weirder. As the region expands into Wisconsin's version of Orlando, some of the quirkier attractions have met the wrecking ball. A few years ago, sacred fiberglass figures from Biblical Gardens were auctioned off to the highest bidder. Xanadu, the House of the Future, met an even more tragic fate. The bubble-shaped Styrofoam structure was bulldozed to make way for a miniature golf course. And what about the energy-efficient Sybarite Underground Home? Buried. The Enchanted Forest? Chopped down. Prehistoric Land? It's history.

So see the Dells now, before the resorts unplug Robot World, sink the Waterski Show, exorcise the Haunted Mansion, and "convert" the Serpent Safari into a handbag shop.

Baraboo
Circus World Museum

Years ago, the Ringling family lived in Baraboo, where their father was a harness maker. Five of the Ringling brothers decided to organize a circus in 1884. It consisted of a trained goat, Zachary the horse, and a few rabbits and chickens. Some show. But before long they were billing themselves as "The Ringling Brothers' Stupendous Consolidation of Seven Monstrous Shows," setting the standard for bombast and bunkum that would put them in the leagues with P. T. Barnum. For example, when they purchased a hyena for their menagerie, its common name was not enough; they dubbed him "The Hideous Hyena *Striata Gigantium*, the Mammoth, Midnight Marauding, Man-Eating Monstrosity."

The Ringling Brothers' Circus wintered in Baraboo from 1884 to 1918, and it was here they bought the Barnum and Bailey Circus in 1906 from Bailey's widow for $410,000, forming the Ringling Brothers, Barnum & Bailey Circus we know today. Five other minor circuses also called Baraboo home, which is why the town calls itself "The Capital of the American Circus" today (though most circuses are now based in Florida).

Consequently, it only makes sense that Baraboo be the location of Circus World Museum. The complex spreads out over 50 acres on the Ringling Brothers' original site. They have more than 170 wagons, a Big Top, magic shows, miniature carnivals, steam calliope concerts, elephant rides, and plenty of clowns to keep the kids in check and the parents creeped out. Best of all, they've got a Freak Show tent with replicas of the Cardiff Giant, the Bearded Lady, Jo-Jo the Dog-Faced Boy, and the original Siamese Twins. Circus World has the world's largest archive of circus material and famous artifacts from the industry, including Clyde Beatty's lion-taming chair, outfits worn by Gunther Gebel-Williams, a balancing chair from the Flying Wallendas, a human cannon used by Frank "Fearless" Gregg, and the tusks of famous elephants.

426 Water St., Baraboo, WI 53913-2597

(608) 356-8341 or (608) 356-0800

Hours: Daily 9A.M.–6P.M. (9:30P.M. summer); Big Top shows, May–August 11A.M. and 3P.M. (and 7:30P.M. July–August)

Cost: Adults $14, Seniors(65+) $13, Kids(3–11) $7

www.circusworldmuseum.com

Directions: Follow signs in town along Rte. 113 (Water St.).

International Crane Foundation

Though cranes have suffered greatly at the hands of human development, they've fared better than the passenger pigeon, though that's not saying much. Much of the thanks for preserving these lanky birds goes to the International Crane Foundation (ICF). They have representatives of all 15 species of cranes, including the endangered whooping crane. These birds come from around the world, not just Wisconsin, and are part of the ICF's breeding and release program.

During hatching season, naturalists are required to "dance" with the females to get them in the mood. These rituals are closed to the public because visitors would distract the cranes and laugh at the staff. When crane chicks are born, handlers limit their contact with the birds to avoid "imprinting." A young chick will imprint the notion that it's a human if allowed to see too many people.

Three tours leave the ICF Center daily, but you're welcomed to take a self-guided walk around the grounds. If you take a tour, ask your guide to show you the mating dance.

E11376 Shady Lane Rd., PO Box 447, Baraboo, WI 53913

(608) 356-9462

E-mail: cranes@savingcranes.org

Hours: May–October, daily 9A.M.–5P.M.; tours 10A.M., 1P.M., and 3P.M.

Cost: Adults $7, Seniors $6, Kids(5–11) $3.50

www.savingcranes.org

Directions: Two roads south of I-90/94 off Rte. 12, heading east.

BARABOO

After leaving Wisconsin for Sarasota, Florida, **John Ringling** was often heard denouncing his hometown as filled with "hick Barabooians."

Devil's Lake near Baraboo was a thriving resort in the late 1800s, but tourism dropped off after people started dying of typhoid fever. Today it is a state park.

A Punctual UFO

Most of the Dells' weirdness can be easily explained, but folks near Baraboo have been sighting the same orange UFO at the same time and place for years. Explain *that*. Weather permitting, it rises from the Baraboo Bluffs and flies off to the southeast between 8:00 and 8:30 A.M., just off Route 113.

Nobody has been able to explain the phenomenon, and like the pot of gold at the end of the rainbow, nobody has been able to approach the craft as it sits on the ground. Could it be aliens emerging from a netherworld porthole at Devil's Lake? Perhaps it's Bigfoot being dropped off on its morning commute? Or is it the active imagination of a bunch of bathtub-gin-soaked circus carnies? Hard to say, but I'm betting on the carnies.

Manchester Rd. and Rte. 113, Baraboo, WI 53913

No phone

Hours: Daily 8:00–8:30A.M.

Cost: Free

Directions: Southeast of the intersection, over the bluffs.

Reedsburg
Museum of Norman Rockwell Art

In the promotional material for this museum, the curators admit there is a better Rockwell museum in Stockbridge, Massachusetts, and that the illustrator never set foot in this small town, but Agnes Moorehead did, and she once modeled for one of his *Saturday Evening Post* covers. They try to entice you by revealing how Rockwell sometimes used nude models—and they weren't all stuffed Thanksgiving turkeys!

There are over 4,000 original covers and illustrations from Rockwell's career on display at the Museum of Norman Rockwell Art. Though best known for his work on the *Saturday Evening Post*, he also did illustrations for *Collier's*, *Boy's Life*, *Leslie's*, *The Literary Digest*, *The Country Gentleman*, *Red Cross Magazine*, and Ma Bell phone books. He even painted several album covers for Pure Prairie League and a portrait of the First Lady used on the sheet music for "Lady Bird Cha Cha Cha."

Framed magazine covers might seem a poor substitute for art lovers, but in many cases, they're the best anyone has of Rockwell's work. Originals are hard to come by because he used cheap materials that quickly deteriorated. The prints are often in better shape than his originals.

When you're done in the museum, the basement of this former church has a well-stocked gift shop with Rockwell reproductions, Rockwell plates, Rockwell figurines, Rockwell mugs—Rockwell you-name-its.

227 S. Park St., Reedsburg, WI 53959

(888) 524-2123 or (608) 524-2123

E-mail: nrmusrdb@mwt.net

Hours: May–October, daily 9A.M.–5P.M.; November–April, daily 10A.M.–3P.M.

Cost: Adults $5, Seniors $4, Kids(13–18) $2.50

www.rockwellart-reedsburg.com

Directions: Two blocks south of Rte. 23, one block east of Rte. V.

Beware the man with a plunger!

Wisconsin Dells
Adventures in Time

Adventures in Time is perhaps the oddest attraction in the Dells. Is it a spook house? Is it a comedy show? Is it a twisted history lesson? God only knows.

The premise makes sense when you enter. For a mere $6.95 you are offered the opportunity to travel through time to a historic era of your choice, led by a helpful teenage Time Pilot. You're ushered into a waiting area that looks like a basement rec room, where things start getting strange. An odd voice talks to you from behind a slightly opened door, its questions punctuated with farting sounds, then asks for your ticket. A Time Pilot arrives and demands you produce the now-gone ticket. When you tell her where it went, she screams at the disembodied voice to return it. The ticket slides out from beneath the door and your adventure begins. *What the hell was that all about?*

You enter a Time Capsule through a secret passage from the rec room, place your hands on a sparking Ouija board–like device, and are asked where you would like to travel in time. You realize whatever chance you had of witnessing the signing of the Declaration of Independence or Elvis in Hawaii are slim when your Pilot warns, "Sometimes this thing doesn't work like it should," bangs on the wooden console, and cautions you about Time Bandits.

Sure enough, the Capsule misfires and you find yourself in 1920s Chicago, but since the Pilot has to pay off a gambling debt to Al Capone, maybe this isn't such a bad stop. She leaves you sitting on a thrift-store couch, but before she does, implores you to scream out "TIME BANDIT!" if anything strange pops up.

What happens next is no great surprise. A Time Bandit jumps in wearing a life preserver and pith helmet, swinging a toilet plunger (who knows why?). It wouldn't be fair to give away the gags you'll endure while chasing this farting goofball through time. But through it all you'll duck artillery fire on a WWI battlefield, gaze at the wonders of ancient Egypt, crash at a psychedelic 1960s hippie pad, belly up to a saloon in the Wild West, all the while terrorized by that plunger guy.

Adventures in Time is strangely entertaining and highly recommended, but if anyone figures it out, could you please explain it to me? I'm no Einstein.

512 Wisconsin Dells Pkwy., Wisconsin Dells, WI 53965

(888) 413-5946 or (608) 253-5278

Hours: June–August, daily 10A.M.–11:30P.M.

Cost: Adults $6.95, Kids(12 and under) $5.95

www.timefantasy.com

Directions: At the intersection of Wisconsin Dells Pkwy. (Rte. 12) and Rte. A.

American UFO & Sci-Fi Museum

The American UFO & Sci-Fi Museum, from its advertisements, sounds like quite an operation. Alien Hall! The Ultimate Roswell Experience! The UFO Research Gallery! Exhibits on the Alien Autopsy and Area 51! A Galactic Gift Shop! All this crammed in a dinky downtown storefront?

Yep. The museum has about a dozen scenes. Most are filled with creature models from *Aliens* and *Independence Day* (made from the same molds as the originals), reproductions of *The Terminator, Mars Attacks, Planet of the Apes, Star Wars,* and *Star Trek.* Two remaining dioramas show an alien autopsy and a zombified painter hovering in space while a "gray" looks on. The Research Gallery consists of laminated photocopies of UFO reports stapled to the walls and a large map of Wisconsin pointing out the state's most celebrated cases.

Before you know it, you're back at the Galactic Gift Shop, wondering. Where was the Roswell UFO? The chips extracted from abductees' brains? The anal probes? Why hasn't a Wisconsin good ol' boy shot, stuffed, and mounted a little green man? Or maybe there was more there than met the eye—perhaps your memory has been erased like those of so many other unfortunate abductees. Check your watch. Are you "missing" an hour?

740 Eddy St., Wisconsin Dells, WI 53965

(608) 253-5055

E-mail: info@ufomuseum.com

Hours: June–August, daily 9A.M.–6P.M.; April–May, September–October, Saturday–Sunday 9A.M.–6P.M.

Cost: Adults $5.95, Seniors $3.95, Kids(6–11) $3.95

www.ufomuseum.com

Directions: Downtown, south of Broadway, one block east of the river.

HITTING THE LINKS IN THE DELLS

For sports fanatics, check out the Dells' miniature golf establishments. Two of the largest are Pirate's Cove and Shipwreck Lagoon. Pirate's Cove (Rtes. B and 12/16) contain five 18-hole courses weaving around 17 waterfalls. Shipwreck Lagoon (213 Windy Hill Rd.) offers only three courses, but it has caves, tunnels, and lookout towers.

Trade in your chariot.

Big Chief Go-Kart World

Go-cart tracks are not unique in the Dells, but Big Chief Go-Kart World is something special. It's America's largest go-cart park, split between two locations. At last count they had 20 tracks, including an elevated course that passes through the side of a 60-foot Trojan Horse, a Poseidon Underwater Track where you traverse tunnels beneath a pond, and a Big Chief Slick Track, oiled up to make things interesting.

Big Chief once had a Native American theme, yet only the name remains. They've replaced tomahawking Indians with Greek gods and added three wooden roller coasters in Park #2: Zeus, Cyclops, and Pegasus. Park #1 is primarily go-carts and retains geography-themed tracks like the San Francisco Freeway and the L.A. Freeway, minus the road rage shootings and slappings from Zsa Zsa.

PO Box 5, Wisconsin Dells, WI 53965

(608) 254-2490

Hours: June–August, daily 10A.M.–10P.M.

Cost: $5.50/ride, 4 rides for $20, $32 for half-day all-ride pass

www.dells-delton.com/bigchief.html

www.dellschamber.com/BigChief/index.htm

Directions: Park #2: On the Wisconsin Dells Pkwy. (Rte. 12) just south of Rte. A; Park #1: On Rte. 1, just east of Rte. 12.

Count Wolff von Baldazar's Haunted Mansion

One of the best recommendations for this walk-through spook house is that it isn't filled with hormone-charged gothic teenagers who jump out of the shadows and scream in your ears. You're also not forced to stick your hands in bowls of cold spaghetti "guts" and peeled grape "eyeballs."

Count Wolff von Baldazar's Haunted Mansion bills itself as nine dungeons of terror, though only one of the rooms actually looks like a dungeon. At the first stop you'll meet a green-skinned witch and her raven sidekick. These low-budget robots warn you there's no turning back, even though you can see the entrance just behind you. Don't worry; just push ahead.

Fumbling through the dark, you'll set off electric sensors, triggering a headless man to begin speaking, skeletons to pop out of nowhere, compressed air to blast you in the face, and a woman's head to rot into a skull before your very eyes! Along the way you'll see graveyards and cobwebs and fluorescent bones. For some reason, the Count doesn't appear until the end of the tour. His queeny ghost hologram sits up in a coffin, rolls his r's and eyes as he cackles about the undead, then settles back into his mortal body for the tape to rewind and the next group to come through.

112 Broadway, Wisconsin Dells, WI 53965

(608) 254-7513

Hours: June–August, daily 9:30A.M.–11P.M.

Cost: Adults $4.95, Kids(12 and under) $3.75

Directions: Downtown, between Eddy and Superior Sts.

The Ducks

Going to the Dells and missing the Ducks is like going to San Francisco and missing the cable cars. A Duck is a WWII–vintage army surplus amphibious vehicle, capable of speeds up to 50 mph on land and 15 mph in water. Hop aboard one of these crafts and careen through the woods with your barely-old-enough driver. Is that water you see up ahead? No problem! Hold on to your camera and loved ones as you slam into the river at the trail's end. If you're really lucky, a Duck just might swamp a canoe or capsize a paddleboat!

The second part of your journey is a tour of the Dells' rock formations. You'll view famous Stand Rock, and perhaps witness a dog jumping onto the tall pillar from the shore. It used to be vaulted by a man in an Indian costume, but today only a pooch is allowed to do it. Who knows how long that will last with heightened concern for our furry friends!

Original Wisconsin Ducks, 1890 Wisconsin Dells Pkwy., PO Box 117, Wisconsin Dells, WI 53965

(608) 254-8751

E-mail: widucks@baraboo.com

Hours: April, daily 10a.m.–4p.m.; May, daily 9a.m.–5p.m.; June–August, daily 8a.m.–7p.m.; September–October, daily 9a.m.–4p.m.

Cost: Adults $14.50, Seniors $11.50, Kids(6–11) $8.75

wisconsinducktours.com

Directions: On the Wisconsin Dells Pkwy. (Rte. 12) just south of Rte. A.

Dells Ducks, 1550 Wisconsin Dells Pkwy., PO Box 11, Wisconsin Dells, WI 53965

(608) 254-6080

E-mail: sfield@baraboo.com

Hours: May–October, daily 9a.m.–6p.m.

Cost: Adults $15, Kids(6–12) $8.50

www.dellsducks.com

Directions: On Rte. 12, east of the Rte. 23 split at the south end of town.

Extreme World

Does your sorry life need a pick-me-up? Are you a rebellious teen who wants to scare the bejeezus out of your too-square parents? Head on over to Extreme World, where adrenaline and fear are the name of the game!

First up is the Skycoaster, where you and up to two friends can "fly" 60 mph over the awestruck crowd, dangling from a harness. There are no upper or lower age limits to ride, but you must be 42 inches tall. Next, throw yourself off the 130-foot Bungee Tower, the Midwest's tallest. Unlike many towers, this one has an elevator to deliver you to the upper platform. Extreme World gives you the option to jump facing forward or backward. Try it both ways!

Even scarier than bungeeing DOWN is bungeeing UP. Strap into the park's Ejection Seat and be slingshotted 150 feet into the air, a full 30 feet above the support towers! And are you tired of all the harnesses and padded seats? Scale the 50-foot Climbing Wall with only a nylon rope between you and the hard, hard ground. Finally, for those afraid of heights but still seeking that special thrill, walk down Alligator Alley and feed a dozen hungry reptiles through tubes in their pens. Go ahead! Why do you think God gave you two hands?? There's one to spare!

1800 Wisconsin Dells Pkwy., Wisconsin Dells, WI 53940

(608) 254-7565

Hours: June–August 10A.M.–Midnight; September–First Snow, Monday–Friday 10A.M.–5P.M., Saturday–Sunday 10A.M.–7P.M.

Cost: Skycoaster(1/2/3 riders) $20/$40/$60; Bungee Tower $40; Ejection Seat $25; Climbing Wall $10/climb; Alligator Alley, Adults $2.99, Kids $1.99

www.extremeworld.com

Directions: On the Wisconsin Dells Pkwy. (Rte. 12) south of Rte. A.

ANOTHER BIG THRILL

Did Extreme World leave you wanting more? That's the problem with endorphin highs—you have to bump up the fright level to get the same thrill. Head on over to Timber Falls (1000 Stand Rock Rd., (608) 254-8414) for **THE SKYSCRAPER**! Imagine a 70-mph, 10-story, two-arm Ferris wheel that pulls four Gs at its bottom arc. Then picture yourself strapped in an open carriage that freely spins upside down, regardless of where you're at in the loop. The Skyscraper will set you back $20 and probably a pair of underwear.

Grave of Belle Boyd, Confederate Spy

Belle Boyd was a hothead, a shameless self-promoter, and a brave defender of unjust causes like slavery and the right for the South to destroy the union of American states. She was hailed in her day, but she's being punished in death—right here in Wisconsin.

This infamous sneak started her career at 17 when a drunken Union soldier tried to push his way into her family's Martinsburg, Virginia (later West Virginia) home. It was the Fourth of July, 1861, and he wanted to hang the Stars and Stripes from the building's upper window. He never made it—Belle shot him in the head. Sound vaguely familiar? It should; Margaret Mitchell lifted the story and put it in *Gone with the Wind.*

A Union commander freed Belle after an interrogation, never questioning her claim that the soldier was there to do worse than hang a flag. Emboldened by the deed, Belle decided to be a full-time Rebel Spy. When Union officers stayed with her family, she'd steal their weapons and hand them over to Confederate forces. When Northern troops were laying a trap for Stonewall Jackson in Front Royal, Virginia, in 1862, Belle crossed battle lines to tell Jackson to attack early before the Union could amass its troops. Jackson won the battle.

This treachery got Belle in big trouble. She spent some time in a Washington prison before another officer/sucker released her to head south, threatening to shoot her if she returned. In Richmond she met Confederate President Jefferson Davis, who sent her on a European mission to enlist England's support for the Southern cause. Belle's ship was captured while trying to run the Southern Blockade. Boyd fell in love with a Union officer on the ship that detained her, coaxed him over to the Rebel cause, then enlisted his help to flee through Canada to England.

Before she could do any more damage, the South lost. Boyd worked the lecture circuit, spent 10 years on Broadway as an actress, and married three times. While on a tour through Wisconsin in 1900, she fell ill and died on June 11 in the Dells. She is now planted in Yankee territory. As fitting punishment for her work against the Union, her grave is festooned with the Stars and Stripes each Memorial Day. Most days it has a Confederate flag, so if you're planning a visit, bring a real flag, the American flag, to stick into her plot.

Spring Grove Cemetery, Broadway & Race, Wisconsin Dells, WI 53965

No phone

Hours: Daily 9A.M.–5P.M.

Cost: Free

Directions: At the east end of Broadway (Rte. 23) from downtown.

H. H. Bennett Studio Museum

Wedged between the T-shirt shops and waffle cone huts in the downtown Dells is one of the most remarkable historical museums in the state: the H. H. Bennett Studio Museum. Never heard of the man or his studio?

Next to Matthew Brady, H. H. Bennett was arguably one of America's premier photographers, developing new techniques for the medium. The Civil War veteran began taking wilderness photographs in the great frontier, but when he wanted to include human or animal subjects they were required to stand very still while he exposed the plate. This was tough enough with people, but even more difficult with deer, and because Bennett's hand had been mauled in the war, the process was even more time-consuming. Out of necessity, he invented a fast-shutter camera that operated with rubber bands. With it Bennett snapped the first stop-action photo in 1886; a thrill-seeker jumping to Stand Rock in the Dells was caught midair. Bennett is also credited as the first photojournalist after he did an exposé on Wisconsin lumbermen in 1886 and documented the life of the local Ho Chunk natives.

The bulk of Bennett's work was "stereo views" of the Dells. When placed in a special device, the images had depth, exactly like ViewMasters. You can see many of these images at the museum housed in his former studio, the oldest continuously operating photography studio in the United States.

Stepping into the museum is like stepping into a Ken Burns documentary. Bennett's images of the Dells have been re-created full-sized and positioned in such a way as to produce the stereo effect, as if you're walking through the images. You'll visit the old portrait studio and the darkroom where he developed negatives and made his prints. An interactive computer system allows you to search through his impressive collection and to experience the 3-D effect with special goggles. The museum/studio still has over 8,000 of Bennett's original negatives, and they will make prints for you—for a price.

215 Broadway, Wisconsin Dells, WI 53965

(608) 253-3523

E-mail: hhbennett@mail.shsw.wisc.edu

Hours: June, daily 10A.M.–6P.M.; July–August, daily 10A.M.–10P.M.; September, daily 10A.M.–5P.M.

Cost: Adults $5.75, Seniors(65+) $5.25, Kids(5–12) $3

hhbennett.shsw.wisc.edu

Directions: Downtown, between Superior and Oak Sts.

STUDIO SLEEPOVER
Haven't had enough of the H. H. Bennett experience? Why not stay in his former home, just around the corner from the museum? It has been restored to it 19th-century appearance, minus the outhouse, and you can bathe in the photographer's old bathtub! (825 Oak St., (608) 254-2500)

Noah's Ark

The hottest temperature ever recorded in Wisconsin was at the Wisconsin Dells on July 13, 1936. That day it hit 114°F. Had Noah's Ark been around at the time, it might have been bearable.

In a town where every resort seems to have its own water park, it's quite an accomplishment to draw visitors to pay for the experience at $25 a head. But thousands of folks flood the park every day to toss themselves down slides on rafting inner tubes. With 33 different slides to choose from, Noah's Ark claims to be the World's Largest Water Park. Some are basic, open to the air, while others, like Black Thunder, flush you through a pitch-black tube faster than a bran muffin with a coffee chaser. Try The Plunge, where you drop 50 feet before skidding out over a pool, or the Kowabunga family slide, where the whole clan rides in one giant raft.

Sick of slides? There's always the Endless River, where you bob along in a circle, roasting in the sun, or the Big Kahuna wave pool, where rubber rafts are capsized every few minutes by a series of mini-tsunamis.

1410 Wisconsin Dells Pkwy., Wisconsin Dells, WI 53965

(608) 254-6351

E-mail: noahsark@midplains.net

Hours: June–August, daily 9A.M.–8P.M. (but times can vary; call ahead)

Cost: All-day pass $24.99, Seniors(60+) $19.99

www.noahsarkwaterpark.com

Directions: On the Wisconsin Dells Pkwy. (Rte. 12) north of Lake St.

Ripley's Believe It or Not! Museum

What tourist trap would be complete without a Ripley's Believe It or Not! Museum? From the street this place looks tame enough. Strange but manageable. You can view a full-sized, wooden Mercedes Gullwing automobile, built by Livio De Marchi and sailed as a boat, without paying admission, but if you want a peek at the rest, fork over the dough. Just around the corner you'll run into a medieval chastity belt, a Tibetan human bone rugen and skull bowl, and a genuine shrunken head from the Jivaro Indians of Ecuador.

And that's just the warm-up. Weird displays surround a plane that appears to have crashed inside the building. Grasshoppers pulling rickshaws, a tattoo surgically removed and preserved by W. K. Foster of Winnipeg, Canada, a python skeleton squeezing the life out of a monkey skeleton, flattened mice pelts, the head of a four-horned Australian "Geep," and the conjoined skulls of a two-headed calf.

Animal oddities seem to be this place's specialty. They've got the stuffed carcass of "Slim," a six-legged cow from Mineral Point, Wisconsin, and "Andy," a footless goose from Hastings, Nebraska, who was outfitted with tennis shoes. And finally, the mummified head of a human animal, Peter Kurten, better known as the Dusseldorf Vampire. This fellow was beheaded in Germany in 1931 after being convicted of killing 9 people (he was tried for 68). His noggin was sliced in half (top to bottom, through the nose), cured like leather, and hung on a meat hook, all in the name of "science." Now you can see it spin in circles in an old icebox—Believe It or Not!

115 Broadway, PO Box 411, Wisconsin Dells, WI 53965

(608) 253-7556

E-mail: ripley@blissnet.com

Hours: April–October, daily 9A.M.–11:30P.M.

Cost: Adults $7.95, Kids(6–12) $4.95

www.conceptattractions.com/html/wismain.htm

Directions: Downtown between Eddy and Superior Sts.

WISCONSIN DELLS RESORT RUNDOWN

OK, so you're overwhelmed with choices of where to stay. Since the beds are pretty much the same, you need to pick a resort on its overall theme, which is often reflected in its water park. Here are a few that stand out in the crowd.

MOTEL	THEME
Alakai 1030 Wisconsin Dells Pkwy. (608) 253-3803 www.widells.com/alakai	*Gilligan's Island* without the coconuts.
Antiqua Bay 655 Frontage Rd. (608) 254-8306 www.antiquabay.com	*Flipper* meets *Yertle the Turtle*.
Atlantis 1570 Wisconsin Dells Pkwy. (608) 253-6606 www.theatlantishotel.com	*The Little Mermaid* gone haywire.
Camelot 1033 Wisconsin Dells Pkwy. (608) 253-3000 www.dellshotels.com/camelot.html	Sir Waterslides-a-lot.
Carousel Inn 1011 Wisconsin Dells Pkwy. (608) 254-6554 www.wintergreen-resort.com/carousel	Lodging on the Candyland gameboard.
Chula Vista 4031 River Rd. (608) 254-8366 www.wisdells.com/chulavista	Cougars and rattlesnakes—terror out West.

WISCONSIN DELLS RESORT RUNDOWN

MOTEL	THEME
Copa Cabana 611 Wisconsin Dells Pkwy. (608) 253-1511 www.copacabanaresort.com	Jah mon! Everything but the ganja!
Grand Marquis 840 Wisconsin Dells Pkwy. (608) 254-4843 www.grandmarquis-dells.com	Island of the Blue Dolphin Lagoon.
Great Wolf Lodge 1400 Black Wolf Dr. (608) 253-2222 www.greatwolflodge.com	Sleeping with Paul Bunyan.
Kalahari Resort 1305 Kalahari Drive (608) 254-LION www.kalahariresort.com	Lions and jaguars and water slides, oh my!

Goody, goody gumdrops! The Carousel Inn.

WISCONSIN DELLS RESORT RUNDOWN

MOTEL

Meadowbrook
1533 River Rd.
(608) 253-3201
dells.com/meadowbrook

Playday
1781 Wisconsin Dells Pkwy.
(608) 253-3961
www.execpc.com/~playday/

The Polynesian
857 Frontage Rd.
(608) 254-2883
www.dellspolynesian.com

Raintree Resort
1435 Wisconsin Dells Pkwy.
(608) 253-4386
www.dellsraintree.com

Treasure Island
1701 Wisconsin Dells Pkwy.
(608) 254-8560
www.WisDellsTreasureIsland.com

The Wilderness
511 E. Adams St.
(608) 253-9729
www.wildernessresort.com

Wintergreen/Polar Island
60 Gasser Rd.
(608) 254-2285
www.wintergreen-resort.com

THEME

A country bear jamboree!

Barney on mushrooms.

Volcanoes and South Seas tikis.

A plastic rain forest.

Long John Silver and buried treasure.

Gold mines and avalanches.

Polar bears and penguins.

Serpent Safari

An old Winnebago legend explains how the Dells' rock formations were formed years ago by a giant snake that dug a path along the river. It must have been a lot larger than Baby, a 27-foot, 403-pound Burmese python on display at Serpent Safari. Currently Baby holds the title of the World's Largest Snake, or at least the largest in captivity, and will get even larger if she swallows a straggler on the tour.

Serpent Safari has celebrity reptiles, like the green anaconda used in the filming of *Anaconda*, or the albino American alligator valued at $1 million. Another alligator, Big Mac, was a local star down in Florida where he ate several household pets before being captured. Serpent Safari adopted the aggressive critter before it was destroyed, and today its guides offer parents $1.50/lb. for misbehaving children. Feeding time is 4p.m. on Sundays.

For true reptile-philes, you can have a photo taken with a large snake draped over your shoulders. But hold on tight! Noah's Ark is just across the street, and if one of those pythons escapes, you know where it's headed.

1425 Wisconsin Dells Pkwy., Wisconsin Dells, WI 53965

(608) 253-3200

Hours: Sunday–Thursday 10a.m.–8p.m., Friday–Saturday 10a.m.–9p.m.

Cost: Adults $6.95, Seniors $5.95, Kids(3–12) $4.95

www.serpentsafari.com

Directions: Across the street from Noah's Ark, just north of Pilgrim St.

WISCONSIN DELLS

A mysterious cougar has been spotted near the Wisconsin Dells along Rte. 16 and Rte. 23.

Back when the Wisconsin Dells was known as Kilbourn City, part of town was known as "Bloody Run" because of the rampant violence.

Somebody's spiked my porridge . . .
Photo by author, courtesy of Storybook Gardens

Storybook Gardens

This attraction was once the sister to Biblical Gardens, but only this god-free venue remains. The vast majority of the scenes on display are Mother Goose rhymes from the days before they were politically corrected. If you want to see Peter, Peter Pumpkin Eater stick his wife in a pumpkin shell, you still can! There are also re-creations of Jack and the Beanstalk, Rock-a-Bye Baby, Humpty Dumpty, Little Miss Muffet, Simple Simon, and Peter Rabbit. The best of the bunch is The Three Bear Family who, with their eyes spinning like pinwheels, look as if Goldilocks dosed their porridge with LSD.

Mixed among the fiberglass characters are teenagers dressed in costumes like Little Bo Peep and the Fairy Godmother. This allows your children to have interactive experiences with their fantasies, if that's your goal.

1500 Wisconsin Dells Pkwy., PO Box 146, Wisconsin Dells, WI 53965

(608) 253-2391

Hours: May–September, daily 9:30A.M.–6P.M.

Cost: Adults $8.99, Seniors $7.99, Kids $8.99

www.dells.com/storybook.html

Directions: On the Wisconsin Dells Pkwy. (Rte. 12) north of Lake St.

Tommy Bartlett's Robot World

Tommy Bartlett's old Robot World was beginning to look dated. After all, who still believes robots will do our housework, cook our food, and give us baths? Would we trust them? And what would happen if they fell under the control of a computer virus? They'd refuse to do the windows, use Hamburger Helper, and talk back when you gave them an order. What kind of Utopia is that?

Tommy Bartlett, visionary that he was, updated the museum shortly before his death, turning it into the Science Exploratory. Your visit still

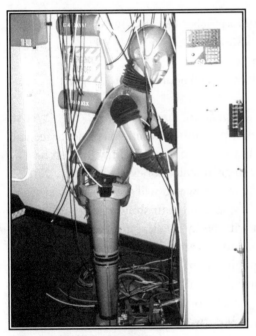

R2D2 made this look so easy . . .
Photo by author, courtesy of Robot World

begins with a futuristic tour through the remnants of the old Robot World, but later on you find yourself learning a thing or two— on vacation!

The tour begins by blasting off to a Space Station. You're treated to a "cathode ray scanner" before entering the "shuttle," a three-floor elevator. The Space Station is run by Tatoo and his sidekick, who quickly lose track of astronaut Buster Leapyear somewhere in outer space. This bungling becomes a theme for the Space Station, and you start to wonder if you're on Russia's Mir. When lights start flashing "Radiation Alert!", a red robot with a Scottish brogue warns you to "Move along before the whole place goes up like a Roman candle!" That's encouraging.

You're dumped out into a collection of hands-on exhibits designed to trick your eyes and surprise your senses. Adjacent to the museum is a gyroscope harness where you can flip yourself silly for an additional fee. It's all preparation for the grand finale: a Mir Space Station module!

Bartlett purchased a portion of Mir from the cash-strapped Russian government, a module that was never attached to that orbiting junk heap. You're welcomed by Dr. Norman Thagard, a Mir astronaut/survivor, via space-age videotape. The module hangs in a large space, at an angle, making you feel unbalanced as you stand inside. Strapped to a wall is a genuine Space Guitar. Now you really are starting to feel ill. You race for the exit and find yourself standing in a Li'l Caesar's pizza outlet. That ought to settle your stomach!

560 Wisconsin Dells Pkwy., PO Box 65, Wisconsin Dells, WI 53965

(608) 254-2525

Hours: June–August, daily 8A.M.–10P.M.; September–May, daily 10A.M.–4P.M.

Cost: Adults $8.75, Seniors(65+) $7, Kids(5 and under) free

www.tommybartlett.com/robotw.htm

Directions: On the Wisconsin Dells Pkwy. (Rte. 12) north of the Rte. 23 split.

Tommy Bartlett's Sky, Ski, and Stage Waterski Show

Don't let this attraction's shameless promotion campaigns discourage you from visiting—it actually lives up to its own hype. Tommy Bartlett has never allowed his waterski show to grow stale, not even with his recent death. It is impossible to describe the show you will see in any given season since it changes every year. Rest assured your show will have all the flare of a 1970s TV variety hour with perky musical numbers, comedy skits, magic acts, dance routines, and lots and lots of sequins.

To get a sense of what you might experience, consider Tommy Bartlett's most recent extravaganza, the Millennium's Ski-Va Las Vegas Revue. The show begins with a overture of Vegas tunes while speedboat operators parade by the viewing stands, waving to the audience. A jeep enters from stage left and a prospector tells you a 30-second history of the origins of Las Vegas, then tears off his beard and clothes to reveal a sparkly outfit. "Let Ski-Va Las Vegas begin!"

The speedboats return, this time pulling showgirls at high speeds. Elvis follows and executes a 360° maneuver around his boat after running the slaloms! Aqua the Clown (that little scamp!) crashes his outboard onto the shore, then ticks off a guy in a gorilla suit who chases him first on land, then on water, and back into a circus cage! Ski-vel Kneivel jumps from the top of Ski-sars Palace without skis, then roars by the audience sliding only on his bare feet!! Next up is the ever-classy Cirque du Swivel, then another clown climbs a 90-foot lamp tower to change a light bulb, all without a net! Aqua returns in a stretch limousine pulling an oversized guitar and pretending to be Wayne Newton! Bugsy Skigal skis by, barefoot, and the Cyber Spacemen compete in a jumping contest—and that's all before intermission!

After you've been given ample time to purchase snow cones and hot dogs, the stage show continues. First up are Michaelangelo and Carolina Nock, who perform death-defying tricks on a spinning Sky Pendulum Wheel, well into the splatter-if-you-fall territory. After they cheat the Grim Reaper, the Argentinian Dancing Gauchos come out, banging drums, cracking whips, and swinging flaming bolos. All three look like Doug Henning, even the woman. The Flying Ashton Family from Australia follow. Dad reclines on a modified weight bench and flips his trusting children end over end through the air with his feet, catching them each time. And straight from the Catskills is Dieter Tasso, who tosses cups and saucers from his toes and catches them on his balding head, in a stack, all the while rattling off vaudeville schtick. Evening shows are topped off with a Dancing Fountain and Lasar-Rama finale!

If you watch this high-spirited hokum for the full two hours and don't walk out of the show smiling, I suggest you check the hole where your soul used to reside. Maybe nothing makes you happy.

560 Wisconsin Dells Pkwy., PO Box 65, Wisconsin Dells, WI 53965

(608) 254-2525

Hours: Shows June–August, 1:00, 4:30, and 8:30 p.m.

Cost: Seats range $11.13–$17.74

www.tommybartlett.com/thrill.htm

Directions: Two miles south of town on Rte. 12.

Wax World of the Stars

If you already thought wax museums were creepy, wait until you see the figures move! In an effort to update the typically static displays, Wax World of the Stars has roboticized or added movement to some of its figures, making it an eerie place indeed. Before entering the main galleries you're serenaded by a female pianist while Marlene Dietrich leans silently over the piano. So impressive is this robot crooner, several tourists have tossed tips into her jar.

Two of Wax World's first rooms have displays that are borderline lecherous. In the first, air blows up Marilyn Monroe's skirt while Humphrey Bogart leers from in the shadows in a trench coat. But no need to shield the kids; Marilyn's wearing an undergarment. In the next room, Snow White is surrounded by seven bug-eyed dwarves, while up in the tree Walt Disney ogles the fairest of them all.

As you move through the museum the wax dummies become more tightly packed together. While viewing Little Red Riding Hood, you can hear Cher belt out "If I Could Turn Back Time." Superman, Batman, and Frankenstein share equal billing in one scene. John F. Kennedy stands over Abraham Lincoln's shoulder in Ford's Theater. Pope John Paul II blesses you while Albert Einstein peeks around the curtain. Captain Kirk and Mr. Spock fade in and out on a transporter. Elvis, in his white Vegas jumpsuit, has been slimmed down to fit in the room with Garth Brooks, Cher, Dolly Parton, Liza Minnelli, Barbra Streisand, Willie Nelson, and Michael Jackson.

Cramped as they are, they fare better than the celebs in the next display. The museum has lopped off the heads of out-of-favor celebrities and parked them on shelves. Who is a bodiless has-been? FDR, John Wilkes Booth, Pope Paul VI, Tricky Dick and Pat Nixon (with glittery blue hair), Chairman Mao, Brigham Young, Jimmy Carter, a buxom Liz Taylor, and a still-black Michael Jackson.

And what's the grand finale to this waxy collection? Princess Di and John Travolta spin in circles on a giant turntable, forever frozen in a dance, just inches from each other. If you look at it just right, Di appears to be backing away from an aggressive Vinnie Barbarino.

105 Broadway, PO Box 411, Wisconsin Dells, WI 53965

(608) 254-2184

E-mail: ripley@blissnet.com

Hours: May–October, daily 9A.M.–10:30P.M.

Cost: Adults $5.95, Kids(6–12) $3.50

www.conceptattractions.com/html/waxworld.htm

Directions: Downtown, just east of the river on Broadway.

Wonder Spot

There are special places in this world where gravity and perception seem out of kilter. Surprisingly, these places always seem to be located in tourist trap towns. In the Dells, it's the Wonder Spot. Chairs cling to walls. People change height. Water and golf balls run uphill. Nobody can walk a straight line. Everything is topsy-turvy and your adolescent tour guides are unable to explain it. Is it caused by a high concentration of magnetic ore in a nearby rock formation? Is it a fluctuation in the gravitational field at the south end of town? Or could it be that this wacky shack has been built on the side of a hill? You decide.

100 Scott Dr., PO Box 462, Lake Delton, WI 53940

(608) 254-4224

Hours: May–September, daily 9A.M.–9P.M.

Cost: Adults $4, Kids(6–11) $2

Directions: At the south end of town on Rte. 12, where it bends to the south.

SOUTHERN WISCONSIN

Yes, Wisconsin is the Cheese State, but Southern Wisconsin supports the biggest wedge of the industry. Cheese fanatics are everywhere: the Historic Cheese Museum in Monroe, the Dairy Shrine in Ft. Atkinson, the Swiss Historical Village in New Glarus. . . .

Businesses are guarded by animals who have expanded to dangerous proportions after feasting for years on the yellow stuff: Igor the Mouse in Fennimore, Bessie the Cow in Janesville, and anonymous rodents outside establishments in Kenosha, Arena, and Madison. Drive into Wisconsin from the south and you'll see its border is defended by Cheese Castles and Cheese Chalets—it's just not safe for those watching their cholesterol level!

This singular dairy focus has had a negative effect on the rest of the tourist industry. Monuments to cheese get so much attention that other roadside attractions are almost overshadowed. Did you know the Lost City of Atlantis has been found in Lake Mills . . . sort of? Have you visited the Mustard Museum, the World's Largest Can of Chili Beans, or the Birthplace of the Gideon Bible? Probably not, because you've never heard of them. If you want to find places like House on the Rock, you really have to search!

Ashippun
Honey of a Museum

Don't know much about the birds and the bees? Honey Acres might be able to assist you—at least halfway. This working apiary has been run by the Diehnelt family since 1852, and they know their bees. Were you aware these stinging insects were originally brought to North America by settlers and were known as the "white man's fly"? You're learning already!

Peer through a glass-enclosed beehive to see them in action. Read displays on pollination and beeswax. Taste honey directly from taps. Check out the 20-minute slide show on Wisconsin's state insect—the bee, of course! And scold Mr. Black Bear, dreaded enemy of nature's pollinator.

Honey Acres, N1557 Rte. 67, PO Box 346, Ashippun, WI 53003

(800) 558-7745 or (920) 474-4411

Hours: November–May, Monday–Friday 9A.M.–3:30P.M.; June–October, Monday–Friday 9A.M.–3:30P.M., Saturday–Sunday Noon–4P.M.

Cost: Free

www.honeyacres.com

Directions: On Rte. 67, two miles north of town.

Bagley
Good-Bye Passenger Pigeons!

There was a time when swarms of passenger pigeons blackened the skies of North America, and Wisconsin was a main stop on the species' annual migration. In 1871, a flock of 136 million descended on Jackson County in the center of the state, blanketing 850 square miles of land.

Overwhelmed settlers felt something had to be done.

The pigeons acted oblivious to predators and were easy targets, and because each nesting pair laid only one egg each year, they couldn't replenish their quickly diminishing population. In less than 30 years they were extinct in the wild.

Conservationists have erected a small monument to the birds in Wyalusing State Park along the birds' former flyway. It is "[d]edicated to the last Wisconsin Passenger Pigeon, shot at Babcock, September 1899. This species became extinct through the avarice and thoughtlessness of man." And howdy.

Though Babcock (in central Wisconsin) claims to be "Where the Last

Passenger Pigeon Was Killed," records indicate the last bird was picked off in Pikes County, Ohio, on March 24, 1900. Some birds remained in captivity, but the final one perished at a Cincinnati zoo in 1914.

Wyalusing State Park, 13081 State Park Lane, Bagley, WI 53801

(608) 996-2261

Hours: Daily 8A.M.–11P.M.

Cost: Three-hour pass $3, daily sticker $7

Directions: Rte. C west of Rte. 18/35; plaque is located at the Green Cloud picnic area.

Beloit
Angel Museum

First things first. According to its literature, the Angel Museum "refrains from promoting religion or a theology of angels." That's a tough sell. It's kind of like collecting stamps but not promoting the Postal Service.

The museum started with the private collection of Joyce Berg. Over many years she collected 12,000+ angel figurines and was about to give some away (to make room for more) when she learned a former Catholic church was about to be demolished. Why not start a museum and use her collection as the "seed"?

The angel-loving public responded with open wings. Open since 1995, Berg's museum can display 6,000 of its collection at any one time, so she's constantly rotating in new cherubs. Oprah donated 570 African American angels she received after asking on her talk show why there weren't any black angels. Apparently, there were.

Berg has porcelain angels, Hummel angels, crystal angels, wooden angels, raw spaghetti angels . . . you name it, somebody's glued wings to it . . . even Joyce Berg. That's right, sometimes she dons a pair of flapping wings and halo to greet her visitors as if they were passing through the Pearly Gates. Perhaps that's the wrong outfit to meet a tour bus of senior citizens.

656 Pleasant St., PO Box 816, Beloit, WI 53512-0816

(608) 362-9099

Hours: November–December and February–April, Tuesday–Saturday 10A.M.–4P.M.;

May–October, Monday–Saturday 10A.M.–5P.M.

Cost: Adults $5, Seniors(55+) $4, Kids(5–12) $3

www.angelmuseum.org

Directions: On Rte. 51, three blocks north of Rte. 81, on the river.

World's Largest Can of Chili Beans

One of the first sights visitors see when entering Wisconsin from Illinois on I-90 is a gigantic can of Hormel Chili with Beans. Could it be garbage left behind by Paul Bunyan on a cookout? Is it part of the nation's strategic reserve of natural gas? Or is it what it seems—an external tank at the Hormel plant, painted as a giant advertisement?

Strike the first theory. Paul Bunyan was long dead before canned chili or the can opener was invented. The second scenario seems unlikely, too. Wouldn't a gas supply like this be stored in a more secure location? That leaves the third option, which seems all too obvious.

But that's maybe what somebody wants us to believe. . . .

Hormel Plant, 3000 Kennedy Dr., Beloit, WI 53511

(608) 365-9501

Hours: Always visible

Cost: Free

Directions: On the west side of I-90, just south of the Rte. 43 Exit.

Blue Mounds
Cave of the Mounds

Cave of the Mounds was discovered on August 4, 1939, on the farm of Ebinezer Bringham. Workers blasting limestone inadvertently opened what is now the entrance to the cave. Realizing tourism was more lucrative than limestone, they developed this hole in the ground into an attraction.

Early visitors had to hike down a wooden stairway, but the steps have long since been replaced with concrete. Down below you'll see impressive stalactites and stalagmites, uncommon in small caves like Blue Mounds because they grow at the rate of one inch every 200 years. You do the math. Your guide will also point out a cephalopod fossil found in the cave. The tour takes about an hour, and during it they'll turn out the lights for the experience of total darkness! Don't worry, they'll turn the lights back on before the kids (or you) start crying.

Due to its long operating history, Cave of the Mounds has been honored as a National Natural Landmark. The temperature down below is 50°F, year round, so if you come in the summer, bring a light jacket, and if you come in the winter, leave the heavy parka behind or you'll work up a sweat.

Bringham Farm, PO Box 148, Blue Mounds, WI 53517

(608) 437-3038

Hours: March–May, Monday–Friday 10 A.M.–4 P.M., Saturday–Sunday 9 A.M.–5 P.M.;
June–August, daily 9 A.M.–7 P.M.; September–November, Monday–Friday 10 A.M.–4 P.M.,
Saturday–Sunday 9 A.M.–5 P.M.; December–February, Saturday–Sunday 10 A.M.–4 P.M.

Cost: Adults $10, Seniors $5, Kids(5–12) $5

www.caveofthemounds.com

Directions: One mile east of town off Rte. ID.

WHO LET THE ELVES LOOSE?

Just down the road from **Cave of the Mounds** is Nissedahle, Norwegian for "Valley of the Elves." Did they escape from Cave of the Mounds? These little critters have been busy, reconstructing a Stavkirke (a 12th-century Norwegian church) originally built for Chicago's 1893 Columbian Exposition, a sod house, and a Stabbur (a storage house on stilts). It's all part of Little Norway (3576 Rte. JG North, (608) 437-8211, www.littlenorway.com), a little bit of Scandinavia in the heart of cheese country.

Boscobel
The First Gideon Bible

Traveling salesmen John Nicholson and Samuel Hill had a vision on September 4, 1898, while sharing Room 19 at the Hotel Boscobel: "A Bible in every guest room in every hotel in America!" And, unlike many religious visions, it has become a reality.

They began by organizing the Christian Commercial Men's Association, better known as the Gideons. It took nine years, but in 1907 the first Gideon Bibles were placed in Montana hotels. Millions of trees and a hundred years later, it's hard to find a room that doesn't have one in a bedside drawer.

The Gideons' name comes from the Book of Judges, and contrary to the Eighth Commandment, you are encouraged to steal their Bible from your room. But if you do, they would like you to confess your sin to the management so it may be replaced.

The Hotel Boscobel has been the scene of other historic events as well. Candidate John F. Kennedy stayed here with Jackie during the 1960

Wisconsin presidential primary. Some believe a child was conceived in their suite. Today, the building houses a bar and restaurant.

Hotel Boscobel, Room 19, 1005 Wisconsin Ave., Boscobel, WI 53805

(608) 375-4714

Hours: Bar, daily 11A.M.–2P.M.; Restaurant, lunch 11A.M.–2:30P.M., dinner 5–9P.M.

Cost: Lunches $5–$10, Dinners $9–$15

Directions: Three blocks east of Rte. 61, south of Bluff St.

Burlington
Angels in the Belfries

God may work in mysterious ways, but one of the strangest ways is as a building inspector. Back in July 1970, parishioners at St. Mary's Catholic Church began to notice a strange glow in the middle of the church's steeple. Was it a swarm of fireflies? A discharge of static electricity? Or was it a message from on high?

Take a guess. That's right, hundreds of the faithful flocked to the church to stand around the intersection and gawk up at the spire, night after night. Sometimes the light was blue, sometimes it was orange, but it was never Packers' green or gold.

Then, as quickly as it appeared, it vanished. Some doubting Thomases decided to check out the steeple from the inside and discovered the builders had miswired its lightning rod. Had the cross on the top been hit by a bolt, the entire structure could have been lit up . . . by flames!

Some interpreted this series of events as a warning from God to save the church. We'll know for sure if the light reappears just before the floorboards are infested with termites or the basement floods.

St. Mary's Catholic Church, 108 McHenry St., Burlington, WI 53105

(262) 763-1500

Hours: Always visible

Cost: Free

Directions: On Rte. P, 1 block south of the Rte. 36 intersection.

BURLINGTON

Burlington celebrates **Chocolate Days** the first weekend following Mother's Day each spring. The event is sponsored by Nestlé Foods, the town's largest employer.

Spinning Top Exploratory Museum

Judith Schulz may very well forget her own name one of these days. Why? More people call her the Top Lady than refer to her as Judith. But don't think she doesn't appreciate the moniker. Schulz has been collecting spinning tops since she was a child and to date has amassed a collection of more than 2,000 and is still going strong. Her hands-on museum has "snake" tops, dreidels, gyroscopes, rev tops, casting tops, doodle tops, bracket tops, sonic satellites, diabolos, a five-pound Malaysian top, and returning tops, better know by their common name: yo-yos. She has tops that blow bubbles, dance like ballerinas, and spin up to seven days without stopping! You can see these twirling toys only if you sign up for one of her two-hour presentations, well worth the time and money.

Schulz is handy with her yo-yos and performs a variety of tricks during your visit. She has the classics, like gravity grippers, sleepers, walk the dog, forwards, and breakaways, but also string tricks like an ice cream cone, a Confederate Flag, and the Eiffel Tower. She performed that last one in front of the Eiffel Tower a few years ago.

For her grand finale Schulz brings out the Chinese Poison Top. Sound scary? It's actually the movie prop from *My Summer Story*, the sequel to *A Christmas Story*, for which she acted as a top consultant and performer. Whenever a top appeared from off screen it had been cast by ever-accurate Schulz. When Disney is dropping thousands of dollars an hour for production, they aren't going to trust the tough jobs to Macaulay Culkin's brother. That's a job for . . . drum roll . . . the Top Lady!

533 Milwaukee Ave., Burlington, WI 53105

(262) 763-3946

Hours: By appointment only

Cost: Adults $6; Hall of Puzzles $3

Directions: At the intersection of Rtes. 11 and 36.

Town Full of Liars

How strange it seems that a town should celebrate the fact that most of its prominent citizens are certified, card-carrying liars. In fact, they actually compete to see who can come up with the most outrageous falsehood. But that's just what they do in Burlington, home of the Burlington Liars Club, founded in 1929 by two local reporters, Manuel Hahn and Otis Hulett. They wrote a fake story about a nonexistent contest between the city's police and fire departments as to who could tell the best lie. The Chief of Police won.

The only thing worse than being accused of telling a lie is to not get the satisfaction of actually telling it. So a year later, when the issue of the contest came up again, the contest really took place. Contestants were charged a dime for each fib and a winner was crowned for the most outlandish statement. Some of the best lies over the years have been commemorated on plaques placed around the city's main business district, such as the one from Tacoma resident John Zelenak outside May's Insurance Agency (300 N. Pine St.): "My wife is so lazy that she feeds the chicken popcorn so that the eggs will turn themselves when she fries them." (To which the modern retort should be, "If you don't like it, fry your own damn eggs!") For a walking tour of the infamous lies, pick up a map at City Hall or the Chamber of Commerce.

The Burlington Liars Club still hosts the World Lying Championships on New Year's Eve each year, or at least that's what they say. To enter, send in your fib and a buck. If you don't hear back, you've either lost or been had.

Burlington Area Chamber of Commerce, 112 E. Chestnut, PO Box 156, Burlington, WI 53105

(262) 763-6044

E-mail: bacc@mia.net

Hours: Plaques always visible; Contest every New Year's Eve

Cost: Free; Lies $1

www.burlingtonareachamber.com

Directions: All around downtown; follow map provided by the Chamber of Commerce.

Columbus
Christopher Columbus Museum

Tucked away on the top floor of an enormous antique mall in Columbus is a private museum to the town's namesake, Christopher Columbus. Most of the 2,000+ items on display are from Chicago's 1893 Columbian Exposition. Statues, glassware, posters, maps, trinkets, needlework, models, books, and tickets document the World's Fair better than anything you'll ever see in Chicago. But because the exhibits wrap around shelves filled with stuff that's for sale, it can be difficult to determine where the museum stops and the store starts. Heaven help you if you bring a Columbian knickknack up to a register.

For true Columbus nuts, visit the fiberglass statue of Chris before leaving town. It was created in 1988 by David Oswald and dedicated on Columbus Day of that year. It stands at the intersection of Rtes. 151 and 16 on the northwest side of town. The work is titled *Columbus Taking Possession*, a characterization many might take issue with.

Columbus Antique Mall, 239 Whitney St., PO Box 151, Columbus, WI 53925

(920) 623-1992

Hours: Daily 8:30A.M.–4P.M.

Cost: Adults $1

www.wistravel.com/columbus/

Directions: One block east of Rte. 151 Business, two blocks north of Rte. 16.

Delavan
A Giant, Clown-Stomping Elephant

If you're no fan of clowns, check out the monument in downtown Delevan. A 10-foot 6-inch replica of "Romeo," the infamous rogue elephant, seems poised to stomp the life out of a clown in this quiet little park. Yet he never does. [The park hasn't always been so sanguine. In 1874, circus balloonist Rodley Palmer took off from this spot, ran into the cornice of the nearby Park Hotel (117 Park Place), and plunged to his death. But that's another story.]

Delevan has a long history with the circus, which is why it calls itself "the Circus City." Baraboo be damned! Twenty different circuses have operated out of Delevan, and it was here the P. T. Barnum show was organized in 1871. Over the years the town has been home to two of the Ringling Brothers and a 12-year-old runaway, Harry Houdini. Many performers and carnies, strong men and bearded ladies, and geeks and dog-faced boys are buried in the local Spring Grove and St. Andrews Cemeteries.

Tower Park, 100 E. Walworth Ave., Delavan, WI 53115

No phone

Hours: Always visible

Cost: Free

Directions: On Rte. 11, three blocks west of Rte. O.

CASSVILLE

Each year in July, Cassville hosts **Twin-O-Rama**, a gathering of twins from around the Midwest and the world.

Built with wine, cookies, and a lot of concrete.

Dickeyville
Dickeyville Grotto

Father Mathias Wernerus had big plans when he was assigned to Dickeyville's Holy Ghost Parish in 1918: He would build a shrine to God and Country. It was originally intended to honor three local men killed in the Great War, but it soon became much more than that. He got the idea from the Grotto of the Redemption in West Bend, Iowa.

Officially called Grotto of Christ the King and Mary His Mother, it took five years to build, beginning in 1925. The grotto's foundation was excavated by hand by the parish schoolchildren who received 10¢, a cookie, and a glass of wine for their day's labor. Most of the work after that was done by Wernerus himself, embedding glass, stones, petrified sea creatures, and crystals into the cement structure. His flock would bring broken glassware that he would melt into brazed chunks and affix somewhere.

The result is a collection of monuments including the Patriotism in Stone shrine to Lincoln, Washington, and Columbus; Holy Ghost Park adjoining the parish cemetery; and the grand Grotto itself. From the front, the Grotto resembles a giant ogre whose mouth is the entrance and whose eyes glare out toward the road. On its left is a Papal flag and on the right an American one.

Now the final question: Why? Father Wernerus once gave a cryptic explanation: "Many reasons urged me to put up 'Religion in Stone' and 'Patriotism in Stone.' The main reason it was done I could not reveal. The Last Day will tell you more about that." Uh, oh. . . .

The Dickeyville Grotto had an enormous impact on folk art in Wisconsin, inspiring the Rudolph Grotto, the Wegner Grotto, the Prairie Moon Museum, and Fred Smith's Concrete Park, all of which are covered in this guide. There is even some evidence that Simon Rodia, creator of the Watts Towers in Los Angeles, worked as a laborer for Wernerus on his way west. Rodia complained that the priest never paid him, and he resented it.

Holy Ghost Church, 305 W. Main St., PO Box 429, Dickeyville, WI 53808-0429

(608) 568-3119

Hours: Always visible; Gift Shop, April–October, daily 9A.M.–6P.M.

Cost: $1 donation encouraged

Directions: On Rte. 61, one block west of the Rte. 151 intersection.

Dodgeville
Don Q Inn

The Plaza? The Waldorf-Astoria? They've got nothing on this place! The Don Q Inn is the flagship in the FantaSuite chain; every room has a theme and a 300-gallon copper cheese vat hot tub! This is the ideal place to spice up a marriage or escape from one.

The names of several of the suites are self-explanatory: Jungle Safari, The Cave, Geisha Garden, The Treehouse, Caesar's Court, Space Odyssey, Northern Lights, Sherwood Forest, and Glasshouse. But others need some explaining. At Tranquility Base you'll sleep in a moon lander. In Up, Up and Away your bed is a balloon gondola. Deer trophies line the walls in Shotgun, and the Swinger's bed is suspended with chains. (Actually, 16 rooms have swinging beds—they're very popular!) The largest suite is an old steeple from a Methodist church. And the most asked-for suite, Mid-Evil, has shackles on the bed and riding crops for the naughty guests.

But there's more at the Don Q than kinky rooms. Parked out front is a Boeing C-97 transport signed by Farrah Fawcett! Inside the motel a mysterious tunnel connects the two wings of the building. And you can hang out in the lobby, where every seat is a barber's chair.

The Don Q was the brainchild of Ron Dentinger, who no longer owns the place. On Saturdays and Sundays at 3P.M., the staff at the Don

Q conducts free tours where you can view most of the rooms that are not currently in use.

3656 State Rd. 23 North, PO Box 199, Dodgeville, WI 53533

(800) 666-7848 or (608) 935-2320

Hours: Tours 3P.M.; check-in 4P.M.

Cost: Tour free; rooms $99 and up, depending on the day and suite

www.fantasuite.com/Location.asp?LocationId=2

Directions: On Rte. 23, north of town.

East Troy
Stevie Ray Vaughan Death Site

Otis Redding wasn't the only rock legend to be killed by the miserable Wisconsin weather.

On August 28, 1990, guitarists Stevie Ray Vaughan and Eric Clapton played a concert at the Alpine Valley Music Theater. Vaughan and three members of Clapton's band hopped into a helicopter headed for Chicago's Midway Airport. Clapton and his entourage took another chopper, but when they emerged from the haze, only their craft remained.

About a mile southeast of where they took off, Vaughan's helicopter slammed into a ski slope in a heavy fog near the top of the main lift. All aboard were killed. Vaughan now holds the dubious distinction of failing to clear one of the few mountains in the entire state.

Alpine Valley, W2501 County Rd. D, East Troy, WI 53121

(262) 642-4400

Hours: Always visible

Cost: Free

www.alpinevalleymusic.com

Directions: Take a lift to the top of Mohawk run, on the left near the top.

Elkhorn
Watson's Wild West Museum

The promotional flyer promises, "You don't have to go to South Dakota to enjoy the Old West." Truth is, you don't even have to go to Beloit! Tucked away in what looks like a typical Midwestern barn (with a covered wagon in front) is a time portal to the 1880s. Step into Watson's Wild West Museum and you're transported to Deadwood or Tombstone or Dodge City. Doug Watson, decked out in cowboy garb, is your host. Rather than let you wander aimlessly through his re-created General Store and Matchless Mine, Watson offers background information, recites cowboy poetry, tells goofy jokes, gives some of his family's history in the region, and quizzes you on Western lore minutia. If you come up with an answer, you just might win a cold bottle of sarsaparilla that he'll slide to you down the bar.

The walls of this cavernous space are filled with authentic general merchandise from the era, including cracker barrels, chewing tobacco, tools, coffee and tea, horse tack, lard, and some 42-year-old pickles. He's also got collections of Lincoln Logs, Big Little Books, Raggedy Ann dolls, guns, and elk trophies. Try your hand at panning gold in the Matchless Mine. Keep what real gold you find, but please return all the fool's gold for the next visitors. Watson wanted to showcase this collection in the famous Bird Cage Theater in Tombstone, but after protracted negotiations the deal was never cut. Arizona's loss is Wisconsin's gain. Watson is even planning to expand this site, as well as the offerings at the bar; lard sandwiches will be on sale soon.

If you've got a large posse (40+), ask about Watson's private parties, where the whole spread can be rented out for a gen-u-ine ho-down. They'll rustle you up some grub, line dancers, and Western singers! Just ask for Doug, Head Honcho.

W4865 Potter Rd., Elkhorn, WI 53121

(262) 723-7505

Hours: May, September–October, Saturday 10A.M.–5P.M., Sunday 11A.M.–5P.M.; June–August, Tuesday–Saturday, 10A.M.–5P.M., Sunday 11A.M.–5P.M.

Cost: Adults $3.75, Kids(4–10) $2.50

www.watsonswildwestmuseum.com

Directions: Just east of Rte. 12/67 on Potter Rd., just north of the Rte. 67 intersection.

EDGERTON

Sterling North, author of the children's book *Rascal*, was born on a farm at N1572 Bingham Rd. and grew up at 409 W. Rollin St. (now a museum), both in Edgerton.

Fennimore
Fennimore Doll and Toy Museum

If you're wondering what to do with the doll collection you inherited from your great-aunt, perhaps you should consider this place. Most of the pieces in this collection are the donations of late local residents Dorothy White and Mildred "Millie" Rudersdorf and current Disney-Pixar animator Jeff Pidgeon, bringing their lifelong hobbies to the general public.

Collectors of today's action figures are unlikely to admit they have a doll fixation, but the Fennimore Doll and Toy Museum doesn't dwell on the distinction. Gathered together are Barbies and *Toy Story* figurines, Mrs. Beasley and John Wayne, Raggedy Ann, and Jack from *The Nightmare Before Christmas*. And they've got plenty of stuff you probably never thought existed, or if it did, are amazed that anyone kept. Do you remember 1970s dolls of *Welcome Back Kotter*'s Horshack and Epstein, *Police Woman*'s Sgt. Suzanne "Pepper" Anderson, Sonny and Cher, or the Six Million Dollar Man and Bigfoot?

Of course, they have a Barbie display. Maybe it's a Barbie Fashion Show or a Barbie at the Beach diorama with Sun-Lovin' Malibu Ken. You never know what you'll find at the Fennimore Doll Museum because every January they rotate in new displays from their collection of more than 6,000 dolls. Next year could have a case filled with Dionne Quintuplets or *Star Wars* action figures—you just have to visit to find out.

1140 Lincoln Ave., Fennimore, WI 53809

(888) 867-7935 or (608) 822-4100

E-mail: dolltoy@fennimore.com

Hours: May–December, Monday–Saturday 10A.M.–4P.M.

Cost: Adults $3.50, Seniors $1.50, Kids(6–18) $1.50

www.fennimore.com/dolltoy/

Directions: At 11th St. and Rte. 61 (Main St.).

FOOTVILLE

Francis Wiggins Ford of Footville wrote *The Little Engine That Could* in 1912.

FORT ATKINSON

Twenty-seven of Fort Atkinson's leading citizens signed a petition to outlaw brassieres in March 1926.

Igor the Mouse

Mightiest Mouse.

It might seem strange to use a rodent to attract customers, but if it worked for Walt Disney, it could work for the Fennimore Cheese Factory.

Igor the Mouse is 12 feet tall and sits on a flatbed trailer in front of the building—perfect for photos. Your slide show viewers will gasp and think, "Geeez, look at the vermin at that place!!" Reassure them the entire cheesemaking process is clean and open to public inspection through bubble windows on a self-guided tour. The "tour" is actually more of a walk around the outlet store, but it's still interesting.

If you're looking for a Styrofoam cheesehead hat, a cheese tie, a set of cheese coasters, or a cheese postcard, this is the place to visit. And they've got plenty of real cheese for sale too, much of it pressed into interesting shapes and coated with wax, like cows, mice, pigs, and the great state of Wisconsin.

Fennimore Cheese Factory, Rte. 61, Fennimore, WI 53809

(888) 499-3778 or (608) 822-3777

E-mail: igor@fennimorecheese.com

Hours: Always visible; Store open Monday–Saturday 9 A.M.–5 P.M., Sunday 10 A.M.–4 P.M.

Cost: Free; cheese extra

www.fennimorecheese.com

Directions: At the south end of town at 16th St.

GENOA CITY

The long-running TV soap opera *The Young and the Restless* is set in Genoa City, Wisconsin. However, the city does not have a monument, nor does it celebrate The Young and the Restless Days.

Kermit in concrete.

Fontana
Concrete Frog

The Concrete Frog in Fontana has seen better days, but since it is made of concrete instead of fiberglass, nobody's planning to bulldoze it just yet. The frog is painted in Packers green and yellow, some of which is flaking off. Its eyes are empty electrical sockets, the bulbs long since bashed out. Over the years the frog has served as a fireworks stand and a putter-hut for the adjacent miniature golf course. Today, the frog is padlocked and the firecrackers are sold from a shack next door, a sad descent from a glorious, hip-hoppety past.

Frog Hollow Miniature Golf, Rte. 67, Fontana, WI 53125

No phone

Hours: Always visible

Cost: $4 per round

Directions: Just north of Fontana Outdoor Sports on Rte. 67, south of the Fontana Blvd. intersection.

Fort Atkinson
Dairy Shrine

You're in "America's Dairyland," so milk lovers should show their respect! Homage can be paid at the Dairy Shrine, a wing of the Hoard Historical

Museum in Fort Atkinson. They've got artifacts from the dairy industry, both past and present, as well as photos of men and women who made Wisconsin the milk, butter, and cheese powerhouse it is today. The journey begins on a multimedia extravaganza tracing the history of the Wisconsin dairy industry. The highlights are a goat- and dog-powered treadmill used to churn butter and a blanket used to cover Elsie, the Borden cow, at the 1939 World's Fair.

The Shrine is only part of the larger Hoard Historical Museum, named for former Wisconsin governor William Hoard, who once advised, "Speak to a cow as you would a lady." (Sexist, yes, but better than "Speak to a lady as you would a cow.") The museum covers every aspect of local history and a few things farther afield. For example, they have a mitt used by Billy Sullivan to catch three baseballs dropped 555 feet from the top of the Washington Monument in 1911, and one of the baseballs, too.

And keep your eyes peeled for the Hoard's rotating exhibits. On a recent visit there was a tribute to Fort Atkinson butcher Ernie Hausen. He won the 1922 National Chicken Picking Championship by denuding a clucker of its feathers in six seconds flat. In 1935 he set a world record at 3.5 seconds!

Hoard Historical Museum, 407 Merchants Ave., Fort Atkinson, WI 53538

(920) 563-7769

E-mail: infohoardmuseum@compufort.com

Hours: September–May, Tuesday–Saturday 9:30A.M.–3:30P.M.; June–August, Tuesday–Saturday 9:30A.M.–4:30P.M., Sunday 11A.M.–3P.M.

Cost: Free

www.hoardmuseum.org

Directions: On Rte. 12 (Merchants Ave.), four blocks south of Rte. 106 and the river.

The Panther Intaglio

A Native American intaglio is the reverse of an effigy mound, where, instead of piling soil up in the shape of an animal, a cookie-cutter hole is excavated. There is only one known existing intaglio in the United States, and that is the Panther Intaglio.

How Increase Lapham (its discoverer) ever recognized the panther shape of this unremarkable earthen depression in 1850 is anyone's guess, but he did. Archaeologists believe the Panther Intaglio was created around 1000 A.D. by the Effigy Mound Culture who lived in the area at the time. They used the hole for religious ceremonies.

Soil sampling reveals there were once 11 intaglios near this site; two were bears and the rest were panthers. The tail of this sole survivor has been filled in by a driveway, but the rest of the shape is faintly visible.

1236 Riverside Dr., Fort Atkinson, WI 53538

No phone

Hours: Always visible

Cost: Free

Directions: On the west end of town on Rte. 106 (Riverside Dr.).

Scenes from my life.
Photo by author, courtesy PEC Foundation

Hollandale
Grandview

Nick Engelbert was a world traveler. Born in Austria, he sailed from Europe to North and South America as a ship's engineer and worked on farms from California to Kansas. But when he met his future bride, Swiss immigrant Katherine Thoni, in Chicago, he decided to settle down. After they were married he went to work with her brother making cheese in Hollandale.

But he never lost his far-off memories. Starting in 1937 and continuing into the 1950s, Engelbert built statues to place around his rural home. With concrete, semiprecious stones, and broken glass, he created Snow White and the Seven Dwarfs, Uncle Sam driving a donkey/elephant team, a Viking in the prow of a boat, Paul Bunyan, the founders of the Swiss Republic, a "monkey tree" with a drunken man at its base, Neptune, a mermaid, an organ grinder, a stork delivering a baby, and a Blarney castle. By the time he hung up his trowel, there were more than 40, and he named his private hilltop park Grandview.

When he could no longer sculpt, he took up painting. He rendered scenes from his life and travels in oil on canvas and Masonite. Only his death in 1962 stopped Engelbert's creative output. Grandview deteriorated through the 1970s and 1980s and weeds grew up around the crumbling figures. The Kohler Foundation rescued his paintings, and in the early 1990s his Hollandale home. Today you can see the restored environment, returned to the way it looked when Engelbert was alive. His paintings are on display at the Kohler Art Center in Sheboygan (see p. 176).

PEC Foundation, 7351 State Highway 39, Hollandale, WI 53544

(608) 967-2140 or (608) 967-2238

Hours: Home, June–August, daily 9A.M.–5P.M.; Grounds, daily 9A.M.–7P.M.

Cost: Free

members.tripod.com/PEC-grandview/index.html

Directions: West of town one mile on Rte. 39.

Hubertus
Holy Hill

A French hermit praying at a wooden cross atop this hill in 1855 was miraculously cured of paralysis . . . and there's no reason you shouldn't expect the same courtesy. At least that has been the hope of thousands of pilgrims who flock to Holy Hill every year. Believing the hermit had experienced a true miracle, the Discalced Carmelite Order of Friars built a church on the site and moved the healing cross to the vestibule.

This place is officially known as the National Shrine of Mary, Help of Christians, which is longhand for Holy Hill. The Shrine Chapel, to the right of the main altar, houses hundreds of crutches and walkers the faithful have tossed aside after receiving miraculous cures. We can assume most of them made it back down the hill, but there's no word on how many were walking and how many were tumbling.

If the shrine isn't special enough, visit the well-stocked gift shop, the outdoor Way of the Cross, or hike the 178 heart-stopping steps to the top of the observation tower and see all the way to Milwaukee.

1525 Carmel Rd., Hubertus, WI 53033-9407

(262) 628-1838

Hours: Daily 8A.M.–4P.M.

Cost: Free

Directions: Four miles west of town off Rte. 167.

Janesville
Bessie the Cow

There's a herd of jumbo fiberglass cows scattered across Wisconsin, but Bessie the Cow is the only one who's been in a Frutopia commercial. For her small-screen debut she wore a Cheesehead hat, but today she is bareheaded.

Bessie is covered in large tan spots and sits on a grassy island between a frontage road and an all-night truck stop restaurant. She provides a great opportunity for gag photos, but whatever you do in front of her you have to be willing to do in front of dozens of truckers and minivans full of impressionable children.

Oasis Restaurant, Motel, and Cheese Shop, 3401 Milton Ave., Janesville, WI 53545

(608) 754-5730

Hours: Always visible

Cost: Free

Directions: Exit I-90 at Rte 26, one block south to Milton Ave., on the right.

White Buffalo Calf Woman

Many centuries ago, a white buffalo calf appeared to two Lakota hunters, one bad and one good, in present-day South Dakota. While they watched, the calf turned into White Buffalo Calf Woman. She floated above the ground and burned the flesh off the bad warrior, then told the good warrior to tell his tribe to expect a message in four days. Among the many prophecies she revealed, she announced that the birth of a white buffalo calf would signal a time of worldwide peace, followed by her return. She left the tribe a sacred peace pipe and told them to keep it until she came back.

Jump ahead 2,000 years to August 20, 1994, on the farm of Dave and Valarie Heider. A female white calf was born and, unlike an albino, had dark eyes and a black nose. The Heiders named her Miracle. When word got around, everyone was flocking to Janesville. Ted Nugent wanted to buy Miracle because of his song "Great White Buffalo," but the Heiders declined.

For White Buffalo Calf Woman's prophecy to come true, Miracle had to turn every color of the human race. Sure enough, Miracle turned black in January 1995, red in June, yellow in November, and is now brown. If she turns back to white—the final step—the Lakota will bring back the pipe. If Miracle turns green, watch out for Martians.

Heider Farm, 2739 S. River Rd., Janesville, WI 53546

(608) 752-2224

E-mail: daval@ticon.net

Hours: Daily 10 A.M.–5 P.M.

Cost: Free; parking $2

www.whitemiracle.com

www.globalphysics.com/lp/Prophecy/white_buffalo.htm

Directions: On the east side of the river, off Avalon Rd. (Rte. 351), northeast of the airport.

MR. LUCKY?

On your drive over to see Miracle, keep a close eye on the north side of Avalon Road. At 2214 W. Avalon, the home of George and Virginia Flint, a certain **"Mr. Lucky"** has stopped in for a visit. Without giving away the surprise, it's safe to say the Flints must be Mr. and Mrs. Unlucky.

Kenosha
Harmony Hall

Barbershop quartet singing, like banjo playing, can't help but make you feel happy . . . for a while. It's the musical equivalent of the hot fudge sundae—one or two doses and you're feeling pretty good, but four or five and you're ready to throw up. Perhaps this is why the upbeat musical form needs a proactive organization to keep it from extinction. The Society for the Preservation and Encouragement of Barbershop Quartet Singing in America (SPEBSQSA) fills that role, and Harmony Hall, on the south side of Kenosha.

The Society's basement museum is small in size but big on pep. They've got artifacts from such well-known foursomes as the Suntones, the Kansas City Barber Pole Cats, the Elastic Four, the Auto-Towners (from Detroit), the Pittsburghers, the Flying L Ranch Boys, and the Slap Happy Chappies. See memorials to William Hanna of Hanna/Barbera cartoons, who promoted barbershop singing on *The Flintstones* with the

Loyal Order of the Water Buffalo Quartet. Finally, step into "the Littlest Theater" and press the Play button on the VCR. The three-foot velvet curtains part and you're treated to newsreels of barbershop conventions from the 1940s. While Hitler's armies were ravaging Europe, it sounds like these crooners endured real hardships. Try getting together to sing about ice cream and Lida Rose with gas rationing. War really is hell!

6315 Third Ave., Kenosha, WI 53143

(800) 876-SING (worth calling, if just to hear the voice mail greeting)

E-mail: info@spebsqsa.org

Hours: Monday–Friday 10A.M.–5P.M.

Cost: Free

www.spebsqsa.org

Directions: North of Rte. 50 (75th St.) on Third Ave.

Orson Welles's Birthplace

Orson Welles never had many kind words for his birthplace, Kenosha. His family moved away when he was only four years old, so it is hard to imagine where he developed his strong negative opinions.

Welles was the son of Richard, the inventor of a new car jack, and Beatrice, chairwoman of the local board of education and accomplished pianist. He was born on May 6, 1915, upstairs in a small house at what was then 463½ Park Ave. (later renamed 7th Ave.). He was reportedly named after stockbroker Orson Wells, life partner of humorist George Ade, who Richard and Beatrice had met on a cruise to Rio de Janeiro. Welles claimed he was conceived at that South American port of call, an embarkation point that sounded more romantic to him than Kenosha.

By all accounts, Orson was a precocious child, even before the family left for Chicago. At 18 months he is said to have told his pediatrician, "(T)he desire to take medicine is one of the greatest features which distinguishes men from animals." Though questionably accurate, he was already mastering the verbal authority that would become his trademark.

6114–6116 7th Ave., Kenosha, WI 53143

Private phone

Hours: Private property; view from street

Cost: Free

Directions: On 7th Ave., just south of Library Park south of 61st St.

Lake Geneva
Andy Gump Statue

When *Andy Gump* premiered in the *Chicago Tribune* in 1917, it was the first daily comic strip that paper ever published. Gump was the type of commoner who would not have been welcomed by the blue bloods of Lake Geneva, but his creator, cartoonist Sidney Smith, was accepted with open arms. Smith built an estate here in 1922 and the *Tribune* gave him this statue in 1924 in gratitude. Smith died in 1935, and the Gump statue sat idle until it was donated to the town by executor Robert Twyman.

205 Wrigley Dr., Lake Geneva, WI 53147

No phone

Hours: Always visible

Cost: Free

www.lakegenevawi.com

Directions: Just south of the Chamber of Commerce Building, in the park, on Wrigley Dr. (Rte. 120).

THE STARS OF KENOSHA

Orson Welles wasn't the only Hollywood star to come from Kenosha, though he was perhaps the biggest.

Three Italian-American actors grew up in roughly the same neighborhood on the south side of town.

Don Ameche was born here on May 31, 1908, and lived at 5714 22nd Ave.

Al *"Happy Days"* Molinaro lived at 2417 53rd St. after greeting the world on June 24, 1919.

And **Daniel J. Travanti**, born in Kenosha on March 7, 1940, grew up at 5129 30th Ave. He graduated from Kenosha's Mary D. Bradford High School in 1958, where he took second place in the Elk's Leadership Contest.

Get it in the caboose. Photo by author, courtesy of End of the Line

End of the Line

You may have long dreamed of riding the rails in a caboose, waving at cars at crossings, watching for hobos. When the railroads stopped using cabooses, your dream died. But there are options. In Lake Geneva you can have the next best thing: spending the night in an old caboose.

The End of the Line opened in 1986 on the old Chicago and North Western tracks running to Lake Geneva. Five cabooses were converted for guests, each decorated with a unique theme and outfitted with a bathroom. Within a few years the motel was expanded to 33 units, seven of which were doubles, and one triple. Owners built a lobby out of three boxcars and filled the space with railroad memorabilia and toy trains.

The End of the Line has attracted high-profile guests like Oprah Winfrey and low-profile guests like Michael *"Family Ties"* Gross. It has also changed much over the years. The cabooses were sold off as condos in the 1990s when the original owner retired. Twenty cabooses are currently available for rent. Most new owners did away with the themes and modernized their cars, or at least made them as modern as an extinct piece of railroad equipment can be.

301 E. Townline Rd., Lake Geneva, WI 53147

(262) 248-7245 or (800) 747-RAIL

Hours: May–October, reservations required

Cost: $59 (Standard, off-peak) to $139 (Villa, peak)

www.caboosemotel.com

Directions: Rte. H south of Rte. 50, east on Townline to the railroad tracks.

Postal Route Tour

The Postal Route Tour on Lake Geneva is unique for two reasons. First, it is the only postal route in the state where letters are delivered by boat. And second, it just might be the only place in the nation where you can watch postal employees actually running to serve their customers.

Your tour aboard the *Walworth II* takes 2.5 hours, and on the way you'll watch the "mailgirls" jump from the boat to the dock, run to each box distributing letters and junk mail (and newspapers on Sunday), then leap back aboard. The boat stays in motion the entire time. The whole process takes about 10 seconds and is repeated about 60 times during the tour.

Mail has been delivered to wealthy citizens on Lake Geneva like this for more than 125 years. If the carriers don't run fast enough they'll miss the boat and end up in the water. That's incentive enough to keep moving, except on blistering summer days. Then, expect a quick dip to keep them from their appointed rounds.

Geneva Lake Cruise Line Docks, Riviera Docks, 812 Wrigley Dr., Lake Geneva, WI 53147

(800) 558-5911 or (262) 248-6206

Hours: June–September, 9:45A.M. departure

Cost: Adults $15.75, Seniors $14.20, Teens(13–17) $12.20, Kids(12 and under) $8.40

www.genevalakecruiseline.com

Directions: One block south and one block west of the intersection of Rtes. 50 and 36.

Lake Mills

Aztalan

It's not every day you can see monuments to human sacrifice and cannibalism. The vacant lots where Jeffrey Dahmer's apartment and Ed Gein's farmhouse stood are unmarked, but Aztalan is the exception to the rule.

An early native culture settled and thrived in this part of Wisconsin from 1100 to 1300 A.D., most likely descendants of those who had abandoned Cahokia in neighboring Illinois. The Pyramid of the Sun and the Pyramid of the Moon at Aztalan are the culture's most prominent surviving relics. It was atop the Pyramid of the Sun that humans were sacrificed to the gods, and it was at the nearby Pyramid of the Moon that others started to take offense. So much so that they drove their cannibalistic brethren off and burned the area to purify it. Anthropologists have rebuilt some of the stockade structures to give modern visitors a sense of what it might have looked like. Still, it loses some of the effect without human bones scattered all around.

Some believe there was something even more remarkable going on at Aztalan. The theories are built on the discovery of several submerged structures in Rock Lake, three miles west of the mounds. A large pyramid, 150 feet long and 12 feet wide with a rectangular base, was first spotted by local fishermen during a 1901 drought when the lake's water level dropped. Word got around town and everyone came out for a look. Kids swam around the structure. Boaters touched the peak with their oars. The water rose again, and nothing much was said until 1976 when a diver reported seeing several conical pyramids beneath the water. Nobody has been able to find them again, though a dragon-shaped mound was discovered beneath the surface in 1998 using sonar imaging.

Author Frank Joseph believes there is a connection between Aztalan and the lost city of Atlantis, and that the cannibal culture driven out of Wisconsin became the Aztecs of Mexico. A local group, the Rock Lake Research Society, has dedicated itself to finding an answer, sponsoring dives to find the now-missing pyramids.

Aztalan State Park, c/o Glacial Drumlin State Trail, 1213 S. Main St., Lake Mills, WI 53551

(920) 648-8774 or (920) 648-4632

Hours: Museum, May–September, Tuesday–Sunday Noon–4P.M.; Park, daily 7A.M.–9P.M.

Cost: Adults $2, Kids(7–17) $1

www.madison.k12.wi.us/whitehorse/ss/history.htm

www.pressenter.com/org/aztalan

Underwater Pyramids: www.rocklakeresearch.com

Directions: Take Water St. (Rte. B) two miles east out of town.

LODI

Tom Wopat, Bo Duke of *The Dukes of Hazzard*, was born in Lodi on September 9, 1950.

Lodi
Home of Susie the Duck

Who is Susie the Duck? Well, she could be any duck, as long as she's an aggressive squatter. The first Susie nested in a cement planter along Lodi's Spring Creek in 1947 and laid her eggs. Locals took a liking to her and named her Susie after the daughter of the local police chief. Maybe it's a statement on what else there is to do in Lodi when a common duck becomes a local celebrity.

Anyway, when fall came, Susie and her brood moved on. The following year, another duck nested in the basket-shaped planter and she, too, was named Susie. A tradition was born. Today, locals hold a contest to guess the date and time Susie's first egg will hatch. Throughout the summer the quacker is given a spot of honor in local events, and when the mallards migrate, she leaves a saddened town. . . .

Goeres Park, Fair and Main Sts., Lodi, WI 53555

No phone

Hours: Always visible

Cost: Free

Directions: In the park where Main St. crosses the creek.

Marshall
Little A-Merrick-A

If you like the atmosphere of the midway but worry about the safety records of traveling carnivals, maybe Little A-Merrick-A is more your speed. The rides are similar to those that are dragged from town to town but are well maintained and permanently attached to the ground.

Like Disneyland, Little A-Merrick-A has it own version of a monorail that encircles the park from a high track. You get a clear overview of not only the rides but also a local cornfield and the town's cemetery. Little A-Merrick-A has a scrambler, bumper cars, a haunted house, a Ferris wheel, kiddie rides, go-carts, miniature golf, and a steam train that rolls two miles over the surrounding countryside past llamas and other wildlife. The strangest ride of the bunch is a roller coaster made out of an old farm silo. You're jammed into a tiny capsule that enters the silo, climbs vertically through the cylinder, and is jettisoned out the top. The track then spirals down around the outside of the silo before screeching to a dead stop. Ride over! You won't find thrills like that anywhere else for $1.50.

700 Main St., Marshall, WI 53559

(608) 655-3181

Hours: June–August, daily Noon–8P.M.; May and September, Saturday–Sunday Noon–6P.M.

Cost: Free to enter, individual rides $1.50, five-hour ride pass $11

Directions: On Rte. 19, just east of the Rte. 73 intersection.

Merrimac
The Merrimac Ferry

The Merrimac Ferry began operation in 1844, transporting people and livestock across the Wisconsin River. The privately owned craft was operated by Chester Mattson, and at the time was dubbed Matt's Ferry. Mattson's business inspired other river ferries, at one time reaching a peak of 500 statewide. Early ferry operators earned their keep because the ferries were hand drawn.

The Merrimac Ferry is the only one in Wisconsin still operating. The state bought out the line in 1933 and eliminated the toll. The current motorized ferry can take up to 12 cars at a time. The crossing takes five minutes and is still the quickest route between Lodi and Baraboo, unless you hit it at the height of the summer season. Then you're better off swimming.

Rte. 113, Merrimac, WI 53561

No phone

Hours: Always running, weather permitting

Cost: Free

Directions: On Rte. 113.

Merton
Paul Bobrowitz, Artist

It sometimes seems that anyone with a chainsaw or a welding torch can make it as an "artist" in Wisconsin. There seems to be an insatiable demand for totem pole bears and yard birds made out of shovels and rakes. But there are a few exceptions, and Paul Bobrowitz is one of them.

You'll find him in as close to the middle of nowhere as you can be, while still being close to Milwaukee. His home and studio are off a cul-de-sac north of Merton. When you pull into his driveway you know you're somewhere unique. Robotic figures made of propane tanks line the lane. The driveway ends at a studio barn covered in metallic suns, moons, and everything else in the universe. The yard is filled with more than 300 pieces of sculpture, many of them kinetic and best appreciated on a windy day. Most of the pieces are for sale, so if you don't see a price tag, ask, or make Bobrowitz an offer.

N93-W29174 Woodchuck Way, Merton, WI 53056

(262) 538-1495

Hours: Call ahead

Cost: Free

Directions: Right (south) on Dieball from Rte. Q, turn right (west) on Woodchuck Way.

Milton
Stagecoach House

Ironically, the historic Underground Railroad was neither a railroad nor underground . . . with one exception: Milton's hexagonal Stagecoach House. Many tales of secret tunnels have been woven around homes and businesses once part of the effort to transport escaped slaves northward, but this is the only place where a tunnel still exists. It connects the main house through a trap door to an outlying log cabin.

The Stagecoach House, today called the Milton House, was the first house in the United States to be made of poured concrete. Joseph Goodrich built the home in 1844. The walls of the six-sided structure were poured a few feet at a time and allowed to harden, the forms were moved up, and another layer was added.

Milton House Museum, 18 S. Janesville St., Milton, WI 53563

(608) 868-7772

Hours: May, Saturday–Sunday 10a.m.–5p.m.; June–August, daily 10a.m.–5p.m.; September–October, by appointment

Cost: Adults $5, Seniors(62+) $4, Kids(5–17) $2

www.miltonhouse.org/milton.html

Directions: At the intersection of Janesville St. (Rte. 26) and Madison St. (Rte. M).

MINERAL POINT

Because the wives of Cornish miners in Mineral Point shook rags out their windows to signal dinnertime, the town became known as "The Shake-Rag City." You can still see their old homes along Tamblyn's Row.

Mineral Point
The Ghost of William Caffee

William Caffee killed a friend in an argument in 1842, and for his actions was hanged outside of Mineral Point's Walker-Grundy House, Wisconsin's oldest inn. Instead of showing remorse or fear, Caffee banged out a tune with two beer bottles on the lid of his coffin on the way to the scaffold.

Years later people would hear the shatter of bottles on the front porch of the house, but no broken glass was found. Doors would lock and unlock when nobody was present. And the cover to a peephole into the main dining area was constantly found off. If you feel like someone, or something, is watching you while you're visiting, you're probably right. Caffee's ghost showed up once, without his head, on the back porch in 1981.

Walker-Grundy House, 234 Madison St., Mineral Point, WI 53565

(608) 987-2884

Hours: May–October, Thursday–Sunday 1–5P.M.

Cost: Donations encouraged

www.mineralpoint.com/hist.html

Directions: Two blocks east of Water Tower Park and the Tourist Information Center.

The Ridgeway Phantom

Mineral Point is a spooky old town, and its most notorious ghost is the Ridgeway Phantom. The general consensus seems to be that the Phantom is the conglomeration of the souls of two young boys killed by rowdies at McKillip's Saloon in 1840. One boy was thrown alive into the fireplace and the other escaped into the woods, only to freeze to death. The killers may have thought it all very funny at the time, but they didn't laugh for long.

Soon a shape-changing spirit began haunting the community of Ridgeway, later renamed Mineral Point. It would show up as a variety of animals, a headless man, a ball of fire . . . you name it. And whenever it did appear, somebody, often a member of the drunken mob, soiled their pants.

The Ridgeway Phantom hasn't been seen much lately, but there's no telling when it might get back into the business. If you see something strange in Mineral Point, chalk it up to the ghouls.

Ridge Road, Mineral Point, WI 53565

Hours: After dark

Cost: Free

Directions: Along Ridge Rd. between Mineral Point and Blue Mounds.

Monroe
Monroe Means Cheese

Monroe brags that it is "Cheese City, USA," and it may have a point. Check out the map in the Historic Cheesemaking Center to see the locations of all the cheesemaking operations in southern Wisconsin; Monroe is the epicenter. Only a minute fraction of these operations still exist, but cheese still runs through this town's veins. Why else would the Monroe High School's team name be The Cheesemakers? And where is Swiss Colony's headquarters? Monroe, that's where!

To keep its heritage alive, Monroe celebrates Cheese Days every other September, and has since 1914. A Cheese King and Queen are crowned at the Turner Hall, cows are milked for sport, children dress up in cheese-themed costumes, and Swiss folk singers yodel their tonsils out. Everywhere you turn you'll find cheese tents, cheese dances, and cheese parades. If you're a brave soul, try a slice of smelly limburger, Monroe's own. The Chalet Cheese Co-op north of town [N4858 County N, (608) 325-4343] is the only place in the United States where Limburger is still made. Take a bite and you'll know why it's an "acquired taste."

Historic Cheesemaking Center, 2108 7th Ave., Monroe, WI 53566

(888) 222-9111 or (608) 325-4636

E-mail: tourism@brodnet.com

Hours: Monday–Saturday 8:30A.M.–3P.M., Sunday 10A.M.–4P.M.

Cost: Free

www.greencounty.org

Directions: At the intersection of Rte. 169 and 21st St.

CHEESY LAWS

Wisconsin's dairy industry is governed by many laws:

If you purchase a meal costing more than 25¢, you are entitled to a one-ounce piece of cheese.

Every piece of apple pie must have a slice of cheese on it.

You need a license to make cheese, and a master cheesemaker's license to make Limburger.

Artificially colored (i.e., yellow) oleo was banned from sale in the state until 1967. Before then, it had been classified as "the yellow stick form of Satan himself" in a proclamation signed by the governor.

Mt. Horeb
Mustard Museum

If you thought mustard was divided into two types, yellow for sports fans and brown for people who ride in limousines, you're sadly mistaken. In actuality, there are more than 3,400 (and more each day!) different types of mustard, and most of them are at the Mt. Horeb Mustard Museum, collected by proprietor Barry Levenson and his wife, Patti.

Start your visit by screening the movie *The Spice of Nations* in the Master Spice Theatre. Mustards from all 50 United States and points beyond fill the shelves around you. Most of the jars in this room are not for sale, but those in the other room are. After a quick survey you'll realize anything can be made into mustard; they've got mustards made of cranberries and apples, beer and BBQ sauce, prickly pears and chocolate fudge. Try spreading *that* on corned beef!

The Levensons also sell products that appeal to customers' goofier sensibilities, like diplomas and T-shirts from Poupon U, or the Naughty, Bawdy, Raunchy, X-Rated, Titillating, Should-Be-Wrapped-in-Brown-Paper, Oughta-Be-Banned, We-Should-Be-Ashamed-but-We're-Not Gift Box that includes such prurient delights as Smack My Ass and Call Me Sally habanero hot sauce, Sweet Mama Jannisse's Sticky Love Sauce, Blow Hard Hot Mustard, Fifi's Nasty Little Secret pineapple jalapeño hot sauce, and Dave's Burning Nuts . . . and those are just the ones we can print.

Levenson, a former Wisconsin state prosecutor, opened this establishment nine years ago and it's still going strong. The museum publishes a newsletter, "The Proper Mustard," hosts an annual Haiku contest and family reunion for people named Mustard, and is an archival repository for all thing mustard-esque, from cartoon strips that mention the condiment to the history of Colonel Mustard of the board game Clue.

109 E. Main St., PO Box 468, Mt. Horeb, WI 53572

(800) GET-MUSTARD or (608) 437-3986

E-mail: curator@mustardweb.com

Hours: Daily 10A.M.–5P.M.

Cost: Free

www.mustardmuseum.com

Directions: Four blocks west of the intersection of Rtes. 78 and ID (Main St.).

The Trollway

Mt. Horeb is a small town, and though they don't have a tollway, they do have a Trollway. The village claims to be "The Troll Capital of the World," and to honor the beasties it has lined Main Street with wood carvings by local artist Mike Feeney. There's the Peddler Troll, the Old Troll, the Sweet Swill Troll, the Chicken Thief, the Tub Troll, the Tourist, the Accordion Player, and the Gardener. Word around town is you're not supposed to take photos of these things, either because the artist requests permission or because a snapshot makes them come alive, and Mt. Horeb could be overrun by these ugly folk. Oooops . . . too late!

Main St., Mt. Horeb, WI 53572

Hours: Always visible

Cost: Free

Directions: Along the main east-west street in town.

New Glarus
Swiss Village Museum

In 1845 a group of 108 Swiss immigrants arrived in Wisconsin to settle 1,280 acres purchased for them by the Swiss government. Economic hardships in Europe made it more cost-effective to export their citizens than to feed them. The group cleared the land, brought in cows, and christened the town New Glarus. A century and a half later, residents are still neutral and prone to yodeling.

On the edge of town is a historic village that re-creates the life of the early settlers. You can see costumed docents blacksmith, farm, go to school, hide money in numbered accounts, and inoculate, cure, wrap, label, and sell cheese.

Twice a year the population pulls itself away from curds long enough to throw two celebrations. In June it's the Heidi Festival Pageant, and on Labor Day weekend it's the William (Wilhelm) Tell Festival. One lucky local boy is chosen to have an apple shot off his head with an arrow.

612 7th Ave., New Glarus, WI 53574

(608) 527-2317

Hours: May, September–October, daily 10A.M.–4P.M.; June–August 9A.M.–4:30P.M.

Cost: Adults $6, Kids(6–13) $2

www.swisshistoricalvillage.com

Directions: On the west side of town at 6th St.

We're trapped!

Decorated Garage

Aluminum siding is a cost-effective material to protect a home or garage, but nothing is as durable as quick-set concrete. That's what Fred Zimmerman used to coat his garage in the 1920s, and it's still holding strong. But out-of-the-sack concrete has an ugly finish, even when painted, so Zimmerman decided to embed objects in the still-wet surface to liven it up. Broken dishes, marbles, stones, metal toys . . . every square inch is filled with the stuff. Fred arranged some of the colorful pieces into American and Swiss flags and a blue star, but for the most part they are randomly placed.

Adjacent to the garage is an encrusted bird house, and in the side yard is a decorated flagpole. The Zimmermans no longer live on the property, but the current residents maintain their wacky shed with loving care.

1319 Second St., New Glarus, WI 53574

Private phone

Hours: Private property; view from street

Cost: Free

Directions: At Second St. and 14th Ave.

Platteville
World's Largest "M"

Given the choice of a letter to paint on the side of a hill outside Platteville's University of Wisconsin campus, what would you choose? A *W* for *Wisconsin*? A *P* for *Platteville*? A *B* for the road it's on? Well, students chose none of these. It's an *M* for *Mines*.

The University of Wisconsin, Platteville is sometimes known as the School of Mines, and they don't like to be confused with those pointy-headed liberal types in Madison, even though Madison starts with *M*. The giant letter was first built in 1937 by students with a lot of time on their hands. The letter is 214 feet wide 241 feet tall. Though the college is full of budding engineers, they could not devise a way to make the M stand upright, opting instead for whitewashed granite stones piled on a cleared hillside. Each year the school's freshmen are required to repaint it, thereby ensuring the survival of the 13th letter of the alphabet, at least in this town.

Hiawatha Pioneer Trail, Platte Mound, County B, Platteville, WI 53818

No phone

Hours: Always visible; illuminated twice a year

Cost: Free

platteville.wi.us/visitors/m.html

Directions: Head west out of town on Rte. B and look for the *M*.

Pleasant Prairie
Kenosha Military Museum

Some collect coins and Beanie Babies. Others, like the Kenosha Military Museum, collect tanks and helicopters. They aren't the kind of collectible you can easily fit in a display hutch, which is why they are scattered in a field off I-94, just north of the state line, as if poised to defend Milwaukee from FIBs, those Friggin' Illinois Bastards.

The KMM has hardware from World War I to Desert Storm. Track the progression of the tank from its tin-can beginnings to a modern get-the-hell-out-of-my-way machine. See armored vehicles from World War II and amphibious landing craft from *Saving Private Ryan*. Flash back to Vietnam with a Huey helicopter. It's all part of the fun that can be had in Pleasant Prairie.

And though this place collects old vehicles, it is also a dealer. They've got duplicates of some of the weaponry and are always interested in sales or trades. No hostile governments, please. Does your local VFW hall need a tank out front to garner some respect? Make them an offer!

11114 120th Ave., Pleasant Prairie, WI 53158

(262) 857-3418 or (262) 857-7933

Hours: Wednesday–Sunday 9A.M.–5P.M.

Cost: Adults $5, Kids(6–18) $3

Directions: Exit Rte. 165 from I-94, follow the eastern frontage road south.

Poynette
Aliens and Oddities of Nature Museum

Have you ever seen a hermaphroditic pheasant? Siamese raccoons? An albino catfish? No? Then head on over to the Aliens and Oddities of Nature Museum at the MacKenzie Environmental Education Center! This tiny four-room shed is a small part of the larger nature complex, but it's the best part. A large display case is filled with stuffed albino critters: a deer, a porcupine, a catfish, a fawn, a possum, a mink, a muskrat, and a squirrel. Another case has three examples of melatonism, the opposite of albinism, where a creature's coloring is completely black. The black red fox is the most striking.

Still another wall of oddities is devoted to hermaphrodites. Three deer skulls, one male, one female, and one somewhere in between, rest in a case. Three stuffed pheasants make a similar point.

In a final display are three jars of mutations. They've got Siamese raccoons, a four-legged pheasant, and a two-headed pig. The pig had the misfortune of being stolen recently on May 20, 1999. Two teenagers later apprehended with the jar claimed they dipped cigarettes in the formaldehyde and smoked them. The pig was returned by the authorities to the museum with fresh formaldehyde.

The "alien" portion of the museum is somewhat disappointing. They don't have stuffed Martians, but examples of foreign species introduced into North America, such as the Chinese ring-necked pheasant. Aliens? Yes. Exciting? No.

MacKenzie Environmental Education Center, Wisconsin Department of Natural Resources, Rte. Q, Poynette, WI 53955

(608) 635-4498 or (608) 635-8105

Hours: May–October, daily 8A.M.–4P.M.; November–April, Monday–Friday 8A.M.–4P.M.

Cost: Free

Directions: Two miles east of Rte. 51 on Rte. Q.

Prairie du Chien
Medical Progress Museum

Were it not for Alexis St. Martin, better known as "the Man with the Hole in His Stomach," nobody would have ever heard of Dr. William Beaumont. St. Martin, a man Beaumont called a "dirty, slovenly fellow, unreliable and given to drink," was shot in the stomach at Ft. Mackinac in 1825. The wound never healed, and Beaumont seized on St. Martin's misfortune to poke around in his stomach during the 1820s and 1830s. Beaumont would place pieces of food on string, push them through the hole in St. Martin's side, and pull them out later for analysis. Through this work he was able to learn how quickly certain foods digested. Beaumont published his findings in 1853. And why did Beaumont never stitch the hole closed? He claimed the shock of surgery might kill the old trapper, and that he was only looking out for his well-being. Small wonder St. Martin was cranky.

Other medical items can be found at this unique museum, including the Transparent Twins. These women's skins are made of Lucite, so you can see their glowing guts. Each body system lights up in succession as they tell you the story of how their organs work to keep them healthy. Nearby a mannequin, trapped in an iron lung, is forced to listen to the twins repeat their message day after day after day. Poor guy.

The museum has other exhibits not related to Beaumont, St. Martin, or medicine. Fort Crawford's most famous Commandant was Colonel (later U.S. President) Zachary Taylor, whose daughter married (later Confederate President) Jefferson Davis, an officer at the fort. She died within three months of their vows. Sauk chief Black Hawk (Ma-ka-tai-me-she-kia-kiak) surrendered at Fort Crawford and was imprisoned here following the Battle of Bad Axe, which ended the Black Hawk War. His cell is gone, but the bars are still on display.

Fort Crawford Medical Museum, 717 S. Beaumont Rd., PO Box 298, Prairie du Chien, WI 53821

(608) 326-6960

Hours: May–October, daily 10 A.M.–5 P.M.

Cost: Adults $2.50, Kids(6–12) $1

www.fortcrawfordmuseum.com

Directions: One block east of the riverfront, four blocks south of the Rte. 18 bridge.

Beam me up, Doc. Photo by author, courtesy of the Evermor Foundation

Prairie du Sac
The Forevertron

Tom Every ran a salvage business for 30 years, but it depressed him; when he finished a job, there was no evidence that anyone had ever been there. So he decided in 1983 to focus his energy on a constructive enterprise, The Forevertron, and began calling himself Dr. Evermor. The Forevertron, a 320-ton sculpture, will transport the "Time-Binding" Dr. Evermor to who-knows-where, maybe Heaven, on a magnetic force beam when his time has come. It is constructed from, among other things, the decontamination chamber from the *Apollo 11* mission, copper kettles from a brewery, a gazebo intended for the Royal Family, a Mississippi River barge, and a mobile home, all sitting on the foundation of a former school.

And that's not the half of it. Using what he calls "historic industrial pieces," Evermor has built a giant spider and a soon-to-be-completed plane-sized wasp. Scattered through a field behind the Forevertron is a 70-piece Bird Band made from discarded musical instruments. The Doctor makes welded creatures from engine parts, which you can purchase for a reasonable price.

And do you think building the World's Largest Metal Sculpture would be a big enough accomplishment? Not for Dr. Evermor! Next on the plate is a 500-acre Historical Artistic Memorial Sculpture Park to be located on the abandoned grounds of the Badger Army Ammunition Plant, across the street from his current digs. The Forevertron will be moved to the site and placed atop the old Compressor Building, what Evermor calls the "heartbeat of the Badger," to form the pupil of an eye-shaped park. As the munitions plant is dismantled, the pieces will be piled in blood-vessel–like berms radiating outward from the center, then covered with soil and landscaped. Atop these berms will be works by various sculptors and open spaces for performance artists. This enormous undertaking will be visible from outer space, an eye aimed at the cosmos.

Sound crazy? Not so fast. . . . The plan has received initial approval from the U.S. Army, which is looking for a way to dismantle its plant; environmentalists, who appreciate Evermor's dedication to recycling on a grand scale; munitions workers, whose labor will be recognized; farmers, who lost their land when the Army first built the plant; and artists, for obvious reasons. Anyone who could bring together these varied interests for a common goal is magical indeed.

Evermor Foundation, PO Box 22, Prairie du Sac, WI 53578

No phone

E-mail: gail@shopstop.net

Hours: April–November, Monday, Thursday–Saturday 9A.M.–6P.M., Sunday Noon–6P.M.; December–March, Saturday–Sunday 10A.M.–5P.M.

Cost: Free

www.drevermor.org

Directions: Seven miles north of town on Rte. 12.

Racine
John Dillinger's Submachine Gun

It was a scene from the Keystone Cops. On November 20, 1933, John Dillinger's gang entered Racine's American Bank and Trust at Main St. and Fifth and demanded all the money. When a teller ignored the hoodlums, he was promptly shot in the arm. Someone tripped an alarm and the bells drew a crowd who, against all common sense, peered through the bank windows at the holdup in progress.

Three police officers arrived at the scene. The first ran into the bank with his machine gun drawn and was captured. The next cop ran inside, was wounded, and lay bleeding on the floor until the crime was completed. The third policeman thought better of going inside and headed in the opposite direction.

To escape, the gang used two employees and the first cop as human shields. The officer was dumped at the edge of town; the other two hostages were released in Waukesha, west of Milwaukee. In all, the bank robbers got $28,000. The local police got Dillinger's 1928 Thompson submachine gun. During the commotion, the gangster had forgotten it at the bank. After Dillinger was captured in Tucson, Arizona, and returned to Indiana, he autographed the stock of the gun.

Today, in the lobby of the Racine Police Department, you can see the gun and the black shoelaces used to tie Bank President Grover Weyland and employee Ursula Patzke to a Waukesha tree. The American Bank and Trust was eventually torn down and a new building, the M&I Bank, stands on the site today (441 S. Main).

Racine Police Headquarters, 730 Center St., Racine, WI 53403

(262) 635-7704

Hours: Always visible

Cost: Free

Directions: Just south of Rte. 32 as it becomes 7th St.

RACINE

Ben Hecht, screenwriter for *Gone with the Wind*, *Stagecoach*, *Lifeboat*, *The Front Page*, *Gunga Din*, *Wuthering Heights*, and *Notorious*, lived in Racine as a child at 1635 College Ave. and later 823 Lake Ave.

Richland Center
Where, Oh Where, Was Little Frank Born?

Frank Lloyd Wright is to Southern Wisconsin what Kurt Cobain is to Seattle: nothing short of a local messiah. But his birth begs the question: In which Richland Center manger was he born on June 8, 1867? No fewer than seven sites have been suggested. A definitive birth record has never been located and Wright himself contributed to the confusion by pointing out conflicting sites on separate occasions. Since the accuracy of his firsthand account is suspect, his input is treated with a grain of salt.

Five candidates are on or just off a five-block stretch of Church St. The most commonly cited location is a home at 518 Church St. It is the only building of the seven still standing, and for that reason is a popular choice of local boosters. Or could Frank have entered the world where the house at 255 Mill St. now stands? Perhaps the parking lot at Park and Seminary Sts., or under the new post office at 213 S. Central? Maybe he was born at a home that stood where Papa's Donuts now sits at 101 S. Church St.? Another possible site stands alone at the south end of town at 810 Park St., today occupied by a one-car garage.

The final suggested birthplace isn't in Richland Center at all, but in neighboring Bear Valley. This location is favored by the head of the local historical society but by almost nobody in Richland Center. Wright's father was a minister and had been called to preside over a funeral in Bear Valley; records show the expectant couple was staying with relatives of his late first wife, and that the funeral was the day after Frank's birth. That's a convincing case, but it has two problems from a tourism perspective. First, the farm where they would have been staying is now gone, and second, it is not located in Richland Center.

All over town, Richland Center, WI 53581

No phone

Hours: Always visible

Cost: Free

www.richlandchamber.com

Directions: Ask around.

RACINE

Racine claims to be "The Most Danish City in America."

Don't jump! Life's not so bad!

Spring Green
Acrobatic Goats

They sing! They dance! They walk the high wire! They're the Acrobatic Goats of Peck's Farm Market!

Okay . . . so maybe they don't sing or dance, but they are acrobatic. Peck's Farm Market has built three towers of increasing height in the goat pens at their petting zoo. Each tower is connected by a narrow wooden ramp, and each platform is linked to the public by a cup on a clothesline pulley. Place a quarter's worth of corn in the cup and wheel it to the top, and watch those frisky goats climb!

These sure-hooved goats are pygmies, which makes the heights seem more ominous and impressive. The tallest tower is at least 10 times a goat's length. Translated, that would be like you scrambling up the ledges of a six-story building for a chocolate bar.

Peck's Farm Market, E3713 Rte. 14, Spring Green, WI 53588

(608) 583-4977

Hours: June–October 8A.M.–8P.M.; goats outside only in good weather

Cost: 25¢ per cup

Directions: East of town on Rte. 14, just east of the Rte. C intersection.

House on the Rock

Hell hath no fury like an architect scorned. When Frank Lloyd Wright dismissed Alex Jordan, Sr., from nearby Taliesin, stating, "I wouldn't hire you to design a cheese crate or a chicken coop. You aren't capable," Jordan decided to get even. And how. Jordan purchased the land overlooking Wright's beloved studio and started building a home to rival Mr. Bigshot's Taliesin, and the project didn't let up until the death of his son, Alex Jordan, Jr., in 1989.

Most of the work was done by young Alex, known to everyone as Junior. The first structure was the actual House on the Rock, a cramped, Asian-esque bachelor pad perched atop Deer Shelter Rock. To blast the top of the rock level, Junior hired drunks and bums in Madison and paid with a bottle of whiskey for the hazardous duty. To demonstrate his sense of style while the work progressed, Junior would drive around Madison and out to Spring Green in a 16-cylinder, 22-foot-long, two-seater black Cadillac convertible. Seeing Alex, Wright must have been insanely jealous or incredibly pissed off. Either emotion would have satisfied the Jordans.

House on the Rock grew out, over, and beyond Deer Shelter into a 30-acre collection of everything under the sun. To see it all, you must prepare yourself to run the Boston Marathon of museums. The self-guided tour snakes through two and one-half miles of displays in dozens of themed outbuildings. House on the Rock won't sell you a ticket less than two and one-half hours before closing time for fear you won't get through it all and they'll have to send out a search party. Among the wonders you'll see are:

- the World's Largest Carousel. It weighs 35 tons, stands 80 feet high, and contains 269 characters, including a cat with a fish in its mouth and a bare-breasted female with a rooster's lower body! No horses though.
- the World's Largest Cannon
- the World's Largest Fireplace. It can burn an entire tree at one time, barbecuing an entire cow.
- the Infinity Room, a glass hallway dangling 150 feet over the Wyoming Valley, unsupported for its final 218 feet
- replicas of England's Crown Jewels
- a 200-foot fiberglass whale battling a giant squid
- chipmunk dioramas in the men's bathroom

- a wooden leg with a gun holster embedded in it
- dozens of questionably authentic Tiffany lamps
- a musical Richard Nixon mannequin in the Circus Exhibit
- the bottled head and hands of a criminal in the Sheriff's Office
- 6,000 Santas placed throughout the attraction at Christmastime. Do they stop at 5,000? No—*it isn't enough!*

How could Jordan afford such a lavish collection of knickknacks? The answer is found in what you don't see: placards detailing where these items came from. Back in the 1970s the Wisconsin Justice Department demanded Jordan remove all signs making unsubstantiated claims about what people were seeing. In reality, many of the "antiques" you see today were purchased at a local K mart and look old only because they're placed at a distance, behind glass. The music that appears to be coming from the mechanical orchestras is often piped in. Much of the ivory is fake, including the impressive Oriental Boat. And who paid for all this junk? Partly you, the American taxpayer, through federal farm subsidies to Jordan not to plant the surrounding land in corn or wheat.

But the bottom line is, *Who cares?* There is no tour in the Badger State that inspires more wonder and awe than the Mighty, Gaudy, Fantabulous Forced March Through the World's Largest Barn of Crapola, better known as House on the Rock. Miss it and you'll die a lesser person.

5754 Rte. 23, PO Box 555, Spring Green, WI 53588

(800) 947-2799 or (608) 935-3639

E-mail: houseontherock@mindspring.com

Hours: March 16–October, daily 9A.M.–7P.M.; November–Early January, daily 9A.M.–6P.M.; January–March 15, Saturday–Sunday 9A.M.–6P.M.

Cost: Adults $19.50, Kids(7–12) $11.50, Kids(4–6) $5.50; off-season $12.50, $7.50, $3.50

www.TheHouseontheRock.com

Directions: Off Rte. 23 between Spring Green and Dodgeville.

SOLDIER'S GROVE
Agnes "Endora" Moorehead once taught school in Soldier's Grove.

WHITEWATER
Actor **Tom Hulce** was born in Whitewater on December 6, 1953.

ALEX JORDAN'S FIRST SCHEMES

Alex Jordan, Jr., was handy with a camera in his early years, but it got him in a lot of trouble. First, he took infrared photos of a stripper in a Green Bay club and was threatened with death when the proprietors found out. He returned the negatives. Junior used the same camera in 1939 to take photos of his lifelong companion, Jennie Olson, having sex with prominent Madison businessmen in an extortion scheme. It worked on several men before the pair were caught, convicted, and sentenced, Jordan with a $500 fine and six months in jail, Olson with $300 and three months. Alex Jordan, Sr., strongly suggested his son spend more time working on the House on the Rock to keep him out of Madison, away from his former victims. For all the salacious details, check out *House of Alex* by Marv Balousek (Oregon, WI: Waubesa Press, 1990).

Taliesin

The second-best architect in this region (after Alex Jordan, Jr.) is, of course, Frank Lloyd Wright. His Wisconsin studio and home, Taliesin, are located in the Wyoming Valley, where you can see them all . . . for a pretty penny. *Taliesin* is Welsh for "Shining Brow" and is a name more fitting for House on the Rock, but Wright took it first. If you take the tour, you will no doubt be barraged with details of Wright's genius, but what you won't hear are the gory details of a mass murder at this very site.

On August 14, 1914, a Barbadan butler named Julian Carleton, pissed off at being canned by Mamah Chaney Borthwick, Wright's mistress, planned his attack at lunchtime. During the meal he walked in, threw gasoline on a dinner guest and set him aflame, split Borthwick's head with an ax, and fled. All exits from the room were blocked except for the one behind which Carleton waited. As guests tried to escape the dining area, he killed them, one by one, with blows to their heads. Before it was over, Borthwick and six others were dead. Carleton ingested muriatic acid and died two months later in jail after a hunger strike.

Wright was out of town and missed the carnage. After he returned, Wright would ramble around, somewhat crazy, in the charred shell of Taliesin while it was being rebuilt. He never quite recovered, and neither did mistress Mamah. She is believed to haunt the Tan-Y-Deri shed out back. Ask the guides about it . . . they never mention the murders in the home's promotional material, nor are they allowed to tell grisly stories during the tour. But you can ask. . . .

Frank Lloyd Wright Visitor Center, Rte. 23 and Rte. C, Spring Green, WI 53588

Contact: Taliesin Preservation Committee, PO Box 399, Spring Green, WI 53588-0397

(608) 588-7900

E-mail: tpc@mhtc.net

Hours: May–October, daily 8:30A.M.–4P.M.; call ahead for reservations and tour departure times

Costs: Hillside Home School $10, Exterior Walking Tour $15, Interior Taliesin House $40, Estate Tour $60

www.TaliesinPreservation.org

Directions: On Rte. 23, two miles south of Spring Green.

SLEEPING WITH FRANK

If you want to spend the night at a **Frank Lloyd Wright** house, there is only one place to do it—at the Seth Peterson Cottage in Mirror Lake State Park. Seth Peterson never stayed in the building he commissioned from the master; he shot himself in 1958 after being dumped by his girlfriend. You can tour the house every second Sunday of the month from 1 to 4P.M.; you can rent the place for short vacations throughout the year. (E9982 Fern Dell Rd., Reedsburg, (608) 254-6551)

SULLIVAN

The town of Rome in the television show *Picket Fences* was based on an unincorporated neighborhood of Sullivan. Parts of the town were shown in the opening credits.

Frank Lloyd Wright's Grave—NOT!

Just down the hill from Taliesen, Frank Lloyd Wright was laid to his not-so-final rest in 1959, beneath a monument of his own design. The stone marker was a rough-hewn hunk of native rock with a cantilevered name-plate. But before the worms got a bite, folks realized they had not put Frank in the ground according to his final wishes, which was to be facing his beloved studio. So Frank was exhumed, turned, and reburied.

Wright's third wife, Olgivanna Milanov, had no intentions of being planted in the cold Wisconsin soil beside her husband, so she ordered that upon her death Wright would be exhumed, cremated, and reburied with her in Scottsdale, Arizona, near Taliesen West.

Milanov died in 1985 of a stroke and her grave-robbing plot was carried out. Though the marker to Wright still marks a grave, nobody's home below. If you want to see a real dead celebrity, actress Anne Baxter has been planted in this small burial ground.

Lloyd-Jones Family Cemetery, Unity Chapel, County Rd. T, Spring Green, WI 53588

No phone

Hours: Always not visible

Cost: Free

Directions: Two miles south of town, just of Rte. 23 on Rte. T.

Union Grove
Great Lakes Dragaway

The trouble with most racing venues is that the average Joe or Josephine isn't allowed to participate. Not so at the Great Lakes Dragaway. If you've got wheels and $22 you can drag all you want on their quarter-mile track. Of course, the place is primarily frequented by serious gearheads, but you'll still see everything from station wagons and K-Cars to dragsters and nitro-burning funny cars. Motorcycles and snowmobiles are also welcome. That's right, a modified snowmobile can eat up a quarter-mile in under 10 seconds, its skids replaced with tiny wheels.

The Dragaway was started by Broadway Bob and has not changed much since it opened—not even the music selection, which contains healthy doses of George Thorogood, Journey, and AC/DC. Sitting in the grandstands, looking out over the cornfields while blue smoke curls up from a Nova's tires to the sounds of Styx, makes for a surprisingly relaxing and entertaining evening. But maybe that's just the beer talking.

City Line Rd., Union Grove, WI 53182

(262) 878-3783

Hours: April–November, Tuesday–Sunday, call for race times

Cost: Adults $11, Racing $22

Directions: East of town on Rte. KR (City Line Rd.).

Watertown
The Nation's First Kindergarten

Friedrich Frobel came up with the revolutionary concept that young children should be prepared for entry into the school regimen, and in 1837 he founded Europe's first kindergarten, "a garden for children." The experiment made an impact on one of Frobel's students, Margarethe Meyer Schurz, who later founded America's first kindergarten on August 26, 1856, in her front parlor in Watertown.

There were only six students in the first class, and two were hers. Lessons were given in German. A friend, Elizabeth Peabody, copied Schurz and opened an English-speaking classroom for tots in Boston. Today, few children enter the first grade without spending some time eating paste, taking naps, and finger-painting with their peers.

Schurz's home was restored in 1956 and the building was moved from downtown to its present site next to the Octagon House. There haven't been classes here for many years, so don't worry about catching the funky odor of vomit-absorbing sawdust.

Octagon House Museum, 919 Charles St., Watertown, WI 53094

(920) 261-2796

Hours: June–August, daily 10A.M.–4P.M.; May, September–October, daily 11A.M.–3P.M.

Cost: Adults $4.50, Seniors $4, Kids(6–17) $2

members.tripod.com/~watertownhs

Directions: Two blocks south on Concord Ave. from Rte. 19, turn west on Western Ave., south on Harvey, then one block east to Charles St.

Williams Bay
World's Largest Refracting Telescope

The telescope at Williams Bay's Yerkes Observatory, with its 40-inch refractor, is the World's Largest Refracting Telescope. It is owned and operated by the University of Chicago, and is located far north of the metropolis to avoid the smog and light pollution of the big city. Few refracting telescopes are still used today; reflecting telescopes are more common, so Yerkes may hold the record forever.

The story of how this telescope was funded is as interesting as anything it has discovered. Charles Yerkes was a public transportation tycoon who owned the streetcars on the North Side of Chicago and built the elevated Loop. He was not above lining his own pockets at his investors' and riders' expenses. In fact, he had spent time in prison earlier in life for misappropriating public funds in Philadelphia in 1871. And though he was rich as Midas, he didn't have the approval of the Chicago social elite, many of whom summered on the shores of Lake Geneva.

Enter U of C President William Harper and astronomer George Hale. They suggested that Yerkes fund the World's Largest Telescope, to be placed on the same shoreline as the socialites' homes. That would certainly win over his critics! After considerable funds had been plowed into the project, the telescope was finished in 1897, and though Yerkes was praised at its dedication, he never was invited to join the Upper Crust.

Yerkes Observatory, 373 W. Geneva St., Williams Bay, WI 53191

(262) 245-5555

E-mail: rdd@hale.yerkes.uchicago.edu

Hours: Saturday tours 10:15A.M., 11A.M., and 12:15P.M.

Cost: Free; donations accepted

astro.uchicago.edu

Directions: On Rte. 67, just east of Theatre Rd.

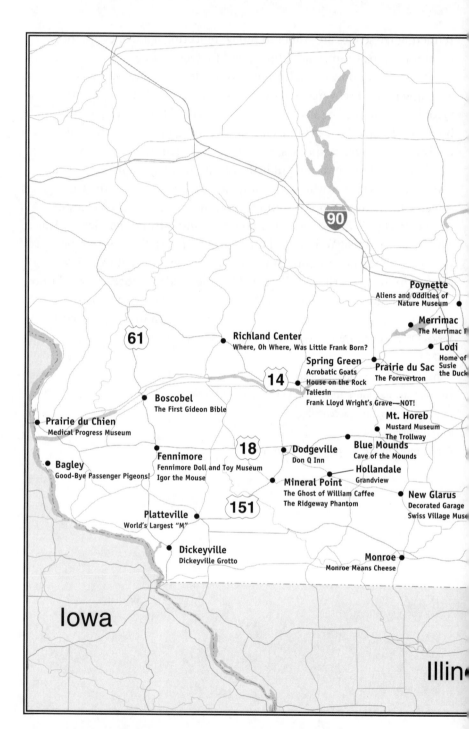

Poynette
Aliens and Oddities of Nature Museum

Merrimac
The Merrimac F

Lodi
Home of Susie the Duck

Prairie du Sac
The Forevertron

90

61

Richland Center
Where, Oh Where, Was Little Frank Born?

Spring Green
Acrobatic Goats
House on the Rock
Taliesin
Frank Lloyd Wright's Grave—NOT!

14

Boscobel
The First Gideon Bible

Prairie du Chien
Medical Progress Museum

Mt. Horeb
Mustard Museum
The Trollway

Blue Mounds
Cave of the Mounds

Dodgeville
Don Q Inn

18

Bagley
Good-Bye Passenger Pigeons!

Fennimore
Fennimore Doll and Toy Museum
Igor the Mouse

Hollandale
Grandview

Mineral Point
The Ghost of William Caffee
The Ridgeway Phantom

New Glarus
Decorated Garage
Swiss Village Muse

Platteville
World's Largest "M"

151

Dickeyville
Dickeyville Grotto

Monroe
Monroe Means Cheese

Iowa

Illin

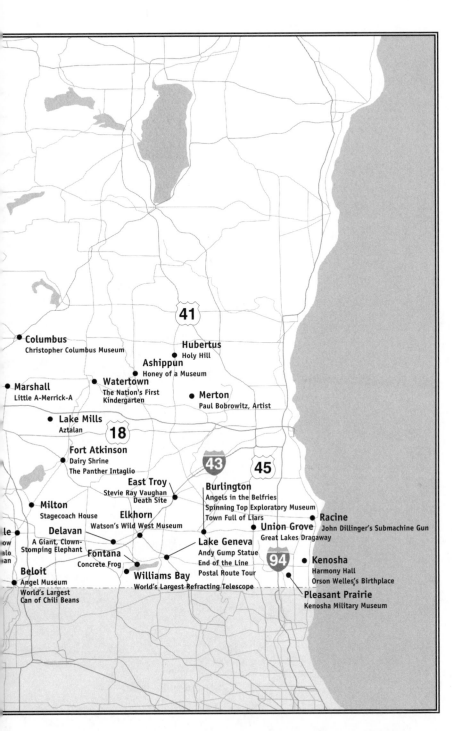

41

Columbus
Christopher Columbus Museum

Hubertus
● Holy Hill

Ashippun
● Honey of a Museum

● **Marshall**
Little A-Merrick-A

Watertown
The Nation's First
Kindergarten

● **Merton**
Paul Bobrowitz, Artist

● **Lake Mills**
Aztalan

18

Fort Atkinson
● Dairy Shrine
The Panther Intaglio

43

45

East Troy
Stevie Ray Vaughan
Death Site

Burlington
Angels in the Belfries
Spinning Top Exploratory Museum
Town Full of Liars

● **Milton**
Stagecoach House

Elkhorn
Watson's Wild West Museum

● **Union Grove**
Great Lakes Dragaway

● **Racine** John Dillinger's Submachine Gun

Delavan
A Giant, Clown-
Stomping Elephant

le
ow
alo
an

Fontana
Concrete Frog

Lake Geneva
Andy Gump Statue
End of the Line
Postal Route Tour

94

● **Kenosha**
Harmony Hall
Orson Welles's Birthplace

Beloit
● Angel Museum
World's Largest
Can of Chili Beans

Williams Bay
World's Largest Refracting Telescope

Pleasant Prairie
Kenosha Military Museum

5

Mad Town Area

Wisconsin Governor Lee Sherman Dreyfus once described Madison as "thirty-six square miles surrounded by reality." Whether it is due to the university or the state lawmakers, Madison has long been known as Mad Town or Mad City, home to Cheese State bureaucrats and radicals, or at least radicals by Wisconsin standards. But blaming the policy wonks and old hippies would be too easy, and not exactly fair. There's something else going on here. Something weird. Something abnormal.

Take, for example, a recent study on rhinotillexomania performed by the University of Wisconsin. Rhinotillexomania is better known by its street name: nose-picking. Researchers wanted answers to such sensitive questions as which finger subjects used and how often they examined their boogers after extracting them. Researchers had no difficulty signing up 1,200 Madison residents as subjects.

Thinking about this study will give you peace of mind as you visit the capital city. Suddenly you won't feel so self-conscious about riding the merry-go-round at Ella's, crying at the death site of Otis Redding, or waiting for a groundhog to tell you what the weather will be like in spring. Next to these booger-digging bureaucrats, you're almost normal.

Almost.

Madison
Bombing at the Army Mathematics Research Center

On August 24, 1970, a 1967 Ford Falcon Deluxe station wagon parked outside Sterling Hall on the UW campus exploded. But it wasn't the car's fault. The blast killed one research scientist, Robert Fassnacht, and injured three others. Sterling Hall was targeted because it housed the Army Mathematics Research Center, and the Vietnam War was raging.

The homemade bomb was detonated by the New Year's Gang, aka the Vanguard of the Revolution, who had three basic demands: (1) release a Milwaukee Black Panther Party official being held in the attempted murder of a policeman, (2) expel the ROTC from campus, and (3) abolish "women's hours" at UW Madison.

The New Year's Gang had named themselves after a previous failed attempt to level the Badger Army Ammunition Plant in nearby Baraboo. On December 31, 1969, they dropped three jars of a fuel oil and nitrogen fertilizer mixture from a low-flying Cessna, hoping to set off a chain reaction at the plant. The plan didn't work.

Unfortunately for Fassnacht, their second plan did work, at least as far as the explosion was concerned. But the unintended consequence of the murder was a backlash against antiwar protests that had grown increasingly violent.

Eventually four men were charged in the crime. Karleton Armstrong was captured in Toronto in February 1972 after trying to get a passport to Algeria under the assumed name of David Weller. (He drew a 23-year sentence.) David Fine was nabbed in San Rafael, California, in 1975 while attending Marin Community College as William Lewes. (He got seven years.) Dwight Armstrong was apprehended in Toronto in April 1977, living as Gary Mitchell. (He also got seven years.) But the final accomplice, Leo Burt, has never been captured.

Sterling Hall was repaired and is still in service today.

Sterling Hall, University of Wisconsin at Madison, Lathrop and Charter Sts., Madison, WI 53706

No phone

Hours: Always visible

Cost: Free

Directions: North on Charter St. off University Ave., just east of the University/Randall Ave. intersection.

GOOD THING THIS ISSUE CAME OUT LATER

The Vanguard of the Revolution might have been able to level the Badger Army Ammunition Plant had they waited a decade. A working blueprint for a hydrogen bomb was published in the *Madison Press Connection* in September 1979. Later, *Madison's Progressive Magazine* attempted to do the same but was blocked by the Pentagon.

MADISON MUSEUMS R.I.P.

Madison was once home to several oddball collections that are now off limits. What a shame these museums have been mothballed or are open only on special occasions.

International Credit Union Museum The Credit Union National Association (CUNA) once maintained a credit union collection at their national headquarters. Your visit started by viewing "The Credit Union Legacy," a 24-projector, multimedia extravaganza in the association's 175-seat auditorium—no need to push, there's room for everyone! After the show you could view dioramas and maps outlining collective debt's checkered history. No longer. CUNA hopes to open the museum again someday.

Madison Museum of Bathroom Tissue Currently "in transit," this privately held collection has rolls "liberated" from the Alamo, the Statue of Liberty, Graceland, Caesar's Palace, and Churchill Downs . . . along with 3,000 other rolls. Admittance was reasonable—just 25 cents and a roll of TP. Until they find a new home, they're closed to the public.

Mystery Critter Display This fabulous collection of strange taxidermy is located in the basement of a reputable business that would prefer to keep a low profile. For determined travelers, consider finding it the ultimate roadside challenge. If you locate it, you're welcome to visit it. Your only clue is that it is located within the Madison city limits. Should you prevail in your quest, you'll find chipmunks riding saddled plastic deer and horses and other rodents dancing in a "Topless Girlie Show," riding a Ferris wheel, or playing cards in a local saloon. Also, a dozen albino squirrels pose in pink Barbie convertibles and monster Tonka trucks.

Eight hands are better than two.

Car-Washing Octopi

To give your car a thorough scrubbing you almost have to be an octopus. As luck would have it, a couple of businesses in Madison do just that: the Octopus Car Washes! Their signs are difficult to miss; a smiling, pistachio-colored octopus grips a pail, sponge, and brush in its writhing tentacles. Whether your car is spattered with bugs or bird doo-doo, this octopus looks up to the job. Yet the octopus stays atop its pole and humans do most of the work on your vehicle.

You would expect other Madison car washes to follow the Octopi's lead. So where's the whale to squirt you with its spout at the Whale of a Wash? Where are the flippered female attendants at the Mermaid Car Wash?

What's so wonderful about Wonder Wash, or magical about Magic Wash?

Octopus Car Wash, 907 S. Park St., Madison, WI 53715

(608) 257-3991

Hours: Always visible

Cost: Free

Directions: On Park St. (Rte. 151) north of the Fish Hatchery Rd. (Rte. D) intersection.

Octopus Car Wash, 1039 E. Washington, Madison, WI 53703

(608) 257-2929

Hours: Always visible

Cost: Free

Directions: On Washington Ave. (Rte. 151) eight blocks northeast of the Capitol Building.

Chris Farley's Tomb

Contrary to what you might have heard, Chris Farley was not buried in "a van down by the river." After the comedian died in the foyer of his Chicago condo on December 18, 1997, his body was returned to Madison, his hometown.

Chris Farley's family lived in the Maple Bluff neighborhood when he was born on February 15, 1964. Farley was the class clown and his idol was John Belushi. Clearly, Farley took the idol worship too far, copying Belushi's excesses in food, alcohol, and drugs. He died at the age of 33 of a heart attack brought on by a long night of partying with a hired stripper.

The location of Farley's tomb in the mausoleum would suggest he was a bishop. Perhaps in Madison he was. He's interred just past the altar, on the left, as you enter the interior mausoleum. A long kneeler in front can accommodate several fans at once.

Resurrection Chapel Mausoleum, 2705 Regent St., Madison, WI 53705

(608) 238-5561

Hours: Monday–Friday 8:30A.M.–4:30P.M., Saturday 9A.M.–Noon

Cost: Free

Directions: At the corner of Franklin Ave. and Regent St.

MADISON

Somewhere on the bottom of Madison's Lake Monona is a chest of gold. It was dumped there by U.S. Army paymasters during a hurried escape from Indians in 1828.

Ella's Kosher Deli & Ice Cream Parlor

The name of this establishment suggests you might find a traditional eatery, but there is nothing about Ella's that's like anything you'd find anywhere else on earth. The food and desserts are average, but the decor is a Mel Blanc acid trip. Animatronic cartoon characters fly overhead on wires, turn, and return for another pass. Mickey Mouse, Bart Simpson, Superman, Batman, and a genie on a flying carpet are some of the tamer robots. Popeye rises into the air on a rocket ship, workshop tools come alive and dance, and three brightly dressed clowns stretch like rubber, changing height before your very eyes. Guitar-plucking cowboys, the Beatles, and Mozart add music to the mix.

If you can take your eyes off the ceiling long enough, check out your table. Each glass-topped table is filled with a collection of toys or interactive games. Those seated at certain tables are given magnetic wands to pull iron-filing beards and hair on the bald heads beneath the glass. Others are filled with marble games or optical illusions. You can also find collections of Pez dispensers, model trains, and yo-yos.

Outside, in the summer, is a fully operational wooden carousel. It was built in 1927 by C. W. Parker of Leavenworth, Kansas. The carousel is in mint condition and can even support full-sized adult riders.

2902 E. Washington Ave., Madison, WI 53704

(608) 241-5291

Hours: Sunday–Thursday 10A.M.–11P.M., Friday–Saturday 10A.M.–Midnight

Cost: Looking is free; food extra

Directions: Just south of Rte. 30 on Rte. 151 (Washington Ave.).

MADISON

The 45-year-old daughter of former Democratic presidential candidate **George McGovern**, Theresa, died in Madison in 1994 after she fell asleep in a snowbank and didn't get back up.

WHA Radio in Madison is the world's oldest continuously operating radio station. It has been broadcasting nonstop since 1917. When it started, its call letters were 9XM and it transmitted a selection of music from Vilas Communication Hall on the UW campus.

The Rebel Dead

When Confederate soldiers were captured in 1862 at Island Number 10 on the Mississippi River, they were transferred to Camp Randall's POW stockade in Madison. Conditions at the camp were similar to prisons on both sides during the conflict: miserable. Many of the Rebs died of disease and were buried in Forest Hill Cemetery. Though these soldiers may be hundreds of miles from home in the cold Wisconsin soil, thanks to Abraham Lincoln they're still buried in the United States. Today, Confederate Rest at Forest Hill is the nation's northernmost Confederate burial plot.

Forest Hill Cemetery is also notable for another reason: It is one of the few urban graveyards in the United States where Native American effigy mounds are part of the land. At the southern corner of the cemetery are two panther-shaped mounds, a goose-shaped mound, and a linear mound, estimated to have been built around A.D. 900–1200. The goose was accidentally "beheaded" by the Illinois Central Railroad in the 1880s, and three other linear mounds were leveled before anyone realized what they were destroying.

Forest Hill Cemetery, 1 Speedway Rd., Madison, WI 53705

(608) 266-4720

Hours: Daily 9A.M.–5P.M.

Cost: Free

Directions: At the intersection of Regent St. and Speedway Rd.

Sid's Sculpture Yard

Sid Boyum has never gotten his due. For years he was Alex Jordan, Jr.'s right-hand man at House on the Rock. Boyum and Jordan's friendship went back to the days when they peddled a product called No Run to university women. When mixed with water it was supposed to keep snagged nylons from running. The claim was true, but No Run turned out to be nothing more than cement.

Though he worked in Spring Green, Boyum lived in Madison for most of his life. Over the years he built 70 sculptures in his backyard and home, many from eastern mythology and many of them sexually suggestive. In the front yard he had a chair shaped like a polar bear, and in the back was a big-breasted sphinx and the Mouth of Hell. In the years leading up to his 1991 death, his home was filled with more than 80 cats.

Boyum's son Steve inherited the home, the sculptures, and the cats. Rather than hide his father's artwork from the public, he restored 13 pieces and moved them to locations around the Atwood neighborhood in the summer of 2000. More of Boyum's works should follow their predecessors.

237 Waubesa St., Madison, WI 53704

No phone

Hours: Always visible

Cost: Free

Directions: Two blocks east of the intersection of Fair Oak and Atwood Aves., north on Waubesa.

Thornton Wilder's Birthplace

Pulitzer Prize–winning novelist and playwright Thornton Wilder was born in Madison on April 17, 1897, at 14 W. Gilman St. He was the only surviving child of a pair of twins and spent much of his first year in a sickly state, carried around on a pillow by his mother, like a golden egg.

At the time, his father was editor of the *Wisconsin State Journal*. The Wilder family moved to 211 W. Gilman, just down the street, when Thornton was an infant, and throughout their time in Madison attended the First Congregationalist Church (1609 University Ave.).

Young Thornton inherited his father's interest in writing, and would hang out at the newspaper office or the local library. The family left town for Hong Kong when Thornton was nine, after his father was appointed American Consul General.

14 W. Gilman Street, Madison, WI 53702

Private phone

Hours: Private residence; view from street

Cost: Free

Directions: Head northwest on Wisconsin Ave. from the State Capitol Building, turn left on Gilman, one block short of the lake.

MADISON

Actress **Tyne Daly** was born in Madison on February 21, 1946.

Both **Vitamin A** and **Vitamin B** were discovered in Madison.

Washin' Up by the Dock of the Lake

Otis Redding recorded "(Sitting On) The Dock of the Bay" on December 7, 1967, and three days later made an unanticipated career move: He died when his plane crashed into Madison's Lake Monona. The song would likely have been a hit had the 26-year-old singer not met an early, tragic death, but as Jim Croce could tell you (if he were alive), the publicity doesn't hurt.

Redding was on his way to Madison from Cleveland to play at The Factory Nightclub and went down three miles short of the runway in the middle of the icy lake. Four band members were also killed, but one, trumpet player Ben Cauley, miraculously survived. Contrary to local legend, all the victims were recovered, so you don't have to worry about stubbing your toe on Otis when you're swimming.

For years there was a three-bench memorial to Redding in Law Park. The benches faced in the direction of the crash site. When the Monona Terrace Convention Center was built, they were moved to the Rooftop Garden.

Rooftop Garden, Monona Terrace Convention Center, 1 John Nolan Drive, Madison, WI 53702

No phone

Hours: Always visible

Cost: Free

Directions: Just southeast of the State Capitol Building, on Lake Monona.

MADISON

The University of Wisconsin at Madison was the first college to ever offer correspondence courses.

The full name of the UW mascot is **Buckingham U. Badger.**

UW law students throw canes over the football goalposts during Homecoming each year. If they catch them on the way down, tradition says they'll win their first cases.

Drivers beware! By law, only baby buggies and three-wheeled vehicles with rubber tires are allowed on the streets of Madison after 8P.M.

Wisconsin State Capitol Building

As State Capitols go, the Wisconsin structure is unique in many weird ways. It has the only granite dome in the United States, which is topped with a gilded statue entitled "Wisconsin." Though it is difficult to distinguish from the ground, this golden, feminine representation of the state wears a badger on her head and has a corncob dangling beside each ear. She was sculpted by Daniel Chester French, who later went on to design the Lincoln Memorial, though Abe didn't end up with such silly accessories.

The highest flagpole to rise from the Capitol roof was the scene of a foolhearted patriotic gesture on Memorial Day in 1911. Citizen Frank E. Smith shimmied up the pole to unwind a flag that had gotten tangled 230 feet in the air. An approving crowd watched from below as Smith unfurled the banner, lost his grip, and plunged to his death.

Inside the Capitol are two special features, both near the Governor's office. First, the 1,000-pound bronze badger just outside once adorned the deck of the USS *Wisconsin*, but the Navy removed it because they worried about shrapnel if the metallic rodent were hit by a shell. The second oddity is a doorknob in the office—it has traveled to outer space! The knob took an uncommon trip aboard the space shuttle *Discovery* with astronaut Daniel Brandenstein in 1985.

Not everyone has been impressed with the Capitol or its knick-knacks. Architect Frank Lloyd Wright once said, "[Y]ou can't put that much stone in one pile without creating some dignity and majesty. Anyway, there it is, and we should make the best of it." From Wright, it was a stellar endorsement.

State Capitol Building, Washington and Wisconsin Aves., Madison, WI 53702
(608) 266-0382

Hours: Monday–Saturday 9, 10, 11A.M., 1, 2, 3, and 4P.M. tours, Sunday 1, 2, 3, and 4P.M. tours

Cost: Free

Directions: On the isthmus between Lake Monona and Lake Mendota.

WAUNAKEE
Waunakee claims to be "The Only Waunakee in the World."

Ooooooh, my aching head!

Suburbs
DeForest
Sissy the Cow and the Partying Pink Elephant

They stare at each other across Interstate 90/94: Sissy the Cow and the Partying Pink Elephant. Pick your side.

Sissy is a clone of Neillsville's Chatty Belle, but unlike her sister, she doesn't talk. The 20-foot-tall Holstein silently guards Ehlenbach's Cheese Chalet, a reputable dairy-based establishment. Folks who shop here get up at the crack of dawn and go to bed early.

The Phillips 66 seems like a harmless enough station, but what's that pink elephant doing out front? You don't end up with that type of hallucination from one too many milk shakes. The Partying Pink Elephant wears sunglasses to protect its bloodshot eyes, and to keep Sissy wondering what he's up to. This place is open 24 hours, wouldn't you know.

The whole stare-down is observed by a large German mouse in climbing attire atop Ehlenbach's tall sign. That rodent is smart enough to stay out of the conflict.

Ehlenbach's Cheese Chalet, 4879 County Rd. V, DeForest, WI 53532

(608) 846-4791

Hours: Always visible

Cost: Free

Directions: Off I-90/94 at Exit 126 north, head east.

Interstate 66, 4995 County Road V, DeForest, WI 53532

(608) 846-9550

Hours: Always visible

Cost: Free

Directions: Off I-90/94 at Exit 126 north, head west.

Sun Prairie
Birthplace of Georgia O'Keeffe

People mentally place Georgia O'Keeffe where she spent the bulk of her creative life, in the Southwest, but it was not her homeland. She was born in Sun Prairie, Wisconsin, on November 15, 1887, the first daughter of Irish immigrants.

Georgia Totto O'Keeffe was the second child of seven and by all accounts her mother's least favorite child. She was a tomboy and, to get back at her sisters for their favorable standing, would bring the girls to the barn and dare them to stick their hands into the cows' mouths, in order to feel their tongues. They did, and Georgia got in trouble. She was also punished by her grandmother for getting dirty while acting on her taste for fresh-tilled soil.

Georgia attended the nearby Town Hall School and was a loner. It took a local art teacher, Sarah Mann, to draw out her creative side. Mann privately instructed the O'Keeffe girls at her home at 173 North St. in Sun Prairie. It must have worked; in addition to Georgia, two of her sisters also became artists.

The O'Keeffe family moved to Virginia in 1904 but left Georgia with an aunt in Madison on Spaight St. O'Keeffe attended Sacred Heart Academy, where she received her most valuable lesson at the hands of her art teacher, Sister Angelique. Georgia had drawn a baby's hand from a plaster cast given to her by the instructor. Though the rendering was accurate, the nun barked at her for drawing it too small. From that point on, O'Keeffe would think and paint large, as if to say, "Take that, you old penguin!"

Town Hall Rd. & County T, Sun Prairie, WI 53590

No phone

Hours: Always visible

Cost: Free

www.sptourism.com/georgia/htm

Directions: Rte. N south from Sun Prairie, east on T to Town Hall Rd.

Jimmy the Groundhog

Pennsylvania's Punxsutawney Phil gets most of the national media attention on Groundhog Day, but for the record, Jimmy the Groundhog is more accurate on the coming of spring. So adamant are the citizens of Sun Prairie that they asked the U.S. Congress to decide who was the nation's official weathercasting rodent. Congress passed a nonbinding resolution giving equal credence to both claims. Some "resolution"— thanks for nothing, gang!

In fairness to Punxsutawney, that community has been celebrating Groundhog Day since 1887. Sun Prairie has been at it only since 1949. That was the year local boosters decided that, because the holiday celebrates the sun coming out on the prairie, they were "the Groundhog Capital of the World." Jimmy hasn't let them down. Speaking statistically, he's 79 percent accurate, while Phil has a lousy 17 percent record. For many years, Jimmy was a stuffed groundhog, which makes his prognostication even more amazing.

Sun Prairie celebrates February 2 each year with a community breakfast at the Round Table Restaurant. The town also has a Groundhog Club, but you can become a member only if you were born on February 2. Those born on other February days are designated mere Woodchucks. Write the chamber of commerce and they'll send you a Groundhog Birth Certificate. It is not valid at U.S. border crossings unless you look like a rodent.

Sun Prairie Chamber of Commerce, 109 E. Main St., Sun Prairie, WI 53590

(608) 837-4547

Hours: February 2, every year; don't bother if it's not Groundhog Day

Cost: Free

Directions: Start at the Round Table Restaurant, 1611 N. Bristol, (608) 837-4547.

6

Eastern Wisconsin

hink of the East Coast of the United States and images of light-houses, overpriced restaurants, and lots of folks reminding one another they're the Upper Crust come to mind. Wisconsin's East Coast is no different. The Badger bluebloods at Kohler's American Club would like you to think they're a better cut of meat, but Kohler is still just a suburb of the Sheboygan bratwurst metroplex. And after a long weekend of antiquing in oh-so-quaint Door County, you still have the shock of driving through Green Bay to get back home.

Don't misunderstand. Wisconsin's East Coast is a wonderful place, not because of its myriad bed and breakfasts or picturesque beaches, but in spite of them. This region gave the world the hamburger and the ice cream sundae. And don't forget toilet paper. Green Bay, Wisconsin, is Toilet Paper Capital of the World! For that reason alone, this corner of the state deserves our undying gratitude and respect.

There is no Toilet Paper Monument in Green Bay, but there is the Hamburger Hall of Fame in Seymour and the World's First Sundae Counter in Two Rivers. So cheer up, and gas up. Eastern Wisconsin is calling to you.

Champion
Mary the Fire Extinguisher

On August 15, 1858, the Virgin Mary appeared to a 28-year-old immigrant from Belgium, Adele Brice, and proclaimed, "I am the Queen of Heaven who prays for the conversion of sinners." Impressed by his daughter's connections, Brice's father built a shrine on the site in Robinsonville (later renamed Champion) where Mary appeared. But that apparently wasn't enough to please the Madonna, because the building was soon threatened with destruction.

In 1871 a massive forest fire raced toward the chapel. Quick-thinking parishioners dropped their buckets, grabbed a statue of the Virgin, and began parading her around and around the shrine. Suddenly, the skies opened and a freak rainstorm doused the blaze, saving the shrine. Or so the story goes.

Brice felt her vision had been vindicated and further devoted herself to Mary . . . but not entirely. Sister Adele was a nun in appearance only, for though she wore a nun's habit in her later years, she never took religious vows. Brice died July 5, 1896, at the age of 66.

Chapel of Our Lady of Good Hope, 4047 Chapel Dr., Champion, WI 54229
(920) 866-2571
Hours: Daily 6:30 A.M.–7 P.M.
Cost: Free
Directions: On Rte. K, just east of the Rte. P intersection.

And you thought a cheesehead hat looked silly.

Green Bay
Green Bay Packer Hall of Fame

The Green Bay Packers are America's most lovable professional football team, which isn't saying much, if for no other reason than their blue-collar backing. They are the nation's only publicly owned professional team, ever since Curly Lambeau bought the franchise in 1919 for $50. Eighty years later the Packers are still in Green Bay, the smallest city with a pro team.

Packers fans are nothing if not rabidly irrational about their team. Just read the brochure for this place: "Buckingham Palace has nothing on the Green Bay Packer Hall of Fame! Where else can you see actual championship rings from Super Bowls I, II, and XXXI?" Good point. And would you ever catch Queen Elizabeth sporting a cheesehead hat? Not likely!

The Green Bay Packer Hall of Fame has everything a Packers fan could want to see. Lockers from the 17 greatest Packers line the walls, as if ready to suit up (without jocks and cups), as well as personal artifacts, like a copy of Paul Hornung's Marlboro cigarette ad. Next, touch a section of the Louisiana Superdome goal post given to Damon's Clubhouse in 1997. "Test Your Skills" in the amusement arcade where you can hone your football skills at pinball and pachinko, or stick the kiddies in a giant motorized Green Bay helmet. Finally, see replicas of the three Vince Lombardi Trophies the team won. Pray it's not 29 years before you see another.

855 Lombardi Ave., PO Box 10567, Green Bay, WI 54307-0567

(888) 4GB-PACK or (920) 499-4281

E-mail: packhof@dct.com

Hours: June–August, daily 9A.M.–6P.M.; September–May, daily 10A.M.–5P.M.

Cost: Adults $7.50, Seniors(62+) $6, Kids(6–11) $5

www.PackerHallofFame.com

Directions: At the intersection of Lombardi and Oneida Sts.

I Like Ike's Railroad Car

One would assume the Eisenhower staff train housed at the National Railroad Museum has been modified since its days as Ike's rolling war office in England. After all, chugging around in a train emblazoned "Dwight D. Eisenhower" is no way to elude the enemy—unless you're on another train. But these are the original, armor-plated London & North Eastern Railroad cars and engine used from 1944 to 1945 by the Supreme Allied Commander. Plaques point to Ike's quarters and his personal shower but fail to detail in which toilet he relieved himself, though there seem to be plenty to choose from.

Ike's train is one of 75 different railroad cars and engines housed at this museum. You'll see Union Pacific's impressive "Big Boy," the largest steam locomotive in the world at 600 tons and 133 feet in length. Check out General Motors's futuristic Aerotrain, a prototype built with Greyhound bus parts. Meet Lydia, Josephine, Winona, and Miss Bud, not staff members but passenger cars. The museum also houses a 72- x 33-foot, HO-scale model railroad being built by local hobbyists. Stop by on Thursday night and you'll see the builders in action.

Included in the price of admission is a ride around a 1.5-mile loop pulled by a diesel engine. The tracks pass over creaking trestles, through repair and restoration areas, and stop briefly at a Hobo Camp. There you'll see "signatures" for Boxcar Betty and Bozo the Clown chalked on boxcars, and learn the difference between a hobo, a tramp, and a bum. (Hint: Be most offended when somebody calls you a bum.) Behind the Hobo Camp is a Haunted House open each October for fund-raisers. Even during the off-season you can spot gothic-clad teenagers in white and black face makeup running around in the woods.

National Railroad Museum, 2285 S. Broadway, Green Bay, WI 54304-4832

(920) 437-7623

E-mail: staff@nationalrrmuseum.org

Hours: January–March, Monday–Friday 9A.M.–5P.M.; April, Monday–Saturday 9A.M.–5P.M.; May–December, daily 9A.M.–5P.M.

Train Rides: May–September 10A.M., 11:30A.M., 1P.M., 2:30P.M., and 4P.M.

Cost: Adults $6, Seniors(62+) $5, Kids(6–15) $4

www.nationalrrmuseum.org

Directions: Ashland Ave. Exit from Rte. 172, north to Cormier Rd., east to Broadway, on the Fox River.

FISH CREEK

Fish Creek holds the **Wisconsin State Championship Cherry Pit Spit** each year at their February Winter Games.

GREEN BAY

"In Green Bay, Wisconsin, 10 bowling shirts are considered a good wardrobe."—Greg Koch

Green Bay is "the Toilet Paper Capital of the World." It is home to both Charmin and Northern Paper companies.

Kewaunee
World's Largest Grandfather Clock

If you think that's big, you should see grandfather.

In general it is not a good idea to leave a fine piece of furniture outside in the rain and snow. But the 35-foot grandfather clock that towers over the Top of the Hill Shop is an exception. Unlike the other handcrafted timepieces made at Svoboda Industries, this one was built to withstand the harsh Wisconsin elements.

It was constructed in 1976 for the nation's Bicentennial, but was not painted red, white, or blue. It's a respectable brown. The face keeps accurate time, though the hands are not powered by the swinging pendulum and weights—it would be too much work to yank the chains every day.

Inside the building is a gift shop where you can find clocks, music boxes, and other collectibles more to your size. If you're the height of the Jolly Green Giant, don't bother asking to buy the World's Largest Grandfather Clock, because a souvenir postcard clearly states it is not for sale.

Geppetto's Top of the Hill Shop, Svoboda Industries, Inc., Rte. 42 North, PO Box 218, Kewaunee, WI 54216-0218

(920) 388-2691 or (800) 678-9996

E-mail: geppetto@svobodausa.com

Hours: Daily 9A.M.–5P.M.

Cost: Free

www.svobodausa.com

Directions: At the north end of town, north of Rte. 29.

Kohler
The Great Wall of China

Why travel all the way to one of the last surviving Communist countries on earth to see the Great Wall when you can see it here, just down the road from Joseph McCarthy's hometown? True, this wall isn't quite the size of the original—you can't see it from outer space—but then again, the original isn't made of sinks, tubs, urinals, and toilets. This Great Wall is built from the latest designs from the Kohler Company, first in bathroom fixtures.

The Kohler Design Center is a fix-it-upper's dream. You can pick up more than a few decorating ideas that won't take 300,000 laborers and 150 years to finish. If you're a true bathroom-phile, come at 8:30 A.M. on a weekday and take the three-hour plant tour. Then visit the Design Center's basement museum dedicated to discontinued models, many of which you can still see in "economy" hotels across the nation.

Kohler Design Center, 101 Upper Rd., Kohler, WI 53044

(920) 457-3699

Hours: Monday–Friday 9 A.M.–5 P.M., Saturday–Sunday 10 A.M.–4 P.M.

Cost: Free

www.kohlerco.com

Directions: On Rte. Y, just south of the Rte. 28 intersection.

This is where ice cream comes from.

Manitowoc
Big Cow

Surprisingly few giant fiberglass cows in Wisconsin are located at or near dairies. They guard gas stations and liquor stores, restaurants, and cheesemobiles. But in Manitowoc, this mammoth Holstein stands watch over the best kind of dairy, an ice cream factory.

Cedar Crest has a malt shop attached to the building that's open every day of the week. You can almost imagine the milk being squeezed from the cow as you lick your cone and gaze out at her. Or perhaps those thoughts are best ignored until you're finished.

Cedar Crest Ice Cream, 2000 S. 10th St., Manitowoc, WI 54220

(920) 682-5577

Hours: Always visible

Store hours: Daily 11:30A.M.–9P.M.

Cost: Free

Directions: Six blocks south of Rte. 10, two blocks from the lake.

Rudy Rotter's Museum of Sculpture

Rudy Rotter began sculpting in 1954, and, boy, has he kept busy. It's not as if he didn't have other pursuits to occupy his time. Rotter was a practicing dentist in Manitowoc and had a family of four children. He also invented a type of sugarless gum and a shoe-shine device that applied white polish like a roll-on deodorant. But Rotter somehow managed to squeeze in the time to pump out 15,000+ works of art, most of which you can still see in his downtown museum.

Influenced by his Jewish heritage, his first piece was Eve emerging from Adam's rib. Other pieces show similar religious themes and often include writings in Hebrew etched into their bases. A good portion of his early works were human figures, mostly female, and usually nude. Early works used stone, plaster, and clay, but his later creations tended to use cast-off materials from local industries, like a wallpaper manufacturer and a trophy factory.

The works are crammed into his Museum of Sculpture in an old three-story warehouse, arranged roughly by subject: the Family Shrine, the Bible Room, Old Russia, the House of the Lord, and a bizarre collection of painted mannequins. They hang on walls, clutter tables, fill shelves, dangle from the ceiling, and are filed in boxes like record collections. It's overwhelming.

Rotter retired from dentistry in 1987, and his arthritis has kept him from doing the difficult, intricate work he once did. His newer pieces integrate markers, spray paint, and random items glued together in interesting combinations. Rotter spends much of his free time at the museum, greeting visitors and making art. And making art. And making art.

701–705 Buffalo St., Manitowoc, WI 54220

(920) 682-6671

Hours: Tuesday–Saturday 9A.M.–Noon, 2:30–5P.M., Sunday 1–5P.M.; call ahead

Cost: Free

Directions: Three blocks north of the river, one block east of Rte. 10.

Dive! Dive! Dive!

USS *Cobia*

The Manitowoc Shipbuilding Company played an important role in World War II submarine production, so it seems appropriate that a maritime museum be located in town. Unfortunately the museum's crown jewel, the USS *Cobia*, was not built in Manitowoc but in Groton, Connecticut, by the Electric Boat Company. None of the 28 subs constructed here between 1942 and 1945 was available.

The USS *Cobia* has been restored to its WWII appearance since its decommissioning. The sub is 311 feet long and needed 80 crew members to operate. It was credited with sinking 13 Japanese ships between 1944 and 1945, mostly merchant marine vessels.

It is hard to appreciate just how cramped submarine service must have been until you stand inside with a tour, then imagine four times the number of crew aboard. Also consider that the men showered once a week (unless they were mess workers) and it makes for a tight, stinky stew. Two stairways have been installed to get tours in and out, but that's all the help you'll get maneuvering from stem to stern. A good portion of the 45-minute tour is watching and helping the senior guests bend their way through the bulkheads.

In addition to the USS *Cobia*, the museum contains an impressive collection of maritime artifacts that will impress gobs and landlubbers alike. Diving suits and miniature ship models, stuffed seagulls and a re-created fishing dock—all that's missing is the Village People.

Manitowoc Maritime Museum, 75 Maritime Dr., Manitowoc, WI 54220-6823

(920) 684-0218

E-mail: maritime@lakefield.net

Hours: April–October, daily 9A.M.–5P.M. (summer 6P.M.); November–March, Monday–Saturday 9A.M.–5P.M., Sunday 11A.M.–5P.M.

Cost: (Museum/Museum+Sub): Adults $3.95/$5.95, Kids(6–12) $2.95/$3.95

www.wimaritimemuseum.org

Directions: Downtown, east of the 8th St. bridge, north of the river.

Peshtigo
Fire Museum and Mass Graves

On the same day as the Great Chicago Fire, October 8, 1871, a much more deadly fire raged through the town of Peshtigo, Wisconsin. Some would say they were asking for it. The town and its mills were cutting 5.7 million board feet of lumber each year; loggers left a quarter again more on the forest floor as waste slash, the perfect fuel for fires, and Peshtigo's town streets were "paved" with sawdust to supress the flying dust.

The inferno began as a forest fire and engulfed the town before anyone had a chance to escape. Reports say the flames consumed the town in 10 minutes and burned out within an hour. Residents dashed for the Peshtigo River, but many did not make it. Some people hid in brick buildings, others in ditches and open fields. All who tried died. Those lucky enough to make it to the river suffered hypothermia or were drowned by livestock swimming to safety.

The heat of the fire was so intense not even the bones of many of the 800+ victims (some say as many as 1,200) remained. For those who weren't already cremated, coffins were built at the Peshtigo Harbor sawmill several miles away, which had miraculously escaped the fire. In all, 2,400 square miles of northern Wisconsin were incinerated on both sides of Green Bay.

In some of the more bizarre tales to come out of the event, a man hanged himself on a well's chain rather than be burned alive. The tabernacle from the Catholic Church was found uncharred by the side of the river where the priest had abandoned it during the hellish inferno. And a looter found in the village after the fire was sentenced to death in a quickly convened court but escaped execution because neither a rope nor a tall tree could be found.

Most of the victims were buried in a mass grave on the edge of town. A church built next to the cemetery just after the fire houses a museum dedicated to the disaster. In it you'll see a few of the relics that survived the tragedy, all charred or melted, and a map showing the fire's deadly path. The cemetery contains a monument and several hundred victims in a mass grave.

Peshtigo Fire Museum, 400 Oconto Ave., Peshtigo, WI 54157

(715) 582-3244

Hours: June–October 8, daily 9A.M.–5P.M.

Cost: Free

www.rootsweb.com/~wioconto/Fire.htm

Directions: One block north of Rte. 41, two blocks west of the river.

Ready for a close encounter.

Poland
UFO Landing Port

Bob Tohak is a welder by trade and a skywatcher by choice. He builds picnic tables and custom trailers, bridges and park benches, but his greatest achievement to date is a 40-foot-tall UFO Landing Port just off his driveway.

Bob has big plans for the port, which is currently half-finished. Today, the former grain silo opens at the top like a flower, making a flat docking surface for a flying saucer. Aliens are protected from falling off with old metal headboards. A large fluorescent sign invites Martians and reminds Earthly visitors, "We're not the only ones." Bob plans on installing flashing lights to beam simple messages into outer space, guiding spacecraft to his backyard. There will also be an interior spiral staircase that opens to a balcony just below the sign so human visitors can get their pictures taken.

You're welcome to view this future historic site from the road, and if Bob's around, he just might show you his submarine (also in progress) or two pet miniature horses. They have their own TV in the barn and love soap operas.

Tohak & Son Welding, 4885 Rte. 29 East, Green Bay, WI 54311

(920) 863-2541

Hours: Always visible; view from road

Cost: Free

Directions: Between Poland and Henrysville on Rte. 29, on the north side of the road.

HAVE THE ALIENS ALREADY LANDED?

Bob Tohak may be too late.

According to *The W-Files* by Jay Rath (Madison, Wisc.: Wisconsin Trails), Martians made contact with Dean T. Anderson near Fish Creek in Door County's Peninsula State Park (Rte. 42) on six different occasions from 1975 to 1976. At first Anderson only spotted UFOs, but then he began making physical contact, usually in the early morning hours. A Martian couple introduced themselves as Sunar and Treena, and corrected Anderson's term for their home planet. It's not Mars, but Muton.

Port Washington
Pebble House

No, this isn't the prehistoric home of the Flintstones—that's in Bedrock. This place is younger, built in 1848 by Elizabeth and Henry Dodge with pebbles they collected along the Lake Michigan shoreline. Its walls are 20 inches thick and covered with stones battered smooth and round by waves over hundreds of years.

The Pebble House was moved to its downtown location in 1985, where it reopened as the city's Chamber of Commerce and Tourist Information Center. You can gather information on local attractions and events during regular business hours.

Port Washington Chamber of Commerce and Tourist Information Center, 126 Grand Ave., Port Washington, WI 53074

(262) 284-0900

E-Mail: mary@portwashingtonchamber.com

Hours: Always visible

Cost: Free

Directions: On Rte. 33, just before it turns north and becomes Rte. 32.

Red Banks
Jean Nicolet Reaches China

Sometimes you have to put the best face on a botched job. Jean Nicolet had been sent in 1634 by the governor of New France, Samuel de Champlain, to discover a Northwest Passage to China. Rumors that an Asiatic tribe (actually, the Winnebagos) lived across a large body of water (Lake Michigan) got Nicolet packing—an embroidered Oriental robe.

When Nicolet, assisted by a group of Hurons, waded ashore near Red Banks he was wearing an elaborate costume festooned with birds and flowers. If that didn't impress the locals, the two pistols he fired into the air did. He then brought out gifts and that whole show with the gown and the guns was forgiven.

Okay, so Nicolet came up a bit short of China, but whatever he did must have made a positive impression because the Winnebagos were loyal to the French for another 150 years. A statue of Nicolet wearing his full-length robe stands near the point where it all happened. The statue was crafted in 1939 by Sidney Bedore.

Jean Nicolet Statue, Rte. 57, Red Banks, WI 54229

No phone

Hours: Always visible

Cost: Free

Directions: View from the wayside on Rte. 57, just north of the Rte. A intersection.

SEYMOUR

A deer attacked the same hunter who had shot it with a bow and arrow near Seymour in 1986, the day after the buck was wounded!

SHEBOYGAN

Sheboygan claims to be "the Wurst Capital of the World," as in bratwurst. Each August they celebrate Bratwurst Days.

Sheboygan began fluoridating its drinking water in 1946, the first Wisconsin town to do so.

Jackie Mason was born in Sheboygan on June 9, 1934.

The Hamburger Hall of Fame today . . .

Seymour
Hamburger Hall of Fame

Folks in Seymour claim the hamburger was invented here by
"Hamburger Charlie" Nagreen. Charlie first flattened his poor-selling,
hard-to-eat fried meatballs and placed them on bread for customers at
the 1885 Seymour-Outagamie County Fair. They were a big hit, and
Charlie sold them every year until he died in 1951.

The town has never forgotten Charlie's contribution to society. Each
year Seymour celebrates Burger Fest with a Bun Run, pickle- and burger-
tossing contests, a catsup slide, stale bun stacking for the kids, and a
Hamburger Parade, among other events. In 1989 they capped off the celebration by frying the World's Largest Hamburger. It had a 5,520-pound
patty and fed 13,000 hungry celebrants. The grill used to cook the patty
still stands on Depot Street, just east of the museum. Should any rival
burg try to top their burger, they'll fire up the grill and set a new record.

If you can't make it for Burger Fest, come for the museum. They've
got thousands of hamburger-esque items, from a Big Boy statue to a
hamburger phone, from burger frisbees to makeup cases. Much of it is
from the collection of the world's biggest burger booster, Jeffrey
Tennyson, author of *Hamburger Heaven*. And because it's a Hall of Fame,
the museum honors greats in the field, starting with Charlie Nagreen and
including Ray Kroc and the White Castle chain.

. . . and the vision for the future. Photos by author, courtesy of The Hamburger Hall of Fame

Currently the museum is housed in a modest storefront on Main Street. But the Hamburger Hall of Fame has big plans for the future. They're trying to raise an estimated $6–$8 million for a new, hamburger-shaped building to attract burger lovers from around the world. The main building will be a four-story burger with cheese with a pile of fries as an entryway and a green, dill-pickle-shaped outdoor pavilion.

126 N. Main St., PO Box 173, Seymour, WI 54165

(920) 833-9522

Hours: June–August, Monday–Saturday 10A.M.–4P.M., Sunday Noon–4P.M.

Cost: Free

www.lodging1.com/advanced/hamburg/index.htm

Directions: On Rte. 55 (Main St.) downtown.

Sheboygan
Stories on the Wall

Viking raiders! Marauding Cossacks! Keystone Cops! They're all here . . . in cement . . . in Sheboygan! No, none of these individuals have had anything to do with the history of the Bratwurst Capital of the World, but they were interesting to Dan Erbstoesser, the man who created them. He also rendered his own version of American Gothic, a log cabin in the woods, and a metalworker pouring molten steel from a cauldron.

Erbstoesser began the bas-relief panels in the 1950s and finished his final piece in 1976. Working slowly over two decades, he completed only four panels along an exterior sidewalk. Each piece was carefully painted and all are still in relatively good condition, considering their location.

548 Whitcomb Ave., Sheboygan, WI 53081

Private phone

Hours: Private residence; view from sidewalk

Cost: Free

Directions: One block north of Wilson Ave. at the corner of Lake Shore Dr. and Whitcomb Ave.

Tellen's Woodland Sculpture Garden.
Photo by author, courtesy of the Kohler Foundation

James A. Tellen, Jr.'s Woodland Sculpture Garden

There are certain weekend warriors that put us all to shame. Thinking his lakeside cabin needed a little sprucing up, James Tellen began creating statues in 1942 to keep him company. Over the next decade and a half he built 14 sculptural tableaus that he placed around his property. Most are strangely realistic and in an evening light look almost human, or elfin.

The entrance to the property is guarded by a Native American chief with a large headdress and a woman with a baby on her back. He's straddling a concrete log fence on which she's leaning. Around the grounds are more full-sized statues with varying subjects: Abraham Lincoln splitting rails, elves playing musical instruments, a man on horseback greeting a woman at a well, the Virgin of Fatima, a goat retreating from a skunk, and more.

The site fell into disrepair after Tellen's death but is currently being restored by the Kohler Foundation. When the project is finished in 2001 the entire site will be open to the public.

5634–5642 Evergreen Dr., Sheboygan, WI 53081

(920) 458-1972

Hours: Always visible; view from road or by appointment

Cost: Free

Directions: One block south of the intersection of Evergreen Dr. and Indian Mound Rd. on the south side of Sheboygan.

Art in the Bathrooms

It's not often a museum asks you to pee on a work of art, at least outside of New York, but the Kohler Arts Center is not a typical art museum. You're not allowed to relieve yourself on any work you choose, just those commissioned for the men's bathrooms. Two artists, Ann Agee and Matt Nolan, designed the tile and fixtures in two men's rooms, including the urinals, inside and out.

The remainder of the museum has expanded greatly in recent years. You can see art on loan from the Kohler Foundation's restorations around the state, most of which are included in this travel guide (The Painted Forest, Grandview, Fred Smith's Wisconsin Concrete Park, The Paul and Mathilda Wegner Grotto, and The Prairie Moon Sculpture Gardens). Their collection also includes rural-life paintings by Nick Engelbert and organic assemblages by Mark Nohl.

John Michael Kohler Arts Center, 608 New York Ave., PO Box 489, Sheboygan, WI 53082

(920) 458-6144

Hours: Monday, Wednesday, Friday 10A.M.–5P.M., Tuesday, Thursday 10A.M.–8P.M., Saturday–Sunday 10A.M.–4P.M.

Cost: Free

www.jmkac.org

Directions: Two blocks north of Pennsylvania Ave., four blocks east of the river, between 6th and 7th Sts.

Sister Bay
Goats on the Roof

The thought of eating a meal while a goat struts around above your head might sound unappetizing, but only if you've never been to Sister Bay. At

Al Johnson puts his goats on a pedestal.
Photo by Annice Tatken

Al Johnson's the food may be Swedish, but the building is all Norwegian. Apparently, in Norway a good place to raise goats is on your sod-covered roof. The roof is peaked and steeper than you'd imagine, so the goats are climbers. Currently three different breeds live on the roof.

Don't worry that they might fall off; they're taken down at night, in the winter, and during storms or high winds.

Al Johnson's specializes in breakfasts and meatballs. They open at 6A.M. in the summer, which makes it a good first stop on a road trip. Still, it's a popular eatery and people may be lining up for their lingonberries before the doors open.

Al Johnson's Swedish Restaurant and Butik, 702 Bay Shore Dr., Sister Bay, WI 54234 (920) 854-2626

Hours: June–September, daily 6A.M.–9P.M.; October–May, daily 7A.M.–8P.M.

Cost: Meals $7–$15

Directions: On Rte. 24 (Bay Shore Dr.). Look for the livestock on the roof.

Two Rivers
Birthplace of the Sundae

Two Rivers claims to be "The Coolest Spot in Wisconsin," not because it is particularly frigid or hip, but because the ice cream sundae was invented here. A local man named George Hallauer inspired the concoction in 1881 by requesting the as-yet-unknown treat at an ice cream parlor run by Edward Berner. Hallauer wanted chocolate sauce poured over his ice cream; until that moment, chocolate sauce was used only in ice cream sodas. The new dish was a hit, but for a while it was sold only on Sundays. Soon people, led by a vocal 10-year-old girl, were demanding it every day of the week, and the name "sundae" was born.

Ed Berner's original parlor stood at 1404 Fifteenth St., but the site is now a parking lot. You can visit another parlor named in his honor a few blocks away on the ground floor of the Two Rivers Historical Society in historic Washington House. Their specialty is a "Washington House Sundae." It's red, white, and (ugh!) blue.

Ed Berner's Ice Cream Parlor, 1622 Jefferson St., Two Rivers, WI 54241

(888) 857-3529 or (920) 793-2490

Hours: November–April, daily 9A.M.–5P.M.; May–October, daily 9A.M.–9P.M.

Cost: Single scoop $1, sundae $2.50

www.lhinn.com/history.html

Directions: At the corner of Jefferson and 17th Sts.

Hamilton Wood Type and Printing Museum

The Hamilton Wood Type and Printing Museum is the first and only wood type collection in the world. Imagine being transported to your high school shop class, without the embittered shop teacher barking at you as you struggled to build a crummy spice rack, and you'll get a feel for this place.

In the days before modern printing techniques, every newspaper, book, and poster was printed using movable type. While metal type was fine for small print, it was hardly cost-effective for large jobs. Posters and headlines needed something lighter and cheaper. That's where wood type was used.

You'll follow the entire process by which a simple log was transformed into a banner headline that might have read, "TITANIC SINKS!" Cross sections were cut and dried, trimmed and planed, sanded and polished, and eventually checked for minute deviations and blemishes. Only a small fraction of each slab made it to the point where it was etched into a giant Z or G using reproduction machines perfected by James E. Hamilton, the man for whom this museum is named.

At the turn of the century, Hamilton's company manufactured more wood type than any other company in the United States. Half a million original "masters" cover the walls and fill the cabinets here in all sizes and fonts. Today, at the museum, printing artists-in-residence use these masters to make elaborate compositions.

1315 17th St., Two Rivers, WI 54241

(920) 793-2490

Hours: Monday–Saturday 9A.M.–5P.M., Sunday 1–5P.M.

Cost: Free; donations encouraged

www.woodtype.org

Directions: Across the street from the Historical Society at 17th and Jefferson Sts., one block east of Rte. 42.

Point Beach Energy Center

Who ever thought a nuclear power plant could be so much fun? Three Mile Island? Don't be a wet blanket! Drive on up to the reactor and hang a right and you'll find a nifty science museum, practically at ground zero! Larry the Lightbulb is your tour guide through the Point Beach Energy Center, or will be until he burns out on the job.

At Point Beach you'll see dozens of interactive exhibits, like a sparking Jacob's Ladder. It discharges a bolt when you trip an electric eye. View a cutaway model of the main building, which looks as if its top was blown off in a Chernobyl mishap. Take a trip "inside containment" to see nuclear fuel rods being pulled out of the core. Yellow danger lights flash in this mock containment chamber, which is so realistic you'll wish you'd pulled on your lead-lined undies.

Best of all is the Energy Detectives' Clubhouse. Four rooms appear to have been modeled on Pee Wee's Playhouse, only in this clubhouse somebody's wasting energy . . . *lots* of it! Who left the water running in the sink? Who installed a 100-watt bulb in the table lamp when a 60-watt would have worked fine? The goal is to get little visitors to spot the culprits and, one would assume, turn them in to the Energy Police.

6600 Nuclear Rd., Two Rivers, WI 54241

(800) 880-8463 or (920) 755-4334

Hours: March–October, daily 9 A.M.–4:30 P.M.; November–February, daily 10 A.M.–4:30 P.M.

Cost: Free

Directions: Ten miles north of town on Rte. 42, turn east on Nuclear Rd.

Waubeka
First Flag Day

Bernard J. Cigrand helped write the Pledge of Allegiance, but that wasn't enough for this zealous patriot. The young Waubeka schoolteacher wanted a day to set aside each year to celebrate Old Glory, so on June 14, 1885, he propped up a 38-star U.S. flag on the desk of his Stony Hill School and declared the event Flag Day.

Why June 14? On that date in 1777, the Second Continental Congress adopted the Stars and Stripes as the nation's official flag. The U.S. Congress had previously declared a Flag Day on the banner's 100th Anniversary, but one day a century wasn't enough for Cigrand. His solitary schoolhouse gesture was a start to a tireless campaign to enact a national Flag Day. Thirty-one years later, on June 14, 1916, President Woodrow Wilson signed the law that made the holiday official.

Stony Hill School, N5595 Rte. I, Waubeka, WI 53021

No phone

Hours: Always visible

Cost: Free

Directions: On Rte. I, just south of the Rte. 84 (Kohler-Fredonia Rd.) intersection.

First Flag Fest.

West Bend
Lizard Mounds

What's a zoomorph? A zoomorph is a physical representation, in this case a dirt effigy mound, of an animal used by Native American cultures during spirit-calling ceremonies. There are 31 large effigy mounds at this small park. Ninety percent of all North American effigy mounds are found in Wisconsin and can take the shape of birds, buffalo, mythical creatures, panthers, bears, and more. Oftentimes a body is found ceremoniously interred within a mound.

Most of the zoomorphs at Lizard Mounds State Park take the shape of (surprise!) a lizard. Others are conical. The mounds are no more than three or four feet high, but they can be as long as 300 feet and would be hard to identify from ground level were it not for the interpretive signs.

Because they are so large and best viewed from above, some have suggested a connection between effigy mounds and prehistoric visits from UFOs. Maybe they're landing markers for flying saucers! But think about it: If early humans were descendants of aliens, why did they build their effigies out of common, everyday dirt? Why not something flashier, like fiberglass? That would really impress their Martian relatives!

Lizard Mounds State Park, Rte. A, PO Box 1986, West Bend, WI 53095

(262) 335-4445

Hours: April–November, daily 7 A.M.–9 P.M.

Cost: Free

Directions: Rte. 144 northeast four miles to Rte. A, turn east and follow the signs.

FantaSuite Hotel Rooms

Unlike its sister hotel, Dodgeville's Don Q Inn, the West Bend Inn looks like a typical motel from the outside. But wait until you get inside. The West Bend Inn has 25 different theme suites, many of them different than what the Don Q offers. Try the Pearl Under the Sea, where you sleep in a giant clam, the Pharaoh's Chambers with a sarcophagus-shaped bed, or Wild, Wild West, where you bunk in a wagon and bathe in a whirlpool horse trough. Talk about romantic!

Do you have secret exhibitionist fantasies? Make the Happy Days Café into your own nudie diner—the whirlpool is a giant coffee cup! Need a little discipline? The Medieval Castle is more of a Medieval Dungeon with wall shackles. Le Cave helps you explore your prehistoric urges, and the Moonlander blasts you into the future. And do most Teepees come with a mirrored ceiling? At the West Bend Inn they do!

West Bend Inn, 2520 W. Washington St., West Bend, WI 53095

(800) 727-9727 or (262) 338-0636

E-mail: wbinn@hnet.net

Hours: Daily, but call ahead for reservations

Tours: Saturday 2:15 P.M.

Cost: Tour free; Fantasuites $99–$199/night, depending on date and room

www.fantasuite.com/Location.asp?LocationId=4

Directions: West of Rte. 45 on Washington St. (Rte. 33).

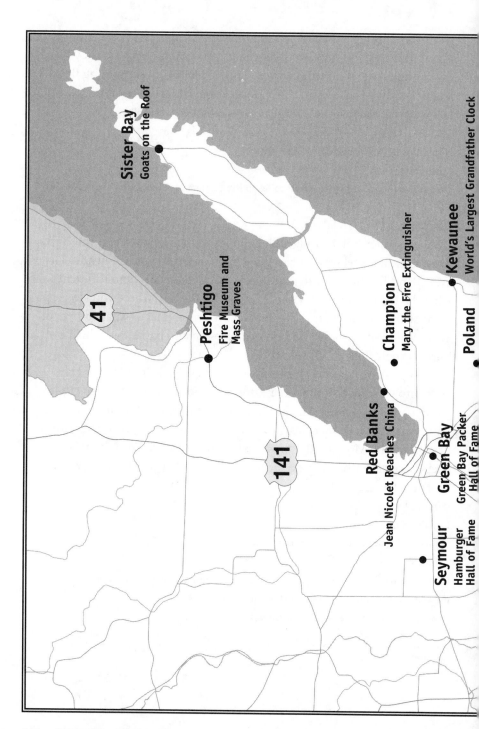

Sister Bay
Goats on the Roof

Peshtigo
Fire Museum and
Mass Graves

Champion
Mary the Fire Extinguisher

Kewaunee
World's Largest Grandfather Clock

Poland

Red Banks
Jean Nicolet Reaches China

Green Bay
Green Bay Packer
Hall of Fame

Seymour
Hamburger
Hall of Fame

41

141

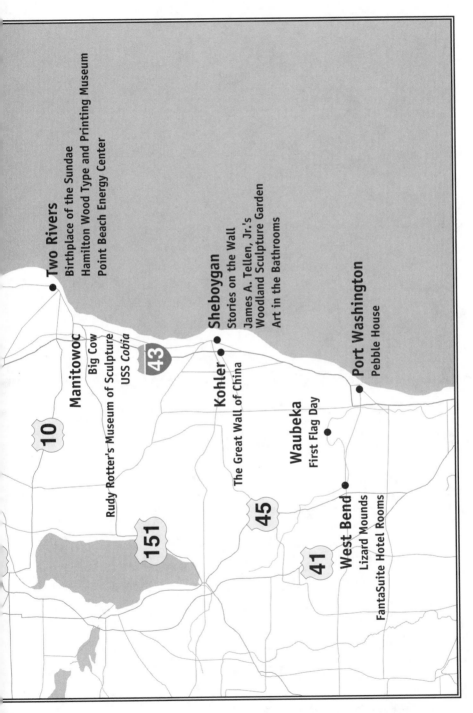

Two Rivers
Birthplace of the Sundae
Hamilton Wood Type and Printing Museum
Point Beach Energy Center

Manitowoc
Big Cow
Rudy Rotter's Museum of Sculpture
USS *Cobia*

43

10

Sheboygan
Stories on the Wall
James A. Tellen, Jr.'s
Woodland Sculpture Garden
Art in the Bathrooms

Kohler
The Great Wall of China

151

Waubeka
First Flag Day

Port Washington
Pebble House

45

West Bend
Lizard Mounds
FantaSuite Hotel Rooms

41

7

Milwaukee Area

Milwaukee is a fun town, and much more international than its beer and brat reputation would suggest. It has been home to such widely divergent personalities as Golda Meir and Liberace, is the birthplace of the typewriter and the Harley-Davidson motorcycle, and has public monuments to ducks and Joan of Arc. Milwaukee has played a role in two failed assassination attempts on presidential candidates, is the hometown of Laverne and Shirley, and has plenty of parking downtown. What more could citizens want?

But though Milwaukee is the most cosmopolitan city in Wisconsin, there's still a bit of the small-town sucker in its blood. Take, for example, a panic that swept the city in 1862. Somehow a rumor got started that Confederate forces were advancing on the city *from the north*. Geography-challenged "refugees" streamed in from nearby Waukesha and the Milwaukee Chamber of Commerce urged citizens to save themselves by fleeing in boats across Lake Michigan. Before the flotilla was launched, somebody consulted a map and questioned the reports from the war front.

Couldn't happen today? What about the strange case of Gary Medrow? This Milwaukee resident was recently arrested for calling local women at random and asking them to pick up family members and carry them around the house. Before he was apprehended, he had convinced dozens of women to submit to his request.

Maybe beer is a factor in all this strange behavior. Milwaukee isn't called Brew Town for nothing. Still, there is plenty of weirdness in Milwaukee that can't be traced back to alcohol. This chapter offers several examples for your amusement.

Where's Alice?

Milwaukee
Cass Street Park

The Cheshire-like cat archway at the entrance to Milwaukee's Cass Street Park is the first of many psychedelic sculptures found around this playground. Kids can climb on the back of a floppy-eared sea serpent or stand on the feet of an Izy Bird. What's an Izy Bird? "Whether you are 2 or 102, short or tall, big or small, black, yellow, white, red, or brown, the Izy Bird reminds us we are all special." Kind of like Mr. Rogers, but with feathers instead of a cardigan.

The whole park has an *Alice in Wonderland* feel to it. Even the light posts have been transformed into big-billed birds. No doubt this will be a gathering place for Boomers and their young grandchildren, and the kids will have to convince their grandparents they are not experiencing some sort of acid flashback.

Pleasant and Cass Sts., Milwaukee, WI 53202

No phone

Hours: Daily 8A.M.–10P.M.

Cost: Free

Directions: North from downtown on Cass St. to Pleasant St.

MILWAUKEE

"Milwaukee" is taken from the Algonquin word *mahn-a-wauk-ee*, meaning "gathering place by the waters."

If you want to legally park for more than two hours in Milwaukee, hitch your car to a horse.

A strike at the Milwaukee Iron Company's Bay View Mill (Superior St. and Russell Ave.) was busted by the state militia on May 5, 1886, when soldiers fired on strikers, killing seven. The workers had been demanding an eight-hour workday.

Actors **Alfred Lunt** and **Lynn Fontanne** are buried in Milwaukee's Forest Home Cemetery (2405 W. Forest Home Ave.). The Pillsbury family, the Pabst family, the Blatz family, and the Schlitz Family are also buried there.

George Carlin was arrested at Milwaukee's Summerfest Festival on July 21, 1972, after performing his "Seven Words You Can't Say on TV" routine. Apparently you couldn't say those words at Summerfest, either. This festival later saw The Plasmatics' **Wendy O. Williams** arrested for obscenity.

Dobberstein's Lourdes Grotto

Before he went off to Iowa to become Mr. Bigshot Grotto-Maker, Paul Dobberstein was a student at St. Francis Seminary in Milwaukee. While training here in 1897, he contracted double pneumonia. He promised the Virgin Mary to build a grotto in her honor if she helped him recover. She did, and Paul kept his word.

Dobberstein's first grotto was a simple stone and concrete cave near his seminary's cemetery. The cave is 10 feet tall and has no special features. Today, it is in disrepair without icons or candles, a sorry state for such an influential piece of Midwestern American folk art. Dobberstein used the skills he developed here to build the massive Grotto of the Redemption in West Bend, Iowa, which in turn inspired Father Mathias Wernerus to build the Dickeyville Grotto in Wisconsin, which in turn spawned the Paul and Mathilda Wegner Grotto, the Rudolph Grotto and Wonder Cave, and so on, and so on. . . . Dobberstein was a true Johnny Grotto-seed, and this was his first.

St. Francis Seminary, 3257 S. Lake Dr., Milwaukee, WI 52325

(414) 747-6400

Hours: Call for permission

Cost: Free

Directions: Just south of Oklahoma Ave.; from the entrance, follow the road to the left to the gymnasium, walk down the cinder road to the cemetery.

Gene & Mary's Holler House

Most bowling alleys serve alcohol, but how many bars have their own lanes? Gene & Mary's Holler House is for the most part a tavern; the bowling alley seems like an afterthought.

The place has only two working lanes and the pins are set by hand. The approach at the Holler House lanes isn't a direct shot, so you must line up crooked to the pins. If you've had a few brews, you'll probably be more crooked than you need to be. In this town filled with bowling alleys, you'd expect there to be enough lanes for leagues. Still, Holler House has hosted its own competitive leagues.

Bowlers from around the country used to come to Milwaukee to visit the Bowling Hall of Fame in suburban Greendale, but that museum has since moved to St. Louis. Only the Bowling Research Center remains, and that's open only by appointment. Second on the visitors' list was always a couple of beers and lines at Holler House. Today the bar is at the top.

2242 Lincoln Ave., Milwaukee, WI 53215

(414) 647-9284

Hours: Daily 4 P.M.–Late; call ahead to see if lanes will be open

Cost: $1.75/line

Directions: At 21st St. and Lincoln, on the north side of Forest Home Cemetery.

Gertie's getting in the way again.

Gertie the Duck Statue

How easily people get distracted! Though World War II was not yet over, a duck captured the nation's attention in the spring of 1945. Workers were rebuilding the Wisconsin Avenue Bridge downtown when they discovered a mother duck protecting a pair of eggs on one of the pilings. Rather than move the mallard, crews halted construction until the eggs hatched. City residents named her Gertie, and when her ducklings burst forward they were christened Pee Wee and Dee Dee.

By the time they were old enough to move on, these babies were paddling through a world free from Hitler, not that they knew it. Their fresh beginning seemed to mirror the nation's postwar determination. A statue of Gertie and her children was erected on the Wisconsin Avenue Bridge in 1997 by the architecture firm of Eppstein Uhen.

Wisconsin Avenue Bridge, Wisconsin Ave. and Water St., Milwaukee, WI 53205

No phone

Hours: Always visible

Cost: Free

Directions: On the north side of the Wisconsin Ave. bridge, between Water St. and Plankinton Ave.

Golda Meir's Childhood Homes

Golda Meir's family, the Mabowehzs, fled pogroms in the village of Pinsk near Kiev in 1906 and ended up in Milwaukee. "Goldie" was just eight years old but already showed personality traits that would lead her to be Israel's first female prime minister. She was enrolled at the Fourth Street Elementary School (now Golda Meir Elementary School, 1555 N. Martin Luther King Dr.) speaking almost no English, but she graduated as valedictorian. Though her parents objected to her continued education, she enrolled at North Division High School (1011 W. Center St.) in 1912 without their blessing. It didn't last long.

When her mother arranged a marriage between Goldie (just 14 at the time) and the 30-something "Mr. Goodstein," Goldie hopped a train to Denver, where her sister was living in a TB sanitarium. Two years later she returned with a husband of her own choosing. The Meirs lived in Milwaukee until 1921.

First Milwaukee Home, 623 W. Walnut St., Milwaukee, WI 53212

No phone

Hours: The home has been torn down

Cost: Free

Directions: Approximately where Walnut St. crosses I-43.

Second Milwaukee Home, 750 N. 10th St., Milwaukee, WI 53233

No phone

Hours: The home has been torn down

Cost: Free

Directions: At 10th St. and Juneau Ave.

MILWAUKEE BABIES

Jeffrey Dahmer: May 21, 1960   **Heather Graham:** January 29, 1970

Woody Herman: May 16, 1913   **Al Jarreau:** March 12, 1940

Steve Miller: October 5, 1943   **Pat O'Brien:** November 11, 1899

Charlotte Rae: April 22, 1926   **Tom Snyder:** May 12, 1936

Gene Wilder (nee Jerome Silberman): June 11, 1935

International Clown Hall of Fame

In most situations, clowns can be spooky or annoying. Not so at the Clown Hall of Fame! What could have been a creepy memorial to long-dead stars who'd been trampled by rogue elephants, blown out of cannons, or smothered in little cars is instead a living tribute to these unique entertainers. Inductees to the Hall of Fame include Emmett Kelly, Sr., Willard Scott (the first Ronald McDonald), Bob Keeshan (Howdy Doody's Clarabell and later Captain Kangaroo), and Red Skelton. Check out the display cases filled with oversized shoes, big noses, and colorful costumes and wigs.

The museum moved to Milwaukee from its former home in an old supermarket in Delevan. At the time a "research center" was attached to the Hall of Fame, as well as a clown college, where they taught people how to make a pratfall, take a pie in the face, and generally act like an ass. On special days you were followed by roving freelance clowns. Today, in the Grand Avenue Mall, only the museum remains. Count your blessings.

Grand Avenue Mall/Plankinton Building, 275 W. Wisconsin Ave., Suite LL 700, Milwaukee, WI 53203

(414) 319-0848

Hours: Monday–Friday 10A.M.–4P.M.

Cost: Adults $2

www.clownmuseum.org

Directions: On the lower level of the Grand Avenue Mall at Wisconsin Ave. and the river.

Jeffrey Dahmer's Place

Jeffrey Dahmer's neighbors thought he was a little strange, and they were right. At odd hours of the night they would hear a buzzing power saw and smell strange odors wafting from his apartment. "I'm building bookcases," or "My refrigerator broke and the meat spoiled," were common excuses. Nobody ever challenged his lame answers, not even the police.

On May 27, 1991, a nude 14-year-old Konerak Sinthasomphone was found wandering on the corner of 25th and State Sts. Police arrived about the same time Dahmer, who had left the drugged boy in his apartment to get a six-pack of beer, returned. He claimed Sinthasomphone was his drunken lover, and the officers helped return him to Dahmer's apartment. Not wanting to get involved in what they wrongly thought was a gay lovers' spat, they overlooked a few obvious red flags: The unit reeked of rotting flesh, the boy was obviously underage and unable to speak for himself, and *he had a hole drilled in his forehead*. Moments after they left, Dahmer strangled the life out of his victim.

The killing spree went on for two more months, claiming four additional victims, until the night of July 22, 1991, when a partially handcuffed man flagged down a police car and claimed a man had tried to kill him. Police found Dahmer in his apartment along with three torsos dissolving in a plastic barrel filled with acid; four heads, seven skulls, and a heart in the freezer; and a penis and two hands in a lobster pot. That's some fairly damning evidence.

Dahmer calmly confessed to killing, dismembering, and/or cannibalizing 16 men and boys in Milwaukee and one in Ohio. The first four Milwaukee murders took place at his grandmother's home; the rest were committed at the Oxford Apartments. In the later years he had been trying to create a zombie sex slave, drilling holes in his victims' heads and injecting them with muriatic acid and narcotics. The experiments never quite worked.

For several years prior to his arrest, Dahmer worked at the Ambrosia Chocolate Factory (Fifth St. and Highland Ave.), first as a mixer and then as a cashier. But as he sank into his own private hell, he became an unreliable worker and was fired only days before his arrest. He found many of his victims by cruising local bars, primarily Club 219 (219 Second St.), but also the Phoenix Bar, the LaCage Club, and the Grand Avenue Mall (275 W. Wisconsin Ave.). Other victims he picked up on the streets, some as far away as Chicago.

After his arrest, Dahmer was housed in the Milwaukee County Jail, where fellow inmates nicknamed him "Chop-Chop Man." Dahmer pled insanity, but the jury did not find him insane. Huh?!? He was given 15 consecutive life terms without the possibility of parole, which wasn't entirely true. His first parole hearing would have been in March 2934.

Dahmer was imprisoned at the Columbia Correctional Facility in Portage. It was here that he "found Christ" and was baptized in the prison's whirlpool by Reverend Roy Ratcliffe. The trouble was, Christ also found him. Christopher Scarver, a convicted murderer who thought he was the million-year-old son of God, beat Dahmer to death with a weight room bar on November 28, 1994, when Dahmer was cleaning a bathroom in a staff locker room. Another convict, Jesse Anderson, also died in the attack.

The families of Dahmer's victims won an $80 million civil verdict against him, but got little more than his fridge, drill, sledgehammer, 80-quart kettle, shower curtain, toothbrush, porno tapes, and a few other things. The items were sold at auction in 1996; most were purchased for $400,000 by several Milwaukee businessmen who had them promptly destroyed.

Oxford Apartments, Apartment 213, 924 N. 25th St., Milwaukee, WI 53233

No phone

Hours: Torn down; vacant lot remains

Cost: Free

Directions: Between State and Kilbourn.

Grandma's House, 2357 S. 57th St., West Allis, WI 53219

No phone

Hours: Private property; view from street

Cost: Free

Directions: One block south of Lincoln Ave.

Columbia Correctional Facility, Inmate 177252—Cell 648, 2925 Columbia Dr., Portage, WI 53901

(608) 742-9100

Hours: Always visible

Cost: Free

Directions: On Rte. 127, north of Rte. 16.

Laverne and Shirley

Laverne and Shirley lived in a basement apartment on Knapp Ave., and while there isn't a Knapp Ave. in Milwaukee, there is a Knapp St. Close enough. Knapp St. runs through a newly gentrified neighborhood just north of downtown and would no doubt price out brewery workers and Lenny and Squiggy types. If living here was one of their dreams, they wouldn't have been able to make them all come true.

Filmed on a Hollywood back lot between 1976 and 1983, the closest Laverne or Shirley got to Brew Town was in the opening credits, where there are quick shots of a few local landmarks, such as Milwaukee City Hall and the Pabst Brewing Company. The latter stood in for Shotz Brewery as the pair's blue-collar employer.

Basement Apartment, 730 Knapp St., Milwaukee, WI 53202

Hours: No basement apartment exists here

Cost: Free

Directions: Between Cass and Van Buren Sts., three blocks north of State St.

Milwaukee City Hall, 200 E. Wells St., Milwaukee, WI 53202

Hours: Always visible

Cost: Free

Directions: Two blocks east of the river, downtown, between Market and Broadway.

Pabst Brewing Company, 915 W. Juneau Ave., Milwaukee, WI 53202

Hours: Always visible

Cost: Free

Directions: Just east of I-43, just south of Rte. 145.

MILWAUKEE

TV's *Happy Days* was set in Milwaukee.

In October 1881, cobwebs blanketed the city of Milwaukee. Witnesses claimed they blew in from the east, across the lake, where land is 100 miles away! The fiber storm was preferable to the 50 pounds of molten metal that fell on Milwaukee on August 22, 1974.

The **Polaris Revolving Restaurant** atop Milwaukee's Hyatt Regency Hotel (333 W. Kilbourn) is the downtown's only revolving restaurant. One full turn takes 45 minutes.

Northwest Airlines Flight 2501 disappeared over Lake Michigan on June 25, 1950. It was flying from New York to Minneapolis. No wreckage was ever found. Fifty-eight passengers and crew disappeared forever. The incident is often cited in speculation about a Great Lakes Triangle.

Milwaukee Mayor Daniel Hoan served the city from 1916 to 1940, a candidate from the Socialist Party. City residents also elected Socialist Victor Berger to the U.S. House of Representatives for four terms beginning in 1910.

The **Boerner Botanical Gardens** in Milwaukee (Whitnall Park, 5879 S. 92nd St., (414) 425-1130) has the World's Largest Collection of Crab Apple Trees.

Don't drink and drive. Drink and *ride.*

Midwest Hiawatha

Modern train travel can be somewhat unreliable. Trains run late, derail, and don't have the glamour of a half-century ago. But the Midwest Hiawatha is an exception. It's never late because it doesn't go anywhere, it never derails because it never moves, and as for style? It's got a train-load worth.

The Midwest Hiawatha was created from several cars of the old Milwaukee Great Northern Railroad. The cars have been sidetracked and converted into a railroad-themed bar. It might sound goofy to go out drinking in a stationary train, but it has its advantages. No need to worry that the rocking, gentle beat will slosh your drink. No conductor marches through the cabin shouting, "Springfield! Next stop, Springfield!" And because you're not in a station, no kid is pestering you to give you a shoeshine.

Milwaukee Great Northern, 366 E. Stewart St., Milwaukee, WI 53207

(414) 481-5480

Hours: Thursday–Saturday 5 P.M.–Midnight

Cost: Drinks $3 and up

Directions: Two blocks east of Rte. 32 (Kinnickinnic Ave.), one block north of Becher St.

The Muskrat Group and the Typewriters

It is hard to imagine there ever was a time when museums didn't have dioramas. But today's standard practice is a relatively new innovation. In 1890, schoolteacher Peter Engelmann suggested placing stuffed animal specimens in a natural setting and talked to taxidermist Carl Akeley about it. The result was the World's First Diorama, the Muskrat Group, still on display on the first floor of the Milwaukee Public Museum. Akeley went on to be known as "The Father of Modern Taxidermy" because he invented many of the processes and methods still in use today.

The Milwaukee Public Museum is a wonderfully weird institution, mixing art, culture, and natural history. Within a display you'll see stuffed creatures, human mannequins in ethnic garb, indigenous art, and excavated artifacts—something for everyone! It also has the World's Largest Dinosaur Skull, a Costa Rican Rainforest, and a full-size re-creation of the old streets of Milwaukee.

The museum is also home to the World's Largest Collection of Typewriters, more than 700, though they're not all on display. The typewriter was invented in Milwaukee between 1867 and 1873 at 318 W. State St. by Christopher Latham Sholes, aided by Carlos Glidden, Samuel Soule, Henry Roby, and Mathias Schwalback. The first proto-type was introduced in 1869 and established what is today known as the "universal keypad." Sholes's efforts were funded by James Densmore, who eventually bought Sholes's interest and made millions with the Remington & Sons Company. Despite his enormous contribution to society, Sholes died poor in 1890.

Milwaukee Public Museum, 800 W. Wells St., Milwaukee, WI 53233

(414) 278-2700

Hours: Daily 9A.M.–5P.M.

Cost: Adults $6.50, Seniors(60+) $5, Kids(4–17) $4

www.mpm.edu

Directions: One block north of Wisconsin Ave. on 8th St. to Wells.

The Safe House

The entrance to this establishment seems harmless enough; a sign on Front St. reads "International Exports, Ltd. Since 1868." But these are no ordinary exporters, for they deal in human cargo, moving spies and secret agents through Brew Town.

"Do you know the password?" That's what they'll ask you when you enter a room with what looks like an old office switchboard. If you're not the clandestine type, you can attempt entry by exhibiting covert behavior; ask your operator what to do. If you pass the test, a secret passageway opens and you're allowed into The Safe House, Milwaukee's not-so-secret watering hole for top-secret agents.

The Safe House's specialty drink menu gets you started: The Incognito, The Silencer, Goldeneye, The Under Cover Girl, and The Spy's Demise. After 6 p.m. you can order The Ultimate Martini that is shaken, not stirred, as it passes through the restaurant in a glowing pneumatic tube. The club is filled with clandestine devices like a CIA phone booth with 99 background sounds to disguise your true location, two Mata Hari outposts where female guests can spy on their dates, a chunk of the Berlin Wall, and a machine gun donated by John Wayne. When you're ready to leave, ask your server to point out the Secret Escape Route.

779 N. Front St., Milwaukee, WI 53202

(414) 271-2007

Hours: Daily 11:30 a.m.–2 a.m.

Cost: Meals $6–12

www.safe-house.com

Directions: One block north of Wisconsin Ave., on the east side of the river.

DON'T ATTRACT SUSPICION!

To be a truly successful double-naught spy you have to avoid situations that might blow your cover. Getting arrested is a good way to be exposed. So if you're snooping in Wisconsin, here are a few laws to obey:

➡ Only one person may occupy a bathtub at a time.
➡ You cannot kiss on a train.
➡ It is illegal to sing in a bar.
➡ To walk on train tracks, you must be either a railroad worker or a reporter.
➡ You may not cut a woman's hair.
➡ It is legal to marry your first cousin, only if the bride is older than 55.
➡ By law, every working lumberjack is entitled to a bathtub.

St. Joan of Arc Chapel

Need a place to cool down on a warm day? Try touching the magic Joan of Arc stone in the Medieval Chapel at Marquette. According to legend, a statue of the Virgin Mary rested on this rock where Joan of Arc prayed just before being burned at the stake. As she rose from her meditation she kissed the rock. Ever since, this stone has been cooler than the stones around it. Don't believe it? Feel it for yourself!

The stone was not part of the original chapel, officially known as the Chapelle de St. Martin de Sayssuel. The chapel once stood 12 miles south of Lyons, France, having been built in the 15th century. The French had abandoned it and Gertrude Gavin, daughter of a U.S. railroad baron, bought it and moved it to her family's estate on Long Island in 1927. The special stone was bricked into the wall to the left of the altar while the chapel was being rebuilt. In 1965 the chapel was donated to Marquette University and moved a second time. Unless services are going on, doubting Thomases are welcome to test the stone, still cold after all these years. First, place your hand on the vertical (nonholy) stone, then touch the holy base.

Marquette University, 14th St. and Wisconsin Ave., Milwaukee, WI 53233

(414) 288-6873

Hours: Monday–Saturday 10A.M.–4P.M., Sunday Noon–4P.M.; services at noon when school is in session

Cost: Free

Directions: Behind the Memorial Library on Wisconsin St.

Spencer Tracy's Boyhood Homes

As a product of Hollywood's Studio System, Spencer Tracy's early life was given a healthy scrubbing by publicists. Born in Milwaukee on April 5, 1900, he was portrayed as a scrappy altar boy when in fact he was more of a hoodlum. By the time he reached eighth grade, he had attended between 15 and 18 elementary schools on the south side of the city, mostly because he had gotten in so many fights with his class-mates. Following an argument with his father, he tried to burn down the family's Prospect Avenue home. It is no longer standing, but not because of Tracy.

When the Tracy family fell on hard times in 1912, they moved to a home on St. Paul Ave. at 30th St. It would be the first of many homes and apartments where the family would live over the years. Only two of those homes remain; they are listed below. In his teen years, Spencer became friends with another teenager, Bill O'Brien, and the two joined the Marines together after the United States entered World War I.

On returning, O'Brien convinced Tracy to study acting with him at Marquette Academy. It was a good move for both of them. Tracy went on to be nominated nine times for an Oscar, winning twice, and O'Brien would change his first name to what people remember today, Pat O'Brien, best known for playing the Irish Catholic priest in every movie ever made.

2970 S. Kinnickinnic Ave., Milwaukee, WI 53207

No phone

Hours: Private residence; view from street

Cost: Free

Directions: Just north of Rusk St.

2447 S. Graham St., Milwaukee, WI 53207

No phone

Hours: Private residence; view from street

Cost: Free

Directions: Between Wilson and Graham Sts.

Teddy Roosevelt Near-Assassination Site

It was a good thing Teddy Roosevelt was both long-winded and near-sighted—both traits saved his life. On a campaign trip to Milwaukee as the Bull Moose candidate for the presidency, Roosevelt was shot by a deranged bartender on October 14, 1912.

The assassination attempt happened outside the Gilpatrick Hotel. Teddy had been stalked through eight states for 2,000 miles by New York tapster John Schrank (who had spent the previous night at the Argyle Lodging House on Third St.). It was here that the would-be assassin finally got within six feet of the Rough Rider. Schrank claimed William McKinley had come to him twice in dreams and implicated Roosevelt in his own assassination. "Let not a murderer take the presidential chair. Avenge my death!" McKinley commanded from beyond the grave. If that weren't reason enough, Schrank was a George Washington fanatic, and hated the idea a lesser man dared run for president for a third term, one term more than the Father of Our Country.

Schrank's .38-calibre bullet hit Roosevelt in the chest but was slowed down by a 50-page speech (folded twice) and eyeglass case in Teddy's breast pocket. The bullet lodged two inches into his chest, touching his lung, but did not hit his heart. The crowd wanted to lynch Schrank, but Roosevelt calmed the mob by talking directly to his attacker. Roosevelt went on to make his speech at the Milwaukee Auditorium before going to Johnston Emergency Hospital, bragging, "[I]t takes more than one bullet to kill a Bull Moose!"

Roosevelt was later moved to Mercy Hospital in Chicago to recover. He died six years later with the bullet still lodged in his chest. Schrank was sent to the Northern Hospital for the Insane in Oshkosh, then transferred to the Central State Hospital for the Criminally Insane in Waupun in 1914. He died there in 1943, angry that another Roosevelt, FDR, had been elected to a third term in 1940.

831 N. 3rd St., Milwaukee, WI 53203

No phone

Hours: Torn down; a new hotel stands on the site

Cost: Free

Directions: On 3rd St. between Kilbourn and Wells

ANOTHER GUN-TOTING STALKER/VOTER

Milwaukee janitor **Arthur Bremer** shot George Wallace in Laurel, Maryland, on May 15, 1972. In the years leading up to his crime, he had worked locally as a busboy and was attending classes at Milwaukee Area Technical College. He had been following various presidential candidates around the nation during the preceding 18 weeks, but Wallace was the first politician he could get close to.

As part of Richard Nixon's infamous "Dirty Tricks" campaign, special counsel Chuck Colson, on Nixon's orders, sent soon-to-be-Watergate burglar E. Howard Hunt to Milwaukee to plant McGovern campaign material in Bremer's filthy apartment. FBI agents had already entered Bremer's apartment for evidence, then left two reporters to ransack the place. Realizing they had made an error in judgment, the FBI returned and sealed the crime scene, barring Hunt from entry.

The best place to park your camel in Milwaukee.

Tripoli Shrine Temple

The temple looms over Wisconsin Ave. like a vision from *The Arabian Nights*. Two stone camels guard the entrance to a North African mosque topped by a 30-foot gold onion dome flanked by two smaller domes, with minarets on each of the building's four corners. No, you're not in Libya, but on the west side of Milwaukee at the state's largest temple for The Ancient Arabic Order of the Nobles of the Mystic Shrine, better known as the Shriners.

Tripoli Shrine Temple was planned and constructed between 1925 and 1928. The interior of the building is as elaborate as the outside, every square inch covered in Islamic-patterned tiles and furnished with matching chairs, tables, and cabinetry. The architectural details of the Temple are described in a self-guided tour book available at the office.

The Temple is the focal point of Milwaukee's most visible fraternal organization, a division of the Masons. The Shriners' primary purpose is to raise funds for children's hospitals specializing in orthopedic afflictions and burns. And if they have some free time to putt around parades in miniature VWs, what's the harm? The Tripoli Temple is also home to the World's Longest Bicycle, though it is not assembled for viewing. The stretched bike, built at Marquette in 1994, is 37 feet long and can transport 36 fezzed Shriners at a time.

3000 W. Wisconsin Ave., Milwaukee, WI 53208

(414) 933-4700

Hours: Call ahead for appointment; self-guided tour

Cost: Free

Directions: At the corner of 30th St. and Wisconsin Ave.

World's Largest Four-Faced Clock

After it was erected, the four-faced Allen-Bradley clock on Milwaukee's south side became widely known as the Polish Moon. This was not intended to imply that local residents felt their immigrant neighbors were punctual or time conscious. Jokes like this don't go over like they used to. . . .

Frankly, it's understandable somebody could mistake this clock for Earth's satellite—this thing is *big*, and no matter where you stand you can always see one beaming face. Today, the Allen-Bradley is still the World's Largest Four-Faced Clock, as well as the World's Largest Non-Chiming Clock. Only London's Big Ben is larger, and it makes a terrible noise.

1201 S. Second St., Milwaukee, WI 53204

No phone

Hours: Always visible

Cost: Free

Directions: Four blocks south of Rte. 59, one block west of Rte. 32.

WAUKESHA
Electric guitar inventor **Les Paul** and his singing wife, **Mary Ford**, were both born in Waukesha, Paul on June 9, 1915, and Ford on July 7, 1924.

Suburbs
Fox Point
Fox Point Art Yard

Mary Nohl is a shining example of human independence in the face of adversity. While her family has owned this beachfront property since 1924 and built a home here in 1943, it wasn't until she began creating yard art in 1968 that a few local boneheads began taking notice. Nohl's organic art has a primitive, Easter-Island-like feel to it, and is made of concrete, driftwood, and items she's discovered on the shore.

Word was passed among the intellectually challenged that Mary was a witch and that the statues she created were somehow involved. The pieces suffered constant vandalism until Nohl was forced to surround her property with a high chain-link fence topped with razor wire.

The only thing witchy about this soft-spoken woman is the word *BOO* embedded in her front steps, put there to ward off further problems. Though sometimes lumped with naive environmental artists, she is definitely not untrained; Nohl is a 1938 graduate of the Art Institute of Chicago and taught for some time in junior high. Her work is extremely personal, and she's never sold a piece of art. And because of a few local jerks, she probably never will.

7328 N. Beach Dr., Fox Point, WI 53217

Private phone

Hours: Private residence; view from street, daylight only

Cost: Free

Directions: Beach Dr. east from Lake Dr. (Rte. 32), take a right at the fork, follow along the shore until it takes a right turn and heads back inland.

Wauwatosa
Hog Heaven

You don't have to see a Harley to know you're in its presence . . . just listen. That signature blop-blop-blop from the V-twin motorcycle's tailpipe is like a Mozart symphony to the ears of Hog lovers everywhere.

The Harley-Davidson Motor Company was founded in a Milwaukee garage in 1903. That year they made only three bikes. But two World Wars made the company a force to be reckoned with, shipping 90,000 bikes to Allied troops in WWII alone. Nostalgic former

GIs fueled commercial sales in the 1950s and 1960s. But as more and more American manufacturers closed their doors or moved overseas, it looked like Harley-Davidson might get back to a three-bike-a-year operation. But, thanks to a hard-working labor force and a loyal customer base, Harley-Davidson survived the recessions of the 1970s and 1980s and is bigger than ever.

Wauwatosa's manufacturing facility is known as the Capitol Drive Powertrain Operations. Weekday tours allow you to see how power-trains are assembled. The facility also makes replacement parts for older bikes. Unfortunately, if you want to see the final assembly of today's models you must travel to a factory in York, Pennsylvania. On a well-tuned Hog you can make the run in eight hours.

Harley-Davidson, Inc., 11700 W. Capitol Dr., Wauwatosa, WI 53222

(414) 535-3666

Hours: September–May, Monday, Wednesday, and Friday 9:30A.M., 11:30A.M., and 1P.M.; June–August, Monday–Friday 9:30A.M., 11:30A.M., and 1P.M.

Cost: Free

www.harleydavidson.com

Directions: At the intersection of Capitol Dr. (Rte. 190) and Rte. 45.

West Allis
Liberace's Birthplace

One of the world's greatest showmen, Waldziu Valentino Liberace, was born in humble West Allis on May 16, 1919. He was the only surviving child of a pair of twins, weighing in at a whopping 13+ pounds. His father was a French horn player with the International Harvester Band at the Schlitz Palm Garden. His mother knew she had given birth to a genius . . . and she was right. At the age of 14 "Lee" got his first gig at Little Nick's (Muskego and Mitchell Sts., Milwaukee) using the stage name Walter Busterkeys, and he went on to win music competitions across the state.

Liberace was very popular at West Milwaukee High School (51st St. and Greenfield Ave.). The school held an annual "Character Day" where students were required to come as a famous or historic person, and Liberace won three years running, first as Haile Selassie, then as Yankee

Doodle, and finally as Greta Garbo. He graduated in 1937 and before long was touring the country. To look around West Allis today, you'd think Liberace took every last rhinestone when he left.

1649 60th St. (formerly 635 51st St.), West Allis, WI 53214

No phone

Hours: Private residence; view from street

Cost: Free

Directions: At 60th and Mitchell Sts., three blocks south of National Ave.

Pagoda Gas Station

With unleaded you get eggroll.

It looks like a Chinese take-out restaurant, this small pagoda with a bright red roof at a busy intersection, but it is actually a former gas station. Wadham's Oil & Grease Company built the structure in 1927, back when automobile touring was all the rage. The goal was to attract customers who were looking for adventure, or at least something different, when they filled their tanks.

At the time it closed its doors, it was known as the Frank Seneca Service Station. Unlike what happens with so many abandoned roadside wonders, the pagoda was restored. Today you can peer through the windows to see what an old station once looked like. It is guarded by a department store dummy in a grease monkey uniform.

Frank Seneca Service Station, 1647 S. 76th St., West Allis, WI 53214

No phone

Hours: Always visible

Cost: Free

Directions: At the corner of 76th St. and National Ave.

8

MONSTER TOUR

$\mathbb{W}$isconsin has long been the stomping grounds for many classic monsters. Ignore the obvious frauds, like the stuffed Merman once on display in a Milwaukee museum. Think instead about genuine ghouls: vampires, werewolves, sea serpents, and Bigfoots, as well as a couple of nasty critters found only in Wisconsin, the Warbinger and the Hodag. And don't forget a human monster, Ed Gein, who still inspires horror movies and nightmares more than 50 years after he first began digging up bodies in Plainfield.

Monster reports vary greatly, depending on the source. Who saw what, when, and where is less important than the fact that somebody saw something, and they saw it in Wisconsin. You might too, on this Monster Tour. Just be sure to lock your car doors. . . .

Various Towns
Bigfoot!

Native Americans call it Windego. Others prefer Sasquatch. To most, it's just Bigfoot.

The first documented case of a modern Wisconsin Bigfoot was in 1910 at **Mirror Lake**. A hairy humanoid followed a 10-year-old girl through the woods, though it never harmed her. In 1936 another was seen digging into an Indian burial mound along Rte. 18 near **Jefferson**.

In the 1960s and 1970s there were a rash of sightings. Farmers were amazed to see a Sasquatch vault a barbed-wire fence near **Fremont** in June 1964. The creature repeated the jumping trick at the intersection of Rtes. 89 and 14 west of **Delavan** in July 1964. Bigfoot was seen twice more in **Fremont**, first on October 19, 1968, and then on November 30 in Deltox Marsh when several hunters were almost knocked off their feet as the monster ran past them. Apparently none of these gun-toting men thought to bag what would be one heck of a trophy. How many sportsmen do you know who have a Bigfoot's head in their basement rec room?

Bigfoot was reported to be in **Benton** in August 1970, **Fort Atkinson** in 1972, **Frederic** in December 1974, **Cashton** in September 1976 (sometime called the Cashton Creature), and **St. Croix Falls** a month later. Children staying in a cabin near **Plainfield** were terrorized by a hairy creature in August 1981. Another Sasquatch was seen squatting over a roadkill on Rte. 106 in **Jefferson County** in the summer of 1992, then attacked a passing car that might have provided it with its squished meal in the first place. A Bigfoot harassed a **Frankfort** family in 1991 and 1992 by eating their chickens and peeping in their windows.

Today, Bigfoot is often sighted near **Rice Lake**. On November 3, 1997, it left 17-inch footprints near the northern Wisconsin town. Another sighting places him at a cabin off Rte. F near **Lugerville** on November 29, 1997. A newspaper delivery man spotted Bigfoot carrying a goat on Rte. H, seven-tenths of a mile west of Rte. K north of **Granton** on March 28, 2000.

But by far the best report of a Wisconsin Bigfoot encounter is described in a book entitled *Story in the Snow* by Lunetta Woods (Lakeville, Minn.: Galde Press, 1997). The book is written from the perspective of Yesoda, a female Sasquatch, who visits a woman and her family in an undisclosed rural location in 1994. Yesoda reveals that she, her lifelong companion Kunta, and others like her are "shape-shifters," taking on the form of any creature in nature. They disguise their tracks as those of rabbits, deer, and various reptiles. Yesoda and Kunta warn the woman's children through dreams that a gargoyle lives in their grain silo. She also reveals that Bigfoots protect the rest of us by moving rocks to align with the "electrical grid pattern surrounding Mother Earth." They sure do keep busy.

Bigfoot Files: www.bfro.net/GDB/state_wi.htm

Directions: Follow the directions listed above, and keep your nose peeled for the smell of a skunk.

Where wolf?

Elkhorn
Werewolf!

Werewolf? Here wolf! This lupine monster has been spotted so often along the same country road in southern Wisconsin that it has been dubbed the Bray Road Beast.

It was first sighted in 1988 by frightened drivers near the intersection of Bray and Hospital Rds. northeast of Elkhorn. The Beast sometimes walked on its hind legs but other times galloped on all four of its human-like appendages. In 1991, locals discovered a sacrificial altar upon which were the remains of several local pets. Were the events connected? Had somebody summoned up sinister forces from Hell?

It appeared so, and the Beast was becoming more aggressive. On Halloween night in 1991, the Bray Road Beast jumped onto the trunk of a teenager's car after she thought she'd run over an animal. It held on for some distance before tumbling off the swerving vehicle, scratching the trunk.

The Bray Road Beast was soon traveling to other locales. In August 1992, a driver on Rte. 106 northbound, just past County Rd. D near Hebron, saw the monster jogging along a cornfield looking for prey. Hebron is 20 miles north of Elkhorn, so the Bray Road Beast should be considered "on the loose."

Then, in February 1993, the Bray Road Beast endorsed State Representative Chuck Coleman for the First Congressional District, then appeared in a campaign photo shaking Coleman's hand. Honestly. Coleman lost the Republican primary, so the Beast wasn't able to frighten voters as it did imaginative teenagers.

Bray Rd., Elkhorn, WI 53121

No phone

Hours: After dark

Cost: Free

Directions: Two miles northeast of the Rte. 43 intersection with Rte. 12, on Bray Rd. at the intersection with Hospital Rd.

Madison
The Mendota Monster!

Loch Ness might be better known, but Lake Mendota's underwater monster gets points for toughing out the frigid northern winters. Reports of a 20-foot-long creature in Lake Mendota have been circulating since the 1860s, when it was first spotted near Governor's Island (northern shore) by a husband and wife. Twenty-odd years later, in 1889, a fisherman near Picnic Point (at the northern tip of University Bay) caught a glimpse of it. Then, in July 1892, it attacked a rowboat carrying mailman Billy Dunn and his wife near Livesey's Bluff, leaving fang marks on a paddle Dunn used to defend himself. Clearly this was not a shy, harmless sea serpent! In 1897 it was blamed for eating a dog swimming in the lake and was fired upon twice by salesman Eugene Heath near the eastern shore. Heath said the bullets bounced off its scales as the creature came after him.

Perhaps the Mendota Monster is just lonely and looking for companionship. A University of Wisconsin student was sunning herself in 1917 on a dock off Picnic Point when she felt something tickling her toes. At first she thought it was her randy boyfriend, but it turned out to be the snakelike tongue of the Mendota Monster! The woman screamed and the creature retreated.

Monster sightings continued into the 1920s, and locals gave it the nickname Bozho, short for Winnebozho. Whatever you call it, it's shorthand for t-r-o-u-b-l-e in a green skin.

Lake Mendota, Madison, WI 53706

No phone

Hours: Summertime best

Cost: Free

Directions: Just north of the UW campus.

Mineral Point
Password? Vampire!

Allen Ludden, future *Password* host and husband to Betty White, was born in Mineral Point on October 5, 1918. When he died in 1981, his body was returned here to spend the rest of its existence with . . . a vampire!

The Mineral Point Vampire was spotted only once, in March 1981, by police in Graceland Cemetery. This bloodsucker was less Anne Rice and more Bela Lugosi. He donned a black cape, had a pale white face, and was extremely tall. Could it have been Ludden, back from the grave? Not likely. Ludden was a short man.

Graceland Cemetery, West Fair St., Mineral Point, WI 53565

No phone

Hours: Daily 9A.M.–5P.M.

Cost: Free

Directions: On the southwest side of town, near the fairgrounds.

Ed was a groundbreaker.

Plainfield
Psycho!

When it comes to psychos, Ed Gein was a groundbreaker.

The product of an overbearing mother, a cruel father, and too much time to himself, Ed Gein was, to put it mildly, odd. Ed's mother Augusta did her best to keep him away from women for Biblical reasons, and in doing so warped her son's psyche. Ed was left to form images of the outside world from dime paperbacks and Mom's advice. Bad strategy.

When his mother died in December 1945, Ed snapped. In 1947 he began robbing women's graves in the Plainfield Cemetery. He dug up Mrs. Sherman, Mrs. Everson, Mrs. Eleanor Adams (whose grave, just in front of Augusta's, was later reopened to confirm Ed's story), Mrs. Bergstrom, Mrs. Evans, and Mrs. Sparks and removed body parts as souvenirs. He also violated the nearby Hancock and Spiritland cemeteries. Ed then began tailoring a human bodysuit for himself. His goal was to become a woman. At night he would put on his macabre outfit, complete with breasts and genitalia, and dance around in the moonlight.

When there weren't enough fresh bodies in the local graveyards, Ed resorted to murder. He is known to have killed two women, but there were perhaps more. The first victim was Mary Hogan, owner of Hogan's Tavern in nearby Pine Grove, just north of Plainfield in Portage County. He murdered her after closing time on December 9, 1954, and brought her home in his truck. It was for a second murder, Bernice Worden, that Gein was eventually apprehended. He shot Worden in her Plainfield hardware store on the opening day of deer season. It was November 16, 1957, and most of the town's men were off hunting. So was Ed. Police traced a store receipt for antifreeze back to Gein at his grisly farmhouse.

Cops discovered Worden hanging from her heels, headless and dressed out like a deer, in Ed's barn. Inside his house were soup bowls made from skulls, chairs and lamps upholstered with skin, a box of salted noses, nine masks made from women's faces and adorned with lipstick, a pair of lips hanging from a window shade, a drum made with a coffee can and two skinned heads, and a bed adorned with bones and skulls on the four bedposts. Mrs. Worden's heart was sitting in a pot on the stove. Her head was in a bag with nails driven into its ears; Ed planned to hang it with twine on a wall. In all, police believed there were the remains of 15 women in the house.

Then there was Ed's mother's room. It had been sealed at her death and wasn't reopened until the police got out the crowbar. Everything was exactly how she left it, but with a thick layer of dust. Ed hadn't touched a thing.

Gein was sent to Central State Hospital, an insane asylum in Waupun (now named Dodgeville Correctional Institute, 1 W. Lincoln St.). An angry local mob torched Gein's home on March 20, 1958, after rumors circulated that it would be purchased at auction and reopened as a House of Horrors. Gein's white 1949 Ford sedan survived. It toured in a Midwest sideshow throughout the 1960s, billed as "The Ed Gein Ghoul Car: The Car That Hauled the Dead from Their Graves." Human evidence collected from the home was buried in 1962 in an unmarked grave at the Plainfield Cemetery.

At a 1968 trial, Gein was found guilty of murdering Bernice Worden but was declared insane in the sentencing phase. He spent his remaining years in the loony bin, transferring from Central State to the Mendota Mental Health Institute in Madison in 1974. He died of respiratory failure on July 26, 1984, and was buried back in Plainfield where it all began . . . next to his dear old mother. His chipped and defaced tombstone was stolen in June 2000 and has not been recovered.

Even if you've never heard of Gein before, you'll recognize him as the inspiration for *Psycho*, *The Texas Chainsaw Massacre*, *Deranged*, and *Silence of the Lambs*. Ed has been transformed into a modern American monster.

Plainfield Cemetery, Fifth Ave., Plainfield, WI 54966

No phone

Hours: Daily 9A.M.–5P.M.

Cost: Free

Directions: Follow frontage road (Fifth Ave.) north along Rte. 51; Ed and his mother's plot are to the right of the central car path, near the back.

Ed's Former Land, Aniwa Lane, Plainfield, WI 54966

Directions: West on Rte. 73, left on Rte. KK, right on Aniwa Lane, between 3rd (KK) and 1st (county line) Aves.

GEINERS

Joke historians believe the origins of the modern "sick joke" can be traced to "Geiners," twisted jokes told around Wisconsin following Ed's arrest. Here are a few.

An "Ed Gein Beer" in Wisconsin is known as one with a lot of body but no head.

Q: What did Ed Gein give his girl for Valentine's Day?
A: A box of Farmer Fannies.

Ed Gein had to keep the heat on in his house or the furniture would get goose bumps.

Hodag or Hoax-dag?

Rhinelander
Hodag!

The Hodag (*Bovine spirituallis*) is a rare and elusive beast found only in the swamps of Northern Wisconsin. It received its name because it looks like a cross between a horse and a dog. The Hodag has a spiny, horned backbone, a serpent's tail, and legs without knee joints. Because of this it cannot lie down and must sleep leaning against a tree. To capture a Hodag, chop down the tree. Hodags eat only white bulldogs, and only on Sunday.

The first reported sighting of a Hodag came from German immigrants led by Gene Shepard near the headwaters of Rice Creek in 1896. Shepard cornered it in a cave and chloroformed it with a rag on a bamboo pole. He then put it on dimly lit display. Shepard's Hodag was seven feet long and three feet tall, and was later discovered to be a cheap hoax: a horse hide stretched over a wooden body with bull horns glued to its back. Its movements were controlled with hidden wires pulled by Shepard. The Hodag was later destroyed when Shepard's resort on Ballard Lake caught fire.

But that wasn't the end of the Hodag. Shortly after the blaze, another Hodag was spotted on the property of George DeBoyle, near Lake Creek, on August 5, 1952. Before being captured, it ripped the shirt off DeBoyle and knocked out Little Donny Decor, a fearless lad. The Hodag was placed in an open-bed cart and brought to town, and today you can see it at the Rhinelander Logging Museum. On close inspection it appears rather . . . wooden.

Enthusiasm for this town's unique critter has not subsided. Maybe Shepard's was a Hoax-dag, but there has to be another one out there somewhere. Today, Rhinelander calls itself "The Home of the Hodag" and has made the monster the high school's mascot. Businesses in town include the Hodag Bar, Hodag Sewing Center, Hodag Express Lube, Hodag Auto Sales, Hodag Learning Center, Hodag Lanes, Hodag Bait & Tackle, and, just in case, Hodag Guns. An enormous fiberglass Hodag has been erected near the Chamber of Commerce building along the river, and every year the town throws a Hodag Festival.

Rhinelander Logging Museum, Pioneer Park, Rte. 8, Rhinelander, WI 54501

(715) 369-5004

Hours: June–August, daily 10A.M.–5P.M.

Cost: Free; donations accepted

www.ci.rhinelander.wi.us/museum/museum

www.rhinelanderchamber.com

Directions: At the intersection of Rtes. 8 and 47.

World's one Warbinger. Photo by author, courtesy of The Bear

Winchester Warbinger!

The Warbinger is a fierce, carnivorous critter, and only one has ever been caught in the North Woods. At first glance it looks like a common deer, but on closer inspection you'll notice it has one red eye and one blue eye (though its electrical wiring has burned out), porcupine quills on its snout, and fangs bloody from a fresh kill.

The Warbinger might be the rarest specimen on the walls of The Bear Bar, but not the only dead animal. Almost all the critters mounted here were felled by a bow and arrow, usually launched by Art LaHa during his filming of *No Land for the Timid*, a hunting film. They've got bears and deer, foxes and beavers, raccoons and minks, pheasants and squirrels, and, of course, the ferocious Warbinger. No land for the timid, indeed!

The Bear Bar, Restaurant & Lodge, Rte. W, HC2 Box 820, Winchester, WI 54557

(715) 686-2280

Hours: Daily 3–10p.m.

Cost: Free

Directions: On Rte. W, just south of the Rte. O intersection.

9

EPiLOGUE

Now for the bad news on Wisconsin's weird roadside attractions: They're an endangered species. For a variety of reasons, there aren't as many as there used to be. Mother Nature takes its toll on the sites, and old age does the same on the proprietors. Property values, "good taste," and cranky neighbors all work against those who look at the world a little differently and want to share it with the rest of us.

Sometimes attractions are put to sleep or abandoned by their creators. A satan-esque art environment called Devil Dance near Pittsville was left to decay, and nothing remains. Only two green men from Dave Siedler's Alien Presence near Tomahawk survive, standing under the eaves of a shed, not much of a presence at all. Ask about the Miniature Village built in Black Earth by Gilman Mikelson and the response is usually, "Here? In Black Earth?" Yet the Lilliputian town does exist, overgrown with weeds, off a county road west of town.

Basic economic laws of supply and demand have killed a few Wisconsin museums and sites. Biblical Gardens couldn't compete with the water parks in the Dells, and fiberglass Jesus statues ended up on the auction block. Spring Green's American Calliope Center tooted its last note, sold off its instruments, and turned the building over to a storefront ministry. The Park Lane Railroad Museum in Dellwood ran off the rails and will not likely reopen. And the Wisconsin Folk Art Museum did its best to attract city slickers with fur-bearing trout, but they couldn't find as many suckers as they used to. It has since closed its doors.

When a business folds, at least somebody out there gets some enjoyment from purchases at the bankruptcy auction. More tragic are cases like Henkelmann's Museum in northern Woodruff. This privately owned collection had animals you wouldn't see in most natural history museums, like three harmonica-playing bears and stuffed squirrels on a turntable, dancing "The Twist." Henkelmann's burned to the ground more than a decade ago. The bears . . . the harmonicas . . . the squirrels . . . all went up in smoke. It was tragic, just tragic.

The Kohler Foundation has coordinated impressive restorations of some of the Wisconsin sites listed in this book, but, with limited resources, has had to focus on locations of artistic or historic merit. That's admirable and appreciated, but who's out there saving the fiberglass cows, the stuffed albino muskrats, and the cheesemobiles? Nobody, that's who. If you don't get in the car and see them now, *today*, you may never be able to tell your grandchildren you ever saw the World's Largest Penny.

ACKNOWLEDGMENTS

The first road trip I ever took was to Wisconsin, just a short trip up through Kenosha and Racine to get away from Chicago for an afternoon. Wisconsin is a beautiful state, and though I am obligated as an Illinois resident to rib its residents, it is hard to escape the fact it produces some of the nicest people in the Midwest. While researching this book I ran out of gas west of Madison, and before I could lock my doors and hike off to a station, a guy named Terry pulled over, drove me to a pump, and brought me back to my car. For all Chicago has to offer, they don't have roadside assistance for spaced-out drivers, and for that reason alone, I love Wisconsin.

This book would not have been possible without the assistance, patience, and good humor of many individuals. My thanks go out to the following people for allowing me to interview them about their roadside attractions: Wilbert Behn (Behn's Game Farm), Fran Burt (Rock in the House), Joan Cook (Wegner Grotto), John Cronce (Jockey International), Tom Diehl (Tommy Bartlett's Robot World), Ted Dzialo (National Freshwater Fishing Hall of Fame), Betty Elliott (Carl's Wood Art Museum), Curt Evans (Chevy on a Silo), Tom "Dr. Evermor" Every (The Forevertron), Ellen Flood (Thunderbird Museum), Connie Ghiloni (Warbinger/The Bear), Catherine Goetz (Hamburger Hall of Fame), Cheryl Harkey (Fountain City Rock Garden), Kenneth Haeuser (Prairie Moon Museum), Paul Hefti (Yard Environment), Brian Holzem (Storybook Gardens), Barry and Patti Levenson (Mustard Museum), Dave Pflieger (World's Largest Grandfather Clock), Richard Hanson (Warner Brothers in Cement), Gordon Johnson (The Painted Forest), Gail "Princess of Power" Lamberty (The Evermor Foundation), Paul and Clarice LaReau (World of Miniature Buildings), Maria McKay (Museum of Woodcarving), Craig Powell (Hamilton Wood Type and Printing Museum), Rick Rolfsmeyer (Grandview), Rudy Rotter (Rudy Rotter's Museum of Sculpture), Jim Schauf (F.A.S.T. Corporation), Ken Schels (Carl's Wood Art Museum), Judith Schulz (Spinning Top Exploratory

Museum), Lisa Stone (Friends of Fred Smith), Fred Theisen (Little Bohemia), Marge Timmerman (Dickeyville Grotto), Bob Tohak (UFO Landing Pad), Peggy Van Gilder (Mocassin Bar), Jim Van Lanen (Hamilton Wood Type and Printing Museum), Bill Vienneaux (Wayward Wind Studio & Gallery), Laura Weingandt (End of the Line), Doug Watson (Watson's Wild West Museum), and Clyde Wynia (Jurustic Park).

Additional thanks go to Nancy Moulton of the Kohler Foundation. Without her fact-checking and editorial advice on the environmental art sites restored by the Kohler Foundation, I might not have given these remarkable works or their creators their proper due.

For research assistance, I am indebted to the librarians in the Wisconsin communities of Amery, Appleton, Eagle River, Fish Creek, Genoa City, Kenosha, Lake Geneva, Lodi, Medford, Mineral Point, Montello, Sparta, and Sun Prairie. Thanks also to the Chambers of Commerce in Bloomer, Burlington, Cumberland, Eagle River, Elmwood, Green Bay, La Crosse, Lake Geneva, Mercer, Mineral Point, Onalaska, Port Washington, St. Germaine, Sauk City, Sun Prairie, Waupun, and Winneconne.

Friends, family members, and complete strangers willingly volunteered to act as models for the photographs in this book: Jim Frost, Richard Hanson, Patrick Hughes, Eugene Marceron, Judith Schulz, Clyde Wynia, and the kids at Children's World in Franklin. Thanks, too, to Annice Tatken for her photo of the rooftop goats in Sister Bay.

To my displaced Cheesehead friends, Gianofer Fields, Julie Froman, Tim Murphy, and Ellen Ryan, I hope I did your home state justice. And to Jim Frost, thanks as always for your support, encouragement, and hours behind the wheel.

RECOMMENDED SOURCES

If you'd like to learn more about the places and individuals in this book, the following are excellent sources.

Introduction

History Just Ahead by the Wisconsin State Historical Society (Madison, Wisc.: Wisconsin State Historical Society, 1999)

Awesome Almanac—Wisconsin by Jean Blashfield (Fontana, Wisc.: B&B Publishing, 1993)

The Wisconsin Almanac by Jerry Minnich (ed.) (Madison, Wisc.: Prairie Oak Press, 1999)

Wisconsin, The Story of the Badger State by Norman K. Risjord (Black Earth, Wisc.: Trails Books, 1995)

Wisconsin Literary Travel Guide by the Wisconsin Library Association (Madison, Wisc.: Wisconsin Library Association, 1989)

Wisconsin Lore and Legends by Lou and John Russell (Menominee, Wisc.: Oak Point Press, 1982)

Wisconsin Lore and Legends, Volume II by Lou and John Russell (Menominee, Wisc.: Oak Point Press, 1982)

Wisconsin Ghosts by Beth Scott and Michael Norman (Minocqua, Wisc.: Heartland Press, 1980)

Sacred Spaces and Other Places by Lisa Stone and Jim Zanzi (Chicago: School of the Art Institute of Chicago Press, 1993)

The W-Files by Jay Rath (Madison, Wisc.: Wisconsin Trails, 1997)

1. Northern Wisconsin

Capone's Hideout and Dillinger's Shootout

Gangster Holidays by Tom Hollatz (St. Cloud, Minn.: North Star Press, 1989)

Carl's Wood Art Museum

A Trapper's Legacy by Carl Schels (Merrillville, Ind.: ICS Books, 1989); *Reflections of the Past* by Carl Schels (Eagle River, Wisc.: Hahn Printing, 1989)

Fred Smith's Concrete Park
The Art of Fred Smith by Lisa Stone and Jim Zanzi (Phillips, Wisc.: Price County
  Forestry Department, 1991)
Museum of Woodcarving
My Brother Joe the Woodcarver by Lucy Barta McKay (Shell Lake, Wisc.: Museum
  of Woodcarving, date unknown)

2. Central Wisconsin
Harry Houdini
The Life and Many Deaths of Harry Houdini by Ruth Brandon (New York:
  Random House, 1993)
Joseph McCarthy
Joseph McCarthy by Arthur Herman (New York: The Free Press, 2000)
Apostle Clock
The Apostles Clock Video by the Oshkosh Public Museum (Oshkosh, Wisc.: 1998)
Sculptureville
Public Sculpture in Wisconsin by Anton Rajer and Christine Style (Madison,
  Wisc.: SOS! Wisconsin, 1999)

3. The Dells
General Dells Guide
The Wisconsin Dells by James Laabs (Madison, Wisc.:
  Prairie Oak Press, 1999)
Circus World
Badger State Showmen by Fred Dahlinger and Stuart Thayer (Baraboo, Wisc.:
  Circus World, 1998)

4. Southern Wisconsin
Passenger Pigeons
Passenger Pigeons by the State Historical Society of Wisconsin (Madison, Wisc.:
  State Historical Society of Wisconsin, 1976)
Dickeyville Grotto
Dickeyville Grotto by Susan A. Niles (Jackson, Miss.: University Press of
  Mississippi, 1997)
Orson Welles
Orson Welles: The Road to Xanadu by Simon Callow (New York: Viking, 1995)

Aztalan
The Lost Pyramids of Rock Lake by Frank Joseph (St. Paul, Minn.: Galde Press, 1992); *Atlantis in Wisconsin* by Frank Joseph (St. Paul, Minn.: Galde Press, 1995)

Mustard Museum
The Wurst of the Proper Mustard by Barry Levenson (ed.) (Mt. Horeb, Wisc.: The Mustard Museum, 1993)

John Dillinger
Dillinger by G. Russell Girardin (Bloomington, Ind.: Indiana University Press, 1994)

House on the Rock
House of Alex by Marv Balousek (Oregon, Wisc.: Waubesa Press, 1990)

Frank Lloyd Wright
Frank Lloyd Wright by Meryle Secrest (New York: Alfred A. Knopf, 1992)

5. Mad Town
Bombing at Sterling Hall
Wisconsin Crimes of the Century by Marv Balousek (Madison, Wisc.: William C. Robbins, 1989)

Thornton Wilder
Thornton Wilder, An Intimate Portrait by Richard Goldstone (New York: Saturday Review Press, 1975)

State Capitol Building
Wisconsin Capitol Fascinating Facts by Diana Cook (Madison, Wisc.: Prairie Oak Press, 1991)

Georgia O'Keeffe
O'Keeffe, The Life of an American Legend by Jeffrey Hogrefe (New York: Bantam Books, 1992)

6. Eastern Wisconsin
Green Bay Packers
When Pride Still Mattered by David Maranis (New York: Simon & Schuster, 1999)

Eisenhower's Train
The Eisenhower Collection of the National Railroad Museum by P. H. Dudley, et al. (Green Bay, Wisc.: National Railroad Museum, 1990)

Rudy Rotter
Rudy Rotter's Spirit Driven Art by Anton Rajer (Madison, Wisc.: Fine Arts Conservation, 1998)

Peshtigo Fire
The Great Peshtigo Fire, 2nd ed. by Rev. Peter Pernin (Madison, Wisc.: State
Historical Society of Wisconsin, 2000)
Hamburger Hall of Fame
Home of the Hamburger Celebration by the Hamburger Hall of Fame (Seymour,
Wisc.: Self-published, 1989)

7. Milwaukee and Its Suburbs
Golda Meir
Golda by Ralph G. Martin (New York: Charles Scribner's Sons, 1988)
Jeffrey Dahmer
A Father's Story by Lionel Dahmer (New York: William Morrow, 1994); *The
Milwaukee Murders* by Don Davis (New York: St. Martin's Paperbacks, 1995);
Massacre in Milwaukee by Richard Jaeger and M. William Balousek (Oregon,
Wisc.: Waubesa Press, 1991)
Spencer Tracy
Spencer Tracy, Tragic Idol by Bill Davidson (New York: E. P. Dutton, 1987)
Teddy Roosevelt
The Attempted Assassination of Teddy Roosevelt by Stan Gores (Madison, Wisc.:
State Historical Society of Wisconsin, 1980)
Liberace
Liberace by Bob Thomas (New York: St. Martin's Press, 1987); *Liberace, An
Autobiography* by Liberace (New York: G. P. Putnam's Sons, 1973)

8. Monster Tour
General Weirdness
The W-Files by Jay Rath (Madison, Wisc.: Wisconsin Trails, 1997); Weird
Wisconsin website: weird-wi.com
Bigfoot
Story in the Snow by Lunetta Woods (Lakeville, Minn.: Galde Press, 1997)
Ed Gein
Deviant by Harold Schechter (New York: Pocket Books, 1989); *Edward Gein* by
Judge Robert H. Gollmar (New York: Pinnacle Books, 1981); *Ed Gein, Psycho*
by Paul Anthony Woods (New York: St. Martin's Press, 1995); *Psycho* by
Robert Bloch (New York: Tom Doherty Associates, 1959)

INDEX BY CITY NAME

Burlington, *cont.*

Town Full of Liars (Burlington Area Chamber of Commerce), 101–102

Cataract

Paul & Mathilda Wegner Grotto, aka A Landscape for Peace on Earth, 37

Champion

Mary the Fire Extinguisher (Chapel of Our Lady of Good Hope), 162

Clintonville

Four-Wheel Drive Museum (Walter Olen Park), 37–38

Cochrane

The Prairie Moon Sculpture Gardens & Museum, 38–39

Columbus

Christopher Columbus Museum (Columbus Antique Mall), 102–103

Couderay

The Hideout, 5

DeForest

Sissy the Cow and the Partying Pink Elephant (Ehlenbach's Cheese Chalet, 157–58)

Delavan

A Giant, Clown-Stomping Elephant (Tower Park), 103

Dickeyville

Dickeyville Grotto (Holy Ghost Church), 104–105

Dodgeville

Don Q Inn, 105–106

Eagle River

Carl's Wood Art Museum, 6–7

Ice Palace (Eagle River Chamber of Commerce), 8

East Troy

Stevie Ray Vaughan Death Site (Alpine Valley), 106

Eau Claire

Paul Bunyan Statue (Paul Bunyan Logging Camp), 8–9

Elkhorn

Watson's Wild West Museum, 106–107

Werewolf, 209–210

Elmwood

UFO Capitol of the World (Elmwood Village Office), 10

Fennimore

Fennimore Doll and Toy Museum, 108

Igor the Mouse (Fennimore Cheese Factory), 109

Fontana

Concrete Frog (Frog Hollow Miniature Golf), 110

Nelson

Warner Brother in Cement, 51

New Glarus

Decorated Garage, 128–29

Swiss Village Museum, 127

Oshkosh

Apostles on Parade (Oshkosh Public Museum), 52

The EAA AirVenture Museum (EAA Aviation Center), 52–53

Pardeeville

World of Miniature Buildings (LaReau's World of Miniature Buildings), 54–55

Pepin

Little House in the Big Woods (Ingalls Cabin), 55

Peshtigo

Fire Museum and Mass Graves, 169–70

Phillips

Wisconsin Concrete Park, 18–19

Plainfield

Psycho (Edward Gein), 212–14

Platteville

World's Largest "M," 129

Pleasant Prairie

Kenosha Military Museum, 129–30

Plover

Get Out, You Drunks! (The Cottage), 56

Poland

UFO Landing Port (Tohak & Son Welding), 170–71

Poniatowski

Center of the Northern Half of the Western Hemisphere, 20

Poplar

Bong Memorial (Memorial Room, Poplar Elementary), 20–21

Port Washington

Pebble House (Port Washington Chamber of Commerce and Tourist Information
   Center), 171

Poynette

Aliens and Oddities of Nature Museum (MacKenzie Environmental Education Center),
   130–31

Prairie du Chien

Medical Progress Museum (Fort Crawford Medical Museum), 131–32

Prairie du Sac

The Forevertron, 132–33

Racine

John Dillinger's Submachine Gun (Racine Police Headquarters), 134

Red Banks

Jean Nicolet Reaches China (Jean Nicolet Statue), 172

Reedsburg

Museum of Norman Rockwell Art, 72–73

Rhinelander

Dead John Heisman (Forest Home Cemetery), 21

Hodag (Rhinelander Logging Museum), 215–16

Richland Center

Frank Lloyd Wright's Birthplace, 135

Ripon

Birthplace of the Republicans (Little White Schoolhouse), 57–58

River Falls

Mollie Jensen's Art Exhibit, 22

Rudolph

Rudolph Grotto and Wonder Cave (St. Philip the Apostle Church), 58–59

Sayner

World's First Snowmobile (Vilas County Historical Museum), 23

Seymour

Hamburger Hall of Fame, 173–74

Sheboygan

Art in the Bathrooms (John Michael Kohler Arts Center), 176

James A. Tellen, Jr.'s Woodland Sculpture Garden, 175–76

Stories on the Wall, 174–75

Shell Lake

The Last Supper (Museum of Woodcarving), 23–24

Sister Bay

Goats on the Roof (Al Johnson's Swedish Restaurant and Butik), 176–77

Sparta

F.A.S.T. Corporation, 59–60

Spooner

Spooner Cowboy (Go-Kart Track), 24–25

Spring Green

Acrobatic Goats (Peck's Farm Market), 136

Frank Lloyd Wright's Grave—NOT! (Lloyd-Jones Family Cemetery), 141

House on the Rock, 137–38

Taliesin, 139–40

Spring Valley

Crystal Cave, 25–26

INDEX BY Site Name

Goats on the Roof (Al Johnson's Swedish Restaurant and Butik), 176–77

Golda Meir's Childhood Homes, 190

Good-Bye Passenger Pigeons (Wyalusing State Park), 96–97

Grandview (PEC Foundation), 112–13

Grave of Belle Boyd, Confederate Spy (Spring Grove Cemetery), 80–81

Great Lakes Dragaway, 141–42

The Great Wall of China (Kohler Design Center), 165–66

Green Bay Packer Hall of Fame, 162–63

H. H. Bennett Studio Museum, 81–82

Hamburger Hall of Fame, 173–74

Hamilton Wood Type and Printing Museum, 178

Harmony Hall, 115–16

The Haunted Lutheran Church, 2

Heap Big Hiawatha (La Crosse Area Convention & Visitor Bureau), 42

The Hideout, 5

Hodag (Rhinelander Logging Museum), 215–16

Hog Heaven (Harley-Davidson, Inc.), 203–204

Holy Hill, 113–14

Home of Susie the Duck (Goeres Park), 121

Honey of a Museum (Honey Acres), 96

Houdini Historical Center (Outgamie Museum), 32–33

House on the Rock, 137–38

I Like Ike's Railroad Car (National Railroad Museum), 163–64

Ice Palace (Eagle River Chamber of Commerce), 8

Igor the Mouse (Fennimore Cheese Factory), 109

International Clown Hall of Fame (Grand Avenue Mall/Plankinton Building), 191

International Crane Foundation, 71

James A. Tellen, Jr.'s Woodland Sculpture Garden, 175–76

Jean Nicolet Reaches China (Jean Nicolet Statue), 172

Jeffrey Dahmer's Place, 191–93

Jimmy the Groundhog (Sun Prairie Chamber of Commerce), 159

John Dillinger's Submachine Gun (Racine Police Headquarters), 134

Joseph McCarthy's Home and Grave, 33–34

Jurustic Park, 46

Kenosha Military Museum, 129–30

The Last Supper (Museum of Woodcarving), 23–24

Laverne and Shirley, 193–94

Liberace's Birthplace, 204–205

Little A-Merrick-A, 121–22

Little House in the Big Woods (Ingalls Cabin), 55

Rock in the House, 40

Rudolph Grotto and Wonder Cave (St. Philip the Apostle Church), 58–59

Rudy Rotter's Museum of Sculpture, 167–68

The Safe House, 196–97

St. Joan of Arc Chapel (Marquette University), 198

Sculptureville, 63–64

Serpent Safari, 87

Sid's Sculpture Yard, 153–54

Sissy the Cow and the Partying Pink Elephant (Ehlenbach's Cheese Chalet, Interstate 66), 157–58

Spencer Tracy's Boyhood Homes, 198–99

Spinning Top Exploratory Museum, 101

Spooner Cowboy (Go-Kart Track), 24–25

Stagecoach House (Milton House Museum), 123

Stevie Ray Vaughan Death Site (Alpine Valley), 106

Stories on the Wall, 174–75

Storybook Gardens, 88

Swiss Village Museum, 127

Taliesin, 139–40

Teddy Roosevelt Near-Assassination Site, 199–200

Thornton Wilder's Birthplace, 154

Thunderbird Museum, 41–42

Tom's Burned Down Cafe, 15

Tommy Bartlett's Robot World, 89–90

Tommy Bartlett's Sky, Ski, and Stage Waterski Show, 90–91

Tony's Fan Fair, 60–61

Town Full of Liars (Burlington Area Chamber of Commerce), 101–102

Tripoli Shrine Temple, 201–202

The Trollway, 127

UFO Capitol of the World (Elmwood Village Office), 10

UFO Landing Port (Tohak & Son Welding), 170–71

USS *Cobia* (Manitowoc Maritime Museum), 168–69

Vampire (Graceland Cemetery), 211

Virgin Mary Apparitions (Queen of the Holy Rosary, Mediatrix of Peace, Mediatrix Between God and Man Shrine), 48

Warbinger (The Bear Bar, Restaurant & Lodge), 216–17

Warner Brother in Cement, 51

Watson's Wild West Museum, 106–107

Wax World of the Stars, 91–92

Werewolf, 209–210